# MISSION
UNDER THE
MICROSCOPE

The National Church Life Survey has been developed and resourced by the Uniting Church Board of Mission (NSW) and the Anglican Diocese of Sydney through its Home Mission Society. It has involved the following denominations:

- Anglican
- Apostolic
- Assemblies of God
- Baptist
- Christian & Missionary Alliance
- Christian Revival Crusade
- Church of the Nazarene
- Churches of Christ
- Congregational
- Foursquare Gospel
- Lutheran
- Presbyterian Church in Australia
- Presbyterian Church in New Zealand
- Reformed Churches of Australia
- Salvation Army
- Seventh-day Adventist
- Uniting Church
- Wesleyan Methodist
- Westminster Presbyterian
- Plus some independent congregations, house churches and Christian communities

Additional support has come from participating denominations and Christian groups including The Bible Society, Christian Blind Mission International, The Uniting Church Investment Fund, African Enterprise, World Vision, Aware Insurance, The Leprosy Mission, Insight Books, Open Doors with Brother Andrew, Drug Awareness Council and ANSVAR.

Do you want further information or resources or would you like to be kept in touch? Simply use the survey hotlines or addresses:

|  | **Uniting Church Board of Mission** | **Anglican Home Mission Society** |
| --- | --- | --- |
|  | PO Box A2178 SYDNEY SOUTH 2000 | PO Box Q137 Queen Victoria Building SYDNEY 2000 |
| **Phone** | 02 285 4594 | 02 261 9500 |
| **Fax** | 02 267 7316 | 02 261 9599 |

NATIONAL
CHURCH
LIFE
SURVEY

# MISSION UNDER THE MICROSCOPE

**Keys to Effective and Sustainable Mission**

PETER KALDOR

JOHN BELLAMY

SANDRA MOORE

*Ruth Powell   Merilyn Correy   Keith Castle*

**National Church Life Survey**

The NCLS has produced a range of resources to assist the church in effective mission. A full set of resources is listed on page 153. The staff of the NCLS work as a team; while team members take on different primary responsibilities, all make a significant contribution. For further information, turn to page 179.

Copyright © 1995 National Church Life Survey

All rights reserved. No portion of this publication may be reproduced in any form or by any means without prior permission in writing from the publisher.

Cartoons and diagrams by Chris Morgan (Chris Cross Art)
Correspondence re cartoons to
PO Box 1939
ASHFIELD NSW 2131

Design by Kym Lynch developed from original concept by Chris Morgan

First printing January 1995

05 04 03 02 01 00 99 98 97 96 95   10 9 8 7 6 5 4 3 2 1

National Library of Australia
Cataloguing-in-Publication entry
Mission under the microscope: keys to effective and sustainable mission: National Church Life Survey.

   Bibliography.
   ISBN 0 85910 705 1.

   1. Evangelistic work. 2. Mission of the church. 3. Church and the world.
   4. Protestant churches – Australia.
   I. Kaldor, Peter.

266.022

Typeset in ITC Stone Serif, Helvetica Condensed and Copperplate Gothic

Published by
Openbook Publishers
205 Halifax Street
Adelaide, South Australia    1519–94

*The authors acknowledge the major
contributions of Bruce Dutton
(Fusion Australia) and Ian Robinson
(NSW Uniting Church Board of Mission)
in the shaping of this publication.*

---

Although more on the edges of church life than might be hoped, the creativity of some congregations is encouraging. These congregations are providing to all denominations a vision of possibility, for those who have eyes to see.

Too often, however, creative mission runs out of steam or doesn't renew itself or the wider church. What is needed is creative mission that is also *sustainable* mission, that builds on the creativity, affecting the wider community and renewing and building the gathered Christian community.

In this changing and diverse society it is vital that congregations put their mission under the microscope, and evaluate their mission strategies for their effectiveness and sustainability, and for their appropriateness to the particular community or group of people for whom they have a concern.

# ACKNOWLEDGMENTS

The National Church Life Survey is the product of the vision, energy and hard work of so many people. Thanks must go to:

- The 60 or so contact people in the 19 participating denominations and more than 1000 people who gave feedback on survey questions, design, pilot testing, manuscripts, printouts and so on.
- The project steering committee – Dean Drayton, John Reid, Harry Goodhew, Silas Horton, Peter Kaldor, Bob Moin, Carolyn Kitto, Geoff Huard and Reg Platt – for their ongoing support at each stage of the project.
- Chris Morgan for the cartoons which help make the statistics and issues come alive.
- Those who have gone to the trouble of reading various drafts of this manuscript in the midst of busy lives.
- Sponsors for their support.
- The thousands of congregational leaders and attenders who completed the survey.

**NCLS Staff Team**
Peter Kaldor (Project Director)
John Bellamy
Keith Castle
Merilyn Correy
Bob Moin
Sandra Moore
Ruth Powell
Joy Sanderson

In a rapidly changing world churches long to be successful. Really to be so they need to discover and sustain the mission to which God calls them. *Mission under the Microscope* is stimulating, balanced and helpful. It will assist churches to analyse and plan in order to become effective mission churches.

*Rev Dr Christopher Walker*
*Consultant for Mission and Evangelism*
*Uniting Church, Queensland Synod*

*Mission under the Microscope* is a forceful reminder that Good News is for sharing and challenges Christians to make God's news heard.

*Robyn Claydon*
*Chair, Lausanne Australia*

Any institution or organisation unwilling to change or adapt will die or become irrelevant. In *Mission under the Microscope*, the NCLS has provided the Australian church with another very useful tool to initiate theologically balanced and creative change in the local congregation. An excellent resource.

*Rev Peter Corney*
*Senior Minister, St Hilary's Anglican Church, Kew*
*and Director, Institute of Contemporary Christian Leadership*

With integrity this book sets a balanced ministry agenda for any congregation seeking to take God's mission seriously. The writers have presented the data we supplied, in ways which help us discover new possibilities for proclaiming the Kingdom in this emerging new world.

*Rev Dennis Obst*
*Mission Director, Lutheran Church, South Australia*

Mission – like life – is all about perspective. True to form, the NCLS provides the data for a clear, broad, realistic perspective on sustainable mission. It's a must for those wanting to be savvy with grass-roots-level evangelism in Australia.

*Rev Michael Frost*
*Morling Baptist Theological College, Sydney*

It's good to see solid, local material that encourages people into mission, that's based on thorough Australian research rather than imported enthusiasm and rhetoric.

*Mal Garvin*
*National Director, Fusion Australia*

Information such as is available in *Mission under the Microscope* is so very helpful as it enables us to recognise the challenges that are ahead of us, and with such a resource of information we can move toward meeting those challenges.

*Brian Houston*
*Senior Pastor, Hills Christian Life Centre, Sydney*

The Salvation Army has made extensive use of the National Church Life Survey research. Congregations with a commitment to growth will find this research to be essential in moving forward in mission.

*Capt. Christine Hewitt*
*Territorial Consultant for Growth, The Salvation Army, Sydney*

# CONTENTS

| | | |
|---|---|---|
| Prologue | **Sustainable mission** | ix |
| Introduction | **What does it mean 2000 years on?** | xiv |
| | Key terms in this book | xxiv |

### PART 1    SIGNPOSTS TO THE KINGDOM

| | | |
|---|---|---|
| Chapter 1 | **Blooming where planted** | 3 |
| | Contacts in everyday life | |
| Chapter 2 | **Where others meet** | 14 |
| | Involvement in community groups | |
| Chapter 3 | **Taking a stand** | 27 |
| | Involvement in social action groups | |
| Chapter 4 | **Involved together** | 37 |
| | Congregational mission activities | |

### PART 2    BEARERS OF THE WORD

| | | |
|---|---|---|
| Chapter 5 | **Readiness to share faith** | 55 |
| | An important prerequisite | |
| Chapter 6 | **Moving beyond the barriers** | 67 |
| | Equipping attenders for faith sharing | |
| Chapter 7 | **Getting on with it** | 82 |
| | Discussing faith and inviting others to church | |

### PART 3    MISSION IN THE CONGREGATION

| | | |
|---|---|---|
| Chapter 8 | **Opening the front door** | 99 |
| | Integrating and nurturing newcomers | |
| Chapter 9 | **Closing the back door** | 113 |
| | Retaining and nurturing the families of attenders | |
| Chapter 10 | **Owning faith** | 127 |
| | Conversion and public commitment | |
| Conclusions | **Mission under the Microscope** | 143 |
| Epilogue | **Making the most of the NCLS** | 153 |
| Appendix 1 | **About the survey** | 155 |
| Appendix 2 | **Additional survey questions** | 159 |
| Appendix 3 | **Congregational mission activities** | 166 |
| | What the churches are doing | |
| Useful references | | 174 |
| The NCLS team | | 179 |

# PROLOGUE
# SUSTAINABLE MISSION

The deacons of a small suburban congregation decided that a good way to reach the community, and provide a valuable community service, was to set up a kindergarten. After much effort from the entire congregation, fundraising and haggling with council, the kindergarten finally came into being. It required effort to administer and maintain. So much so, that attenders had little time to get involved in its life, to form relationships with the parents of children who attended or to establish links back into other aspects of congregational life.

While a valuable contribution to the wider community, as a bridge between congregation and community it required so much maintenance that there was no time for anybody to walk across it! Further, the lack of meaningful contact with the kindergarten sometimes created distrust among members of the kindergarten board and those in the church. The congregation failed to recognise the importance of relational as well as institutional bridges with the wider community.

It could have been different . . .

The leaders of a congregation in a regional centre were keen on the latest church growth literature. It advised congregations to make their building easily visible to passers-by, brighten their worship centre, produce quality printed literature and have an organised welcoming program. At great cost, the church was transformed, yet few new attenders joined, especially attenders without a church background. The leaders discovered that the congregation's members didn't have the skills or confidence to share their faith with others or invite them to church. Strategies for welcoming and integrating newcomers are important, but only if newcomers are visiting the church in the first place. The welcoming kits gathered dust in the foyer.

It could have been different . . .

Youth workers attached to a large congregation were very successful in connecting with the culture of kids on the street. Through their commitment and actions, the street kids caught glimmers of Jesus. Yet the youth workers could not find a church into which the young people could fit. The funding congregation was not culturally appropriate . . . and was unwilling to change. Disillusioned by the lack of young people in the church, the congregation began talking about pulling the plug on the funding.

However, the youth work team were unwilling to let the matter lie. They organised an evening at one of their homes, where the kids could discuss matters of faith in an informal and positive environment. One of the elders from the congregation became a strong advocate for the project, organising a prayer support network. A year later the elders council and the congregation began discussing the possibility of a new worship service.

What do these three congregations have in common? All had a heart for mission. All were willing to try new things and to invest their time, hard work and financial resources in mission activities. However, the problems associated with these projects demonstrate that it is one thing to explore mission possibilities and another to develop sustainable models of mission.

## A NEW ERA

In this era of rapid change and increasing choice, of insecurity and redefinition (Mackay, 1993), creative and sustainable mission is needed. Whether they like it or not, the churches have moved into a new era. The notion of Australia as a Christian country is disappearing. Social reasons for church attendance have declined. Traditional bridges with the wider community – such as Sunday school – are proving inadequate channels for connecting the Christian faith with the increasing social diversity of Australia.

Church attenders cannot assume that others they talk to in the wider community will be familiar with Christian teachings or jargon, or that they will automatically feel comfortable when visiting a congregation. Indeed, even existing attenders may feel little compulsion to stay involved with a congregation just because it was part of their upbringing, if it is not meeting their needs. In contemporary society there are a great many options for leisure, feeling part of a community or making sense of life.

Loren Mead suggests that the churches are being stretched between a great vision of the past and a new vision not yet fully formed. 'Our present confusion about mission hides the fact that we are facing a fundamental change in how we understand the mission of the church' (Mead, 1994, 5).

These are traumatic, yet invigorating, times. Traumatic, because many of the old ways no longer seem to be effective. Congregations are being challenged to move from a time where maintaining an open door was an adequate mission strategy to one where they must engage more intentionally with society.

Invigorating, because congregations following their calling are discovering exciting new options and ministries. Traditional styles of congregation are being augmented by new models: congregations that meet in schools, community centres and homes; congregations that serve special interest or ethnic groups; congregations that are exploring contemporary styles of worship or make creative use of small groups; congregations developing a more intentional mission focus, seeking to understand the communities they feel called to serve, building different bridges of relationship with those in the wider community. Such creativity has often emerged where congregations or groups of Christians have struggled together to discover their reason for existence, purpose and call.

## SUSTAINABLE MISSION

Such creativity is a positive sign for the churches, providing models which other congregations can learn from and apply to their own situations. Yet how do good ideas become part of a sustainable mission strategy? Too often evangelism strategies are spoken of without reference to nurture; social action initiatives are pursued in isolation from a theology of the gathered body of believers and its growth; church growth principles are implemented without reference to the specific needs of unchurched newcomers or groups that are hard to reach.

The different aspects of a mission strategy exist in relationship with each other. Congregations need to evaluate all aspects of what they do and how these relate together. Creative mission strategies are more likely to be sustainable if issues of context or community involvement are not considered in isolation from questions of nurture and the equipping of newcomers and existing attenders to live out their faith.

Of course, this is easier to say than to do. Key people move on or get involved with other groups. There will be many instances where a congregation or Christian group cannot provide all that is needed for sustainable mission and nurture. It is vital for congregations to reflect on all aspects of their life and ministry to discern directions for a positive future.

## MISSION UNDER THE MICROSCOPE

*Mission under the Microscope* seeks to:
- explore a number of important aspects of the mission of the church. The book looks at the extent to which attenders interact with others in the wider community, and how involved they are in community groups, social action or congregationally sponsored mission activities. It explores how comfortable they are about discussing their faith with others and how congregations can equip them in this area. It also examines the extent to which attenders invite others to church, what can be done to assist newcomers to fit into church life and the importance of assisting attenders to own their faith publicly.

- highlight the relationships that exist between these different aspects of mission. The research in this book will demonstrate that these aspects of mission do not exist in isolation, but are related to each other.

The main source of information for this book is analysis of the 1991 National Church Life Survey (NCLS). However, a survey of church attenders such as the NCLS cannot be prescriptive or comprehensive on all these issues. For instance, it does not include the perspectives of those in the wider community or those who have dropped out of church life. Nevertheless, the results provide a wealth of insights into effective mission strategies.

*Mission under the Microscope* can help congregations in two ways. First, it provides readers with a framework with which to evaluate their congregation's life and mission. It provides an overview of the church at large as a backdrop against which individual congregations can compare themselves.

Second, the survey results provide pointers for congregations in each of the critical areas of mission covered in this book. Wherever possible, suggestions are provided to assist congregations to move forward.

## JUST A MATTER OF MODELS?

While this book is about describing trends, patterns and principles, it is important to acknowledge at the outset that God is at work in the world. The mission of the church will not be accomplished by technological sophistication alone or unthinking adherence to a set of rules propounded by sociologists or growth gurus! The real world seldom fits neat theoretical models.

As this book was being finalised, an NCLS team member went to a reunion of people involved in an inner-city mission team. It was a ministry that had been very successful in its contacting and care, yet it had failed to integrate people into any churches or develop an appropriate gathered community of believers. In retrospect, it was far from a model of sustainable mission.

Part of the ministry included support to street teenagers. Steve was a very difficult teenager who dropped out of school, was hooked on drugs and broke into and stole from the homes of those in the ministry. The team provided love and support and taught him to read. Yet it seemed to have little impact at the time and Steve was last seen on one of his regular stints in prison.

To everybody's surprise, Steve was at the reunion, accompanied by a wife and two young children. In a stable job for more than five years, Steve came to say thankyou. During one of his periods in gaol, he received letters from a Christian expressing her care for those in prison. After parole he made contact with her and the rest is history!

Some sow, others reap! Sustainable mission may result from the faithful activity of two or more unrelated groups following their sense of call. One reader of an early draft of this book commented that some of the mission activities she had been involved with had seemed crazy and unsustainable at the time, yet in her view: 'God had worked through them, people had come to faith and she had learnt a lot!' In reflecting on the mission of their congregations and how the aspects relate together, people must not ignore their callings and passions, but rather explore how best to express them.

May all those who read *Mission under the Microscope* find it a useful sociological resource. May those with a Christian faith remember that God is not confined by trends, statistics, golden rules or key principles.

It is our fervent hope that *Mission under the Microscope* will be a useful resource to aid the mission of the church.

Peter Kaldor<br>
John Bellamy<br>
Sandra Moore<br>
on behalf of the NCLS team

## INTRODUCTION

# WHAT DOES IT MEAN 2000 YEARS ON?

A key issue for any organisation in the '90s is how well it implements its mission. Few people who spend hours helping their community or company achieve its mission know that they are using a word which was adapted by the early church to define its purpose.

The word *mission* is derived from the Latin word *missio*, which means 'sent'. In John 20, when Jesus, the resurrected Lord, greeted his frightened disciples, he said: 'As the Father has sent me, so I send you'. The disciples were empowered by the Spirit to be a 'sent' or a 'mission' people, who were to announce God's decisive action to the planet.

Archbishop Temple once pointed out that the church is one of the few institutions created in the interests of non-members! The Great Commandment and Great Commission point to this outward focus:

'You shall love the Lord your God with all your heart, and with all your soul, and with all your strength, and with all your mind; and your neighbour as yourself.' (Luke 10:27)

'Go therefore and make disciples of all nations.' (Matthew 28:19)

The first Christians formed a worshipping community that provided both instruction in the faith and help for those who lacked the means of support. Church leaders not only nurtured this new community; they also sought to disseminate the faith and establish new worshipping communities. To the Jewish communities and to the whole Roman world, they became bearers of the good news of Jesus Christ and signposts to God's kingdom in both word and deed.

## THINKING ABOUT MISSION

Today, different traditions have different emphases as to what constitutes mission and its place in the life of the church. These differences are in part theological and in part contextual. Yet there is much common ground as well.

In the early 1800s, national governments in Europe recognised for the first time non-conformist religious groups as denominations. During the 19th century many denominations developed. Citizens were able to choose which denomination they would belong to, whereas previously they belonged to the national church of the land or joined another church group at the risk of being denied access to many positions in society.

The growing availability of choice and of denominations, alongside many other contextual factors, gave rise to different theological and missional emphases; some churches emphasised the importance of evangelism in the conversion of individuals in society, while others emphasised the social responsibility of the churches in the wider community.

## Evangelism

The gospel or *good news* refers to the coming of the kingdom of God in Jesus Christ. The Lord Jesus' life, teaching and works, culminating in his death and resurrection, reveal the kingdom of God to humanity (Walker, 1988, 1).

The essence of evangelism is the proclamation of the gospel. To 'evangelise' is to communicate the good news about Jesus to those who do not know him. The proclamation of the gospel carries with it an invitation to repentance and recognition of the lordship of Jesus Christ. It brings with it forgiveness of sins, a call to discipleship and new relations with God (Stromberg, 1983, 18; Samuel and Hauser, 1989, 213).

## Social concern

Social concern can take a variety of forms. For many Christians it involves living their lives for the good of society, and includes acts of service to meet human need. Churches have become some of the largest private sector providers of social services and welfare in Australia.

For some, the gospel implies going beyond works of service to changing the structure of society. For instance, the World Council of Churches has affirmed the need to participate in struggles for justice in different parts of the world.

Such social action seems to have a higher priority among people from the Developing World, where issues of injustice and suffering can be seen in more clarity. Christians in the Developing World have also been in the vanguard of a shift in attitude among evangelical Christians towards social action, as expressed at successive Lausanne Conferences on Evangelism (Samuel and Hauser, 1989, 200–207).

## Holding the tension

These different emphases have generated debate within the churches. Holding an appropriate tension between evangelism and social action has not always been easy.

Some have sought to resolve this tension by speaking of 'holistic evangelism' which includes care for the body as well as the soul. Others see social action as evangelistic in itself: when social concerns are

THE ANNUAL MISSION'S BIKE RACE WAS A HIGHPOINT FOR EVERYONE. EVERYONE EXCEPT THE "WORD ONLY" TEAM FROM ST. LUKE'S AND THE "DEED ONLY" TEAM FROM ST. MICHAEL'S.

addressed, the gospel may receive a better hearing. Still others dismiss evangelism without social action as an inadequate response to the needs of people, favouring social action as the greater priority.

In contrast, those who consider evangelism to be the major priority often see personal salvation as the greatest human need and at the heart of God's mission mandate for the church. They are sometimes wary that an agenda of social change may jeopardise the fulfilment of this basic mandate.

What do Australian church attenders think? As was noted in a previous NCLS publication, *Winds of Change* (p 61), some 16% place their priority on evangelism alone, 39% on evangelism with social action, 14% on social action with evangelism and 5% on social action alone. Clearly, attenders have different priorities for the mission of the church; however, the majority see a need to hold the two aspects in some sort of balance.

In writing this book, it was recognised that readers would have different understandings of mission. Nevertheless, there is also much in common; most Christian traditions accept the importance of both word and action.

The NCLS included indicators of both evangelism and social concern. Indeed, on the ground, mission activities often incorporate both evangelism and social concern. Although congregations may have a particular priority, the two aspects frequently become intertwined. In the writing of *Mission under the Microscope*, it was impossible to prevent a degree of such intertwining.

## AND WHAT OF TODAY?

How can congregations fulfil their mission in an era of change? What do the Great Commandment and the Great Commission mean in a time of changing family structures and in a society with consistently high levels of unemployment? Who is a neighbour in a global village? What does 'go to all people everywhere' mean in a technological age when the ends of the earth are on the doorstep? How do the churches effectively communicate the gospel to the diverse ethnic, socio-economic, generational and interest groups that comprise Australian society?

The data on newcomers to church life, presented in *Winds of Change* (p 263), show that Australians are willing to consider the Christian option if it is presented in a credible way. The challenge for the churches is to present the gospel appropriately to the Australian community.

In dealing with change, some church leaders have been caught flat-footed. Some believe the particular models and methods of mission they have been brought up with should remain for all time, and they are unnerved by the need for new directions and new ways of mission.

Yet, while the Great Commission and the Great Commandment are timeless, the way they have been lived out has changed from era to era. The mission of the church has taken many forms as the church has related to different people, cultures and contexts. As an agent of mission, the church has been underground cells in times of persecution, parishes in the Roman Empire, monasteries in hostile environments, community centres of meaning and hope, places of refuge, guardians of truth and conveyors of compassion. New forms and shifts in priorities were needed to adapt to life in the Middle Ages, to the Enlightment and to the changes in the Industrial Revolution (Bosch, 1991, 181).

In every age and context, however fallibly, the church has given shape to its mission in different ways. In the present age, new models of mission and ministry are needed once again.

## SUSTAINABLE MISSION

The Great Commission and Great Commandment highlight the outward focus of discipleship. At the same time, there is also an emphasis from the inception of the Christian church on the gathered body of believers.

The early church was an important place for nurture, accountability and discernment of God's will. Newcomers were encouraged to join into its life. As they did, the church itself recognised its need to change and adapt to incorporate newcomers appropriately while maintaining authenticity to the gospel. The church's struggle over the place of circumcision and the law, recorded in the book of Acts, is an early example of this (Acts 15).

The NCLS acknowledged the importance of both an outward focus and the gathered body of believers by suggesting that congregations interact with their communities in two primary ways.

First, a congregation can assist people to understand and grow in the Christian faith by encouraging its members to become involved with those in the wider community where they live and work and providing, by word and deed, signposts to God's kingdom. In *Winds of Change* (p xix) this has been termed the *incarnational* aspect of the church's interaction with the wider community.

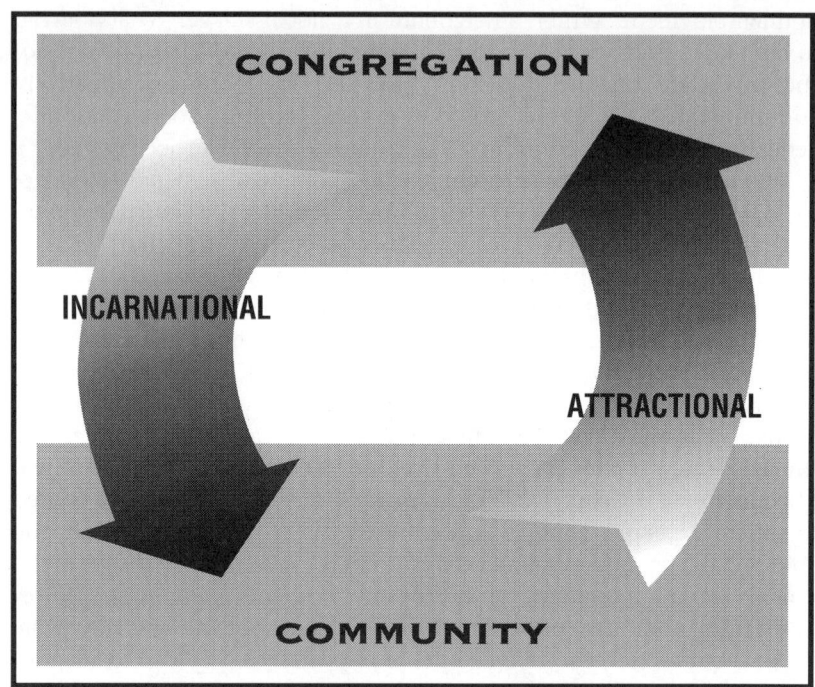

Second, a congregation can encourage exploration of the Christian faith by attracting people from the wider community into its life and worship. People may be invited by church attenders to explore the faith in the congregation, or they may be attracted to the congregation for other reasons.

This aspect of the church's life and mission has been called the *attractional* aspect. It also includes the nurturing of existing attenders and their families, as well as newcomers without a background in church attendance.

A sustainable mission strategy takes seriously both the incarnational and attractional aspects and their relationship to each other. It is likely to involve several key components.

## CONTACT WITH THE WIDER COMMUNITY

A necessary prerequisite for mission is that a congregation is in contact with the community for which it has a concern. A congregation with little community contact is likely to become a closed system, and one probably headed for decline.

Contact with the wider community can happen in various ways. It can be **personal** or **impersonal**. Personal activity includes any action in which a person involved with the congregation comes into direct contact with a person in the wider community. Impersonal activities are more 'arms-length', such as advertising, letterbox drops or letter-writing campaigns.

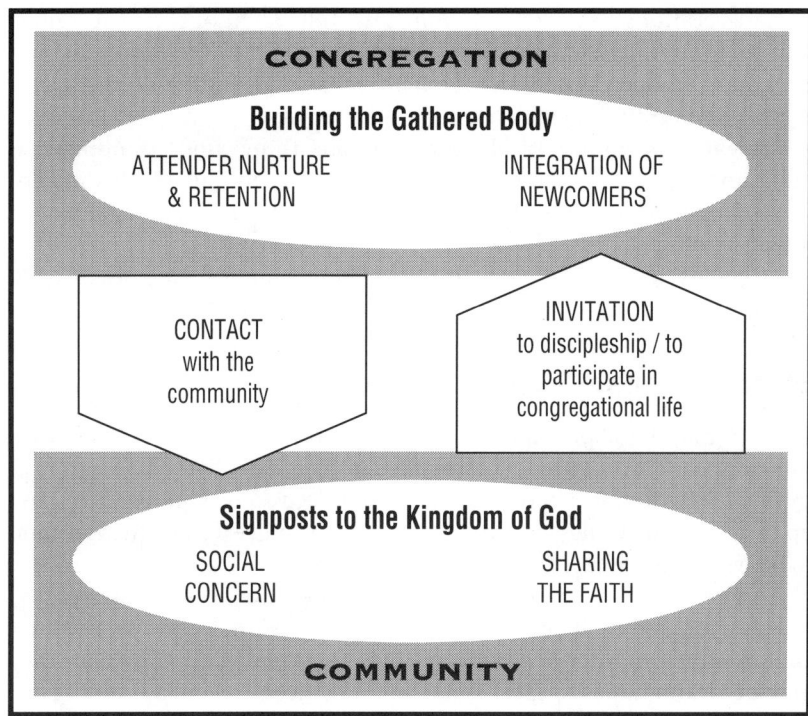

There are many possible avenues for personal contact. First, attenders are involved with other people in their workplace, home life, and interests. Such contexts can provide opportunities for discussing faith, offering love and care, modelling right relationships, contributing to the country's future directions and so on.

Second, attenders can be involved individually in community groups and organisations, including local community care groups, social action and lobby groups, overseas aid and justice groups.

Third, a congregation can organise mission activities such as evangelistic programs, visitation programs and community care activities.

Congregations may pursue wider contact in many different ways. At one end of the spectrum are congregations that have an array of structured mission/service activities; at the other are congregations whose main focus is equipping their attenders to 'bloom where they are planted' within their natural social networks.

Then again, there are many congregations with little outward focus or contact with the wider community.

As part of evaluating their levels of wider community contact, congregations may need to discern more consciously those with whom they are called to be in mission. In some cases this may be a local area; in others, congregations may have a more regional focus. Still others may have a concern for a particular group of people.

Congregations also need to examine the full extent of personal contact that their attenders have with others in the community. Becoming and remaining an open system may be hard or easy, depending on the nature of the community in which a congregation exists.

Knowing a community of concern is one thing; understanding it is quite another! Every community and culture is unique, with different needs, hopes, struggles and styles of expression. Contact is a vital part of understanding.

Attenders' levels of contact with the wider community are discussed in Part 1.

## BEING SIGNPOSTS TO THE KINGDOM

Contact may be a prerequisite for sustainable mission, but it is not a sufficient condition. Attenders are called in their daily lives to be signposts to God's kingdom in word and deed. They need to be equipped to stand up for Christian values, to live out their faith in everyday situations and to be willing to discuss their faith with others.

Congregations need to encourage attenders to be signposts to the kingdom of God in all aspects of their lives – at work, home, in the local community or in interest groups to which they belong. As Christians they may need sometimes to speak out about injustices, to lend a listening ear, or to provide love and care. Aspects of this are examined in Part 1.

Congregations also need to equip attenders to assist others to explore faith and to talk about their faith. Many attenders have difficulty in this area. This is explored in Part 2.

## BUILDING THE GATHERED BODY

Helping others to explore matters of faith can occur in two ways. People in the wider community coming into contact with church attenders may be encouraged to explore faith within the context of their everyday lives. Alternatively, or in addition, they may be invited to explore matters of faith within the life of a congregation.

At its heart, the Christian faith has an important corporate dimension. Jesus told his disciples: 'Where two or three are gathered in my name, I am there among them' (Matthew 18:20). The various sectors of the church affirm the idea that a response to the gospel involves joining a community of faith. For instance, the World Council of Churches sees that the responsibility of the church is to 'continue sowing seeds until there is a church in every human community' (Stromberg, 1983, 79). Raymond Fung describes it as an invitation to outsiders to worship God, which may precede or follow an invitation to discipleship (1992, 4).

Writers in the evangelical stream identify the incorporation of people into churches as an outcome of evangelism (eg Engel and Norton, 1975; Gibbs, 1981, McGavran, 1988). As Australian author Peter Corney observes, evangelism is not complete until people have been 'grafted into the church and taught to obey Jesus' commands' (1991, 21).

How do new attenders come to join a community of faith? The majority join as a result of personal invitation and relationship. This is explored in Chapter 7.

## INTEGRATING NEWCOMERS

In times past, many congregations believed that people in the wider community had a Christian upbringing and understood their language, traditions and teachings. 'Mission' was out there, somewhere geographically remote. The issue of integrating newcomers without a church background simply wasn't on the agenda.

In more recent times, congregations have started to realise that there are missionary frontiers in their own backyards. However, often there has been little thought put into integrating and nurturing newcomers who are culturally different from other attenders.

Congregations need to examine how they are integrating and nurturing newcomers into congregational life. The level of newcomers provides a measure of the extent to which a congregation is actually connected to the wider 'unchurched' sections of the Australian community. This issue is explored in Chapter 8.

SEACLIFF BAPTIST CHURCH, WITH A SPECIAL MINISTRY TO LEMMINGS, WERE JUSTIFIABLY PROUD OF THEIR INTAKE OF NEWCOMERS.

## RETAINING AND NURTURING EXISTING ATTENDERS

While newcomers are a vital sign of hope, existing attenders and their families form the backbone of the churches. Retaining and nurturing this core is essential and sometimes as difficult as integrating newcomers. The large declines in attendance in the late '60s and '70s was the result of the defection of a large core of 'baby boom' attenders, who felt the faith of their childhood was not touching the issues of their adulthood or resonating with the hopes of their generation.

Congregations need to reflect on where attenders go once they leave their congregation. Are they joining another one? And if not, why? Some communities have highly mobile populations. Congregations in such areas will find their attenders move on frequently. Retaining attenders within the life of the church may involve helping them to link up with a new congregation in their new community. Levels of retention, particularly of the children of attenders, are the subject of Chapter 9.

Another critical aspect for both newcomers and existing attenders and their families is the extent to which attenders come to own their faith and make it real in their lives. It has been said that people own their values when they do so publicly. Many congregations offer attenders opportunities to make public commitments to their faith. Attenders who own their faith are more likely to take it seriously and be strengthened through it. The importance of owning faith is discussed in Chapter 10.

## MOVING FORWARD IN MISSION

Congregations need to evaluate each aspect of their mission and ministry and how they relate to each other, to identify strengths and areas for further growth. The accompanying table suggests some key issues, each of which is dealt with in a chapter of *Mission under the Microscope*.

---

**Sustainable mission: some key issues**

- What are the levels of contact between attenders and the wider community?
- How involved are attenders in community groups of different sorts?
- To what extent are attenders concerned about and involved in social action in their community and the wider society?
- How involved are attenders in congregational mission activities?
- How comfortable are attenders talking about their faith?
- What are the barriers to attenders sharing their faith and how can they be helped to move beyond them?
- How willing are attenders to invite others to church activities?
- How well are newcomers being integrated into the life of the congregation?
- What are the levels of retention of existing attenders and their families?
- How can attenders be helped to own and grow in their faith?

---

In evaluating their ministry and mission, congregations need to bear in mind the impact of external factors on their corporate life. Some external factors which need to be considered include local factors, such as the ethnicity and socio-economic character of the local community, and national factors, including trends such as secularisation, pluralism and materialism (Hoge and Roozen, 1979).

There is much research which suggests that context affects church life. For instance, the *Who Goes Where?* study suggests that church attendance rates in Sydney are several times higher in certain types of local community than in others (Kaldor, 1987, 83). Many researchers have explored the impact of the external environment on the growth and decline of churches (eg Hoge and Roozen, 1979; Currie, Gilbert and Horsley, 1977; Roof, 1978).

Effective mission planning, then, will not just be about internal change and programs within the congregation. It will also be about gaining an appreciation of the wider community and the impact it can have on church life.

## ABOUT THIS BOOK

*Mission under the Microscope* invites readers on a journey of reflection on key aspects of creative and sustainable mission. It follows the different components of the model just described, sharing results, implications and priorities for mission that emerge.

*Part 1, Signposts to the Kingdom*, looks at attender involvement with the wider community, including patterns of involvement with:
- other people generally;
- community organisations other than the church;
- environmental, peace and justice, overseas aid and morals groups;
- congregational mission activities.

In *Part 2, Bearers of the Word*, the focus shifts to evangelism. The chapters in this part deal successively with:
- attenders' attitudes towards discussing their faith with others;
- moving beyond the barriers to faith sharing;
- patterns of faith sharing and inviting others to church.

*Part 3, Mission in the Congregation*, looks at issues of integration into congregational life, including:
- how newcomers are integrated into congregational life;
- retaining and nurturing existing attenders and their families; and
- the importance of owning faith.

# KEY TERMS IN THIS BOOK

*Mission under the Microscope* is part of a series of publications from the NCLS covering different facets of church life. While every endeavour has been made to keep jargon to a minimum, it is inevitable that in a series of books some terms and concepts will be used that were developed in a previous work.

Some readers will be familiar with the NCLS and previous publications. For others, this may be a first contact. For those unfamiliar with the NCLS, details of the survey are provided in Appendix 1.

A range of terms related to church background reappear throughout this book. To understand the discussion for each topic, readers will need to be familiar with these terms, which are described below. The relevant survey questions used in creating these categories are shown in Appendix 2. There are a number of additional survey questions referred to in this book which are also outlined in Appendix 2.

It should be noted that the statistics in the tables may not add to 100% because of rounding error.

---

**Denomination**

The denominations involved in the NCLS were, for simplicity, grouped into four categories:

**Mainstream** (heritage of being an established or state church in another country): Anglican, Uniting, Presbyterian, Lutheran.

**Pentecostal:** Assemblies of God, Foursquare Gospel, Christian Revival Crusade, Apostolic.

**Large Protestant** (based on overall size in Australia): Baptist, Churches of Christ, Salvation Army, Seventh-day Adventist.

**Small Protestant** (based on overall size in Australia): Congregational, Wesleyan Methodist, Christian & Missionary Alliance, Reformed Churches, Church of the Nazarene, Westminster Presbyterian.

## Patterns of faith

While many variables were available to explore patterns of faith, one indicator of attitude to the Bible has been frequently used.

**Literalists:** people who believe the Bible is the word of God to be taken literally word for word.

**Contextualists:** people who believe the Bible is the word of God which needs to be read in the context of the times to understand its implications for us today.

**Valuists:** people who believe the Bible is a valuable book, parts of which reveal God's word to us or that it is a valuable book with much to teach us. (Responses for these two categories were too similar to separate.)

Attender attitudes towards 'speaking in tongues' and the influence of various theological traditions have also been used in exploring patterns of faith.

## Congregational involvement

A summary index was derived based on indicators of congregational involvement.

**Non-worshippers:** people who do not regularly attend worship services.

**Infrequent worshippers:** people who attend worship services less than monthly.

**Frequent worshippers:** people who attend services at least monthly, but do not attend any other activities.

**The more involved:** people who attend worship services at least monthly and also attend other groups within the life of the congregation. These attenders spend on average less than six hours a week in congregational life.

**The highly involved:** people who attend worship at least monthly, are involved in other groups and spend six or more hours per week in congregational life.

**The employed:** people employed by the church, including clergy and ordained persons, as well as a wide range of lay workers.

## Background of attenders

Attenders' length of attendance and history of involvement:

**Visitors:** people visiting the congregation in which they completed the survey forms.

**Newcomers:** people who have attended their present congregation for fewer than five years and who previously were not attending regularly anywhere else.

**Switchers:** people who have attended their present congregation for fewer than five years and previously were attending a congregation of a different denomination.

**Transfers:** people who have attended a congregation for fewer than five years and previously were attending a congregation of the same denomination.

**Long-term attenders:** people who have attended their present congregation for more than five years.

PART 1

# SIGNPOSTS TO THE KINGDOM

When observers of church life talk about effective congregations, they too often equate effectiveness with numerical growth. Certainly most quantitative research has adopted this approach. While important, numerical growth on its own does not provide an adequate measure of congregational 'connectedness' with the wider community.

The NCLS included indicators of wider community contact and involvement. These are the subject of this part. It also included some questions about discussion of matters of faith, which are the focus of Part 2.

As was noted in the Introduction, there are various avenues for attenders to be involved in wider community life. In their everyday lives, attenders are in contact with people in the workplace, in the home and in the neighbourhood. Attenders can get involved in community groups of various sorts, including welfare, care and social action groups. They can be involved in congregationally sponsored mission activities, either evangelistic or with a social care/action emphasis. A chapter is devoted to each of these avenues of contact.

These measures are not comprehensive but are indicators of congregational involvement in the wider community. Taken together, they can provide a picture of levels of contact with the wider community and some aspects of the nature of that involvement. They provide a starting point for further reflection.

CHAPTER 1

# BLOOMING WHERE PLANTED

**Contacts in everyday life**

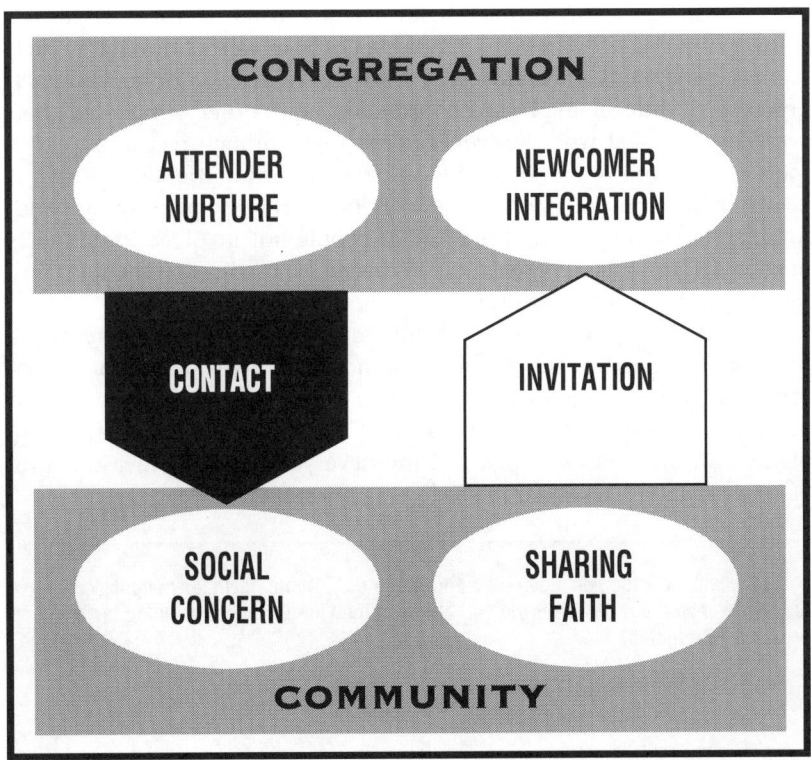

Significant contact with others in the community is an important starting point for mission. Schools, tertiary institutions and workplaces are vital contact points, which may play a key role in a congregation's mission strategy.

Congregations can be in contact with the wider community in a myriad of ways. Some of this contact is formal; for instance, through church services, mission activities and Sunday schools, as well as through church schools, playgroups and counselling services. The vast majority of contact, however, is informally between attenders and other people in their everyday lives – at work, university or school, through recreation clubs, sport or community groups, and with neighbours and friends.

Informal community contact may often be a starting point for mission. Attenders who have little contact with people not involved in churches may be helping their congregations to become closed systems, cut off and separate from the community.

The NCLS explored levels of attender involvement in the wider community, including the degree of contact and where it takes place. Most importantly, it explored the relationship between levels of contact and mission, to demonstrate how important it is for attenders to 'bloom where planted' in the various contexts of their everyday lives. To measure level of contact, the NCLS asked the following question.

> **Look back over the last week (at work, home etc). About how many people *not involved with any churches* did you talk with individually about anything for *at least* 15 minutes?**
>
>     a. none
>     b. 1–2 people
>     c. 3–5 people
>     d. 6–10 people
>     e. 11–20 people
>     f. over 20 people

This question is an indicator of contact only. The 15-minute time frame was used because it was considered significant enough for attenders to remember. Most people could not begin to count the number of contacts they have if brief encounters such as in shops and banks and on public transport are included. However, people can sometimes make meaningful contact in a shorter time, while some long conversations may be relatively insignificant.

## IN CONTACT WITH THE COMMUNITY?

The good news is that the Australian church is in contact with those in the wider community. Attenders have contact with an average of 6.6 non-churchgoers each week. However, looking at the average can be a little misleading.

At one extreme, 12% of attenders have significant contacts with more than 20 non-church people each week. These attenders would include people whose work involves significant interaction with others, such as journalists, health workers and managers. At the other extreme, 16% of attenders do not have any contact with non-church people, while another 23% have contact with only one or two.

*Some 16% of attenders do not have any contact with non-church people*

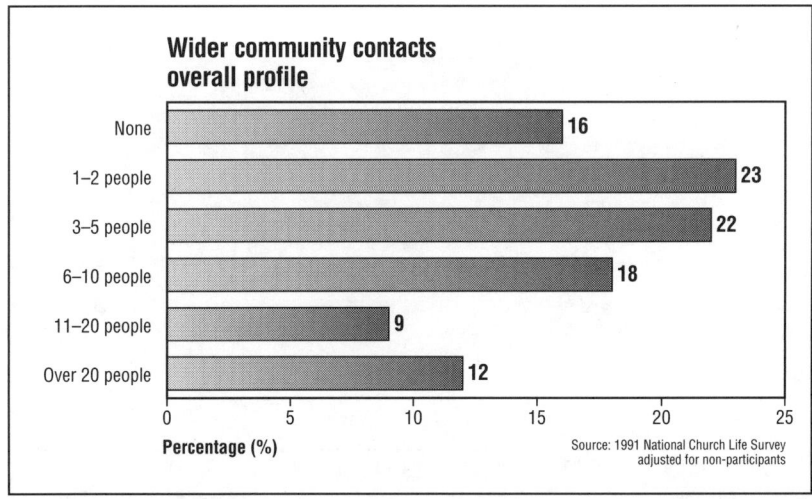

Figure 1.1

This is a significant issue. If the church needs to be where the people are, then attenders must be in contact with the wider community. Yet four out of 10 attenders have little such contact.

This data is not only relevant to mission; it also has important pastoral implications. No doubt some attenders with low levels of wider contact have a supportive network of church friends and family. However, some may be isolated and lonely, seeing few people each week. Others may have many casual contacts, but lack relationships of any depth.

Obviously, not everyone is able to increase their level of contact. Some people, because of age or illness, may need care from their congregation. Others, such as those under severe stress, may need personal space.

Congregations where attenders have little wider contact may want to consider starting activities that put attenders in touch with others. Examples include over-60s clubs, mothers' groups and youth ministries, but the options are as vast as a congregation's imagination and need to be developed to suit the make-up of the particular congregation and the community or group for which it has a concern. Congregational-based activities are examined in Chapter 4.

Alternatively, such congregations can encourage attenders to get to know better those in their street or workplace, or to get involved in community groups or networks at work or clubs. Attender involvement in such groups is the subject of Chapters 2 and 3.

## THE YOUNG HAVE MORE CONTACT

The number of contacts attenders have with non-churchgoers is strongly related to their age. Attenders aged 15 to 19 years have an average of 9.4 contacts each week, compared to 7.2 for attenders aged 40 to 49 years and just 4.1 for attenders aged over 70 years.

Figure 1.2

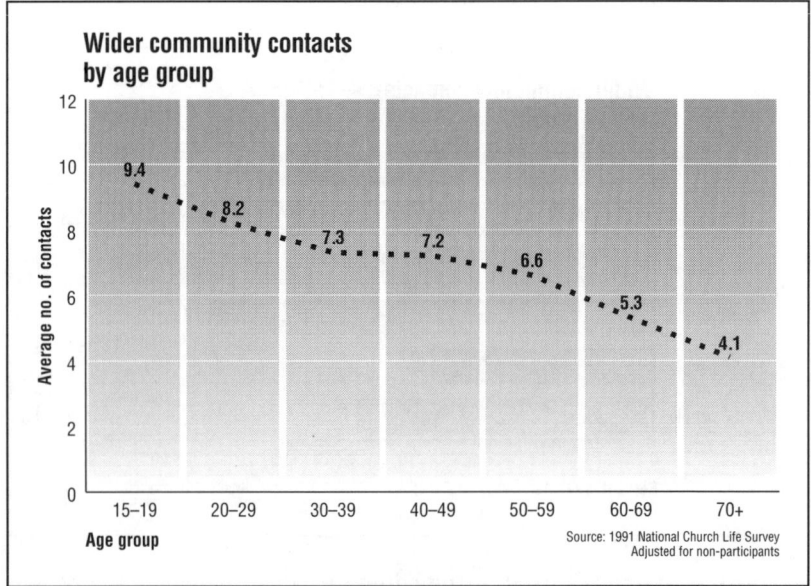

This is in line with some other research. For instance, researchers Larson and Bradney found that the amount of time people spend with coworkers and strangers decreases from the 20s onwards, declining significantly after retirement, while the amount of time spent alone increases with age (1988, 118).

Young people can have an important role in mission. Their number of contacts, combined with enthusiasm and openness, can make them important links to the wider community. While it may sometimes be threatening, leaders and congregations with a heart for mission will want to encourage young people and give them a voice in creating a church environment which they can own and want to share with their friends.

## VITAL CONTACT POINTS

Two of the most fruitful places for wider community contact are schools and tertiary institutions. School and tertiary students have an average of 9.1 contacts each week, well above the average of attenders overall.

Workplaces are also significant. In *Growing an Everyday Faith*, Ian Robinson (1991, 98) points out that work is the place where the church most often meets the world in a significant way. The NCLS confirms this. Full-time workers (8.3), part-time workers (7.4) and the self-employed (7.1) have considerably more contacts than attenders with family responsibilities (5.1), unemployed people (5.1) or retired people (4.6).

*Schools and workplaces are vital contact points*

| Wider community contacts by type of employment | Average no. of contacts |
|---|---|
| **Overall** | **6.6** |
| Full-time salary earner | 8.3 |
| **Part-time worker** | **7.4** |
| Self-employed | 7.1 |
| **Retired** | **4.6** |
| Unemployed | 5.1 |
| **Student** | **9.1** |
| Family duties | 5.1 |

Source: 1991 National Church Life Survey attender data adjusted for non-participants

Figure 1.3

Many Christian groups have recognised the importance of the workplace as a mission field. Ray Bakke, who lectures and writes on urban ministry, notes the importance of the workplace to urban people. Bakke urges church leaders to visit people at their workplace, both to help them to minister in their work environment and to increase understanding of the issues they face there (Bakke, 1987, 152–153).

Some groups are seeking to address this issue by organising networks of business people to develop a vision for their community and implement Christian values in the workplace. Christian professional associations hold events to which members can invite their colleagues, while Christian fellowships meet in some large organisations. More recently, there have been moves to put chaplains into workplaces and to attach them to sporting teams.

Congregations also need to operate creatively in the midst of work environments, be they city office blocks or industrial areas. Attenders may find value in mid-week worship services, discussion groups or activities that they can attend with their friends. Such options would help attenders who are reluctant to invite work colleagues to their own church if their

NADINE, WHO HAD BEEN SEARCHING FOR A WAY TO WITNESS IN HER WORKPLACE, QUICKLY REALISED THAT THIS WAS NOT IT...

colleagues live half a city away. This will be particularly true if attenders are part of a locally focused congregation where a work colleague may feel an outsider.

At the same time, *Winds of Change* (p 94) suggests that people may be more willing to travel larger distances to attend church than many might expect, just as they do for sporting fixtures, concerts and other events. Outsiders may be more willing to travel and visit congregations than attenders are to invite them.

Helping attenders connect their faith with the issues of the workplace is an important priority for congregations and their leaders. The NCLS has found that 68% of employed attenders feel their faith and church involvement helps them greatly in their home life, but only 48% feel it helps greatly in their work life.

## DENOMINATION MAKES LITTLE DIFFERENCE

As was shown in *Winds of Change*, there is a strong link between denomination and many facets of church life. However, in the area of contacts, denomination makes little difference. Attenders generally have similar levels of contact with non-church people, regardless of their denomination and the numerical growth of their congregation. The exceptions are the Seventh-day Adventist (5.3), Lutheran (5.5) and Reformed (5.5) Churches, where attenders generally have lower levels of contact with outsiders.

Similarly, NCLS data suggests that, on average, attenders' levels of contact are much the same regardless of their view of the Bible or attitude to speaking in tongues. The level of contact is only slightly related to

Figure 1.4

| Wider community contacts by denomination | Average no. of contacts |
|---|---|
| **Overall** | **6.6** |
| Anglican | 7.2 |
| Apostolic | 6.8 |
| Assemblies of God | 6.8 |
| Baptist | 6.7 |
| Christian & Missionary Alliance | 6.7 |
| Christian Revival Crusade | 6.8 |
| Church of the Nazarene | 6.2 |
| Churches of Christ | 6.5 |
| Congregational | 6.6 |
| Foursquare Gospel | 6.4 |
| Lutheran | 5.5 |
| NZ Presbyterian | 6.6 |
| Presbyterian | 6.4 |
| Reformed | 5.5 |
| Salvation Army | 6.5 |
| Seventh-day Adventist | 5.3 |
| Uniting | 6.7 |
| Wesleyan Methodist | 6.6 |
| Westminster Presbyterian | 6.3 |
| House Churches | 9.1 |
| **Type of denomination** | |
| Mainstream | 6.8 |
| Pentecostal | 6.8 |
| Large Protestant | 6.4 |
| Small Protestant | 6.2 |

Source: 1991 National Church Life Survey attender data adjusted for non-participants

congregational size and is unrelated to numerical growth of a congregation.

## INVOLVEMENT DOESN'T REDUCE CONTACT

A positive finding of the NCLS, discussed in *Winds of Change* (pp 131–137), is that the majority of attenders make friends within their congregation. The down side of this might be that as attenders become integrated into congregational life, they gradually lose touch with people in the wider community who are not part of a church. If this were so, attenders who are highly involved in church could be expected to have lower levels of contact with non-church people since they spend more of their time with one another.

The NCLS suggests that this is not the case. In fact, the reverse is true. Attenders who spend more than six hours each week in congregational activities have an average of 7.9 contacts, compared to an average of 6.6

for attenders generally. There may be several explanations for this. First, involvement in church may motivate attenders to be involved in mission. Many sharing/study groups encourage wider concern and regularly pray for non-church contacts and wider social issues. Highly involved attenders may seek wider contacts as part of their personal commitment to mission.

Alternatively, the link may be a function of personality. Some people are more likely to join groups and organisations and to thrive on contact of all types.

Whatever the reason, these findings undercut suggestions that attenders who are highly immersed in congregational life will become cut off from the wider community. Instead of binding them, congregational participation can give attenders the motivation to be involved in the wider community and the support they need to discuss their faith with others.

## INVOLVEMENT IN COMMUNITY GROUPS

Apart from everyday life contacts, attenders can make wider contact through involvement in community groups or congregational mission activities. The number of contacts attenders have with non-church people increases with their involvement in community organisations. Attenders

REV. TAYLOR WOULD OFTEN RELIVE THAT FATEFUL "COMMUNITY INVOLVEMENT" SERMON IN WHICH HE OMITTED TO MENTION COMING BACK TO CHURCH.

who have some involvement with a community organisation have an average of 7.2 contacts, compared to 5.3 for attenders with no such involvement. Attenders who are involved in both community welfare and social action groups have an average of 9.3 contacts with non-church people each week, compared to 6.3 for attenders who are not involved in either type of group. Attenders who are involved in community groups may be able to play a key role in their congregation's mission strategy.

While all groups are valuable sources of contact, some are associated with higher levels of contact, including professional associations (10.1), political organisations (8.6), school groups (7.9), sporting organisations (7.4), charities and service organisations (7.3) and arts/amateur theatre groups (7.5).

## CONTACTS AND EVANGELISM

A high level of contact with the wider community does not of itself equate with standing for Christian values, discussing faith or inviting others to church. Indeed, in a survey such as the NCLS it is not possible to evaluate fully the impact of attenders' contacts with others. That would require a view from the community rather than from the perspective of attenders.

The NCLS included a range of questions on discussing matters of faith with others. One question probed how comfortable attenders feel about discussing their faith and whether they look for opportunities to do so. Attenders who are comfortable discussing their faith, and who actively seek opportunities to do so, do not necessarily have more community contacts than attenders who prefer not to talk about their faith.

However, while readiness to discuss faith is not related to levels of contact, opportunities to do so are. Attenders with higher levels of contact are more likely to share their faith with more people. A third of attenders who have only one or two contacts each week have shared their faith with a few or several people in the past year, compared to 44% of attenders who have 20 contacts or more.

*Attenders with higher levels of contact are more likely to share their faith*

In addition, attenders who have successfully invited someone to church in the past year are likely to have more contacts than those who have not. Attenders who successfully invited someone to church have an average of 7.9 contacts per week, compared to 6.5 among those who invited someone without success and 6.1 among those who do not encourage others to attend. This link remains when age is taken into account.

While this is not a strong relationship, attenders with higher levels of contact are more likely to be effective in this aspect of mission. By broadening the number and range of contacts they have, attenders increase the chance of meeting people who may like to discuss matters of faith or who are open to an invitation to attend church.

\* \* \* \*

# A NECESSARY PREREQUISITE FOR MISSION

Contacts are a necessary prerequisite for mission. Not only are higher levels of contact related to involvement in a range of community contexts; they are also related to increased levels of sharing faith and inviting people to church activities.

While overall levels of contact are encouraging, a relatively high percentage of attenders have little community contact. This suggests that some congregations may largely be cut off from the wider community. In such circumstances, a congregation's mission initiatives are less likely to be effective, since attenders have little opportunity to stand for Christian values, to share their faith or invite others to church.

Congregations would do well to examine the extent to which attenders are involved in the wider community. The importance of encouraging attenders to 'bloom where they are planted' cannot be underestimated. Small groups and teaching need to address such issues, provide role models and give encouragement.

Congregations that have low levels of contact will need to think carefully about how to establish bridges with the wider community. In some cases, congregationally sponsored mission activities may be a useful step forward. In others, it may be important to help attenders realise the importance of broadening their everyday life contacts.

Some training courses on mission focus on 'how to' without examining the context of people's lives. Training also needs to emphasise the importance of establishing meaningful contacts with the wider community.

### The chemistry of affirmation

Paul, an elder at an inner-city Uniting Church congregation, was challenged at a conference on urban ministry to make a point of visiting attenders at their workplace.

'Most visiting takes place at home or in hospital', he says. 'Visiting people at their workplace can be very affirming, especially for blue-collar workers whose workplace is a world away from the often white-collar, professional church setting.'

Paul has visited attenders in all sorts of work environments, including offices, a police station and an industrial chemical plant. 'My two-hour tour of the chemical plant helped me understand Angus's very male working environment. My computer button seemed a long way from the button which would shut down this high-temperature, high-pressure, high-cost machinery. Making a mistake is expensive. Angus has to monitor the plant for hours on end, so that he can shut down parts of the plant at the right time if needed. I suddenly understand the boredom yet pressure of his job.'

Paul says the visit was a real breakthrough with Angus, who commented that he felt he was being taken seriously and felt more understood. 'By neglect, the church often gives the impression that the Christian life is separate to work. Given that most people spend so much time at work this needs to be addressed, for pastoral and missional reasons. The workplace is one of the main contacts Christians have with non-Christians. Church attenders need to feel affirmed in their mission there.'

In seeking to be involved in mission, attenders should not overlook the value of day-to-day contacts. All forms of contact and relationships are important, including a visit to a local shop, a chance encounter or a casual conversation. Congregations may want to help attenders see their workplace or school as a key part of the congregation's mission. Too often congregations assume a local geographical focus, and attenders may feel that wider involvement is not relevant.

If any further evidence for the importance of contacts needs to be given, the statistics reported in *Winds of Change* (p 161) on what prompted newcomers without a church background to join a congregation are telling. The majority of newcomers join through a personal invitation. Far fewer join because of the visibility or reputation of a congregation. As attenders bloom where they are planted, the gospel can be made real to others through their lives, actions and words.

Contact is, however, a starting point, not an end point. High levels of contact, of themselves, do not make for effective mission. Attenders need to look at the quality of their existing contacts, as well as quantity. There is little point in encouraging more contact if attenders are not able to live out their faith in a positive way or are uncomfortable talking about their faith with existing contacts.

---

**Significant contact with others in the community is an important starting point for mission. Schools, tertiary institutions and workplaces are vital contact points, which may play a key role in a congregation's mission strategy.**

- Overall, church attenders have plenty of contact with the Australian community. However, levels of contact vary widely. An eighth of attenders have contact with more than 20 non-church people each week, while a sixth of attenders have no outside contact at all.

- Many attenders appear to be cut off from the community. While this may be necessary for some, for others it may be a source of loneliness or insularity. While not all attenders can be in contact with the wider community, congregations which are committed to mission need to encourage their attenders to form relationships with people not involved with the churches.

- Young adults have more contacts than those who are older. They can play a key role in the mission of the church if they are comfortable with and confident about their faith and their congregations.

- School, university and the workplace are important sources of contacts, as are community groups and organisations. These can also form a pivotal part of a congregation's mission strategy.

- Far from being cut off from the world, attenders who are highly involved in their congregations also have more contact with the wider community.

- Attenders with higher levels of contact are more likely to share their faith with others or to have successfully invited someone to church in the past year.

CHAPTER 2

# WHERE OTHERS MEET

## Involvement in community groups

Community groups can be a useful avenue for attenders to get involved in wider community life. The types of group chosen by attenders at different stages in their lives provide congregations with a range of mission opportunities.

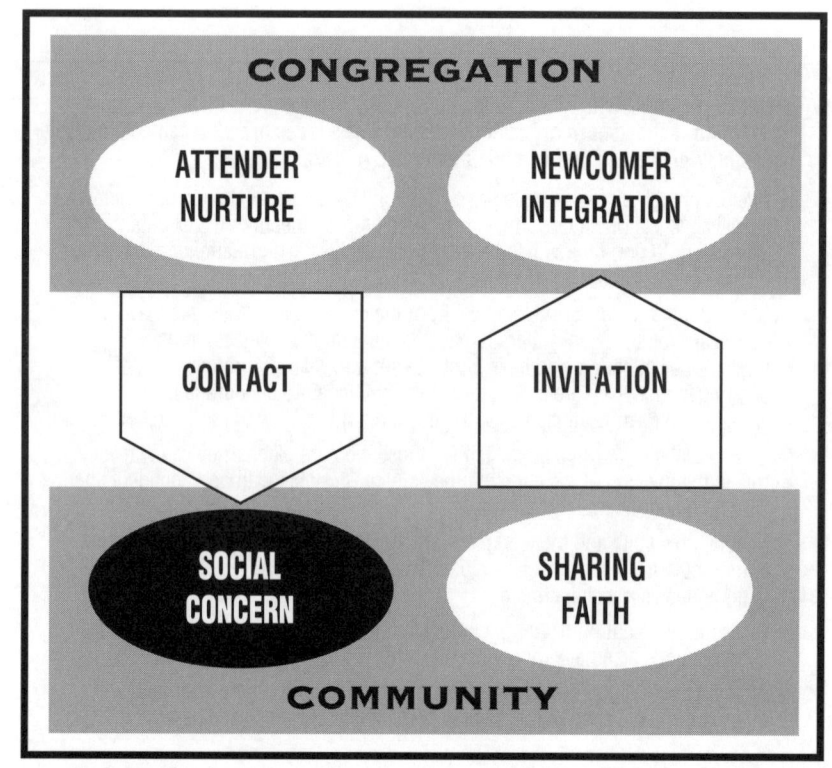

**CONGREGATION**

- ATTENDER NURTURE
- NEWCOMER INTEGRATION
- CONTACT
- INVITATION
- SOCIAL CONCERN
- SHARING FAITH

**COMMUNITY**

Fran is an older teenager in a small country town. There's not much to do at night, so she really looks forward to Friday night basketball organised in the community hall. It's fun, and she has made some new friends as a result.

Peter has long had a concern for the environment. Encouraged by his wife and those in his home group, he decided to get involved with the lobby group concerned about pollution in the local catchment. His role with the group has become more significant in the past year when, as the spokesperson, he had to fight hard for stricter environmental controls.

It was when Steve's son joined the scouts that Steve decided he should get involved. He attended some training weekends and became a leader. His son is grown up now, but Steve continues his involvement.

He may be getting on, but Frank still enjoys a game of football with the local club. Besides, it's a good chance to get to know people outside of the church.

The local Chamber of Commerce has been an important group for Clara, particularly in view of her line of business. It has also given her important insights as her church planned some new developments.

\* \* \* \*

As part of their everyday lives, or as a result of their needs or their beliefs, attenders may become involved in community groups of many kinds. Some community involvement may be relatively insignificant; on other occasions it may result in significant contacts, in personal care and growth for others, or in helping to shape the future directions of society.

In this and the following chapter, aspects of involvement in the wider community are explored. To gain an indication of the level of involvement of church attenders in community groups and organisations, the NCLS included the following question.

> **Are you actively involved in any of the following community groups/organisations? (Circle a maximum of two)**
> a. Service organisations (eg Lions, Rotary, YMCA)
> b. Resident groups (eg Neighbourhood Watch)
> c. Political parties/organisations
> d. Charitable organisations (not part of your local church)
> e. Large clubs (eg RSL)
> f. Sporting or recreation organisations
> g. Leisure groups (eg Senior Citizens club)
> h. Parents' & Citizens'/school committee
> i. Play groups/mothers' groups
> j. Amateur theatre/arts
> k. Professional/business associations
> l. Other (please specify)
> m. None of the above

Figure 2.1

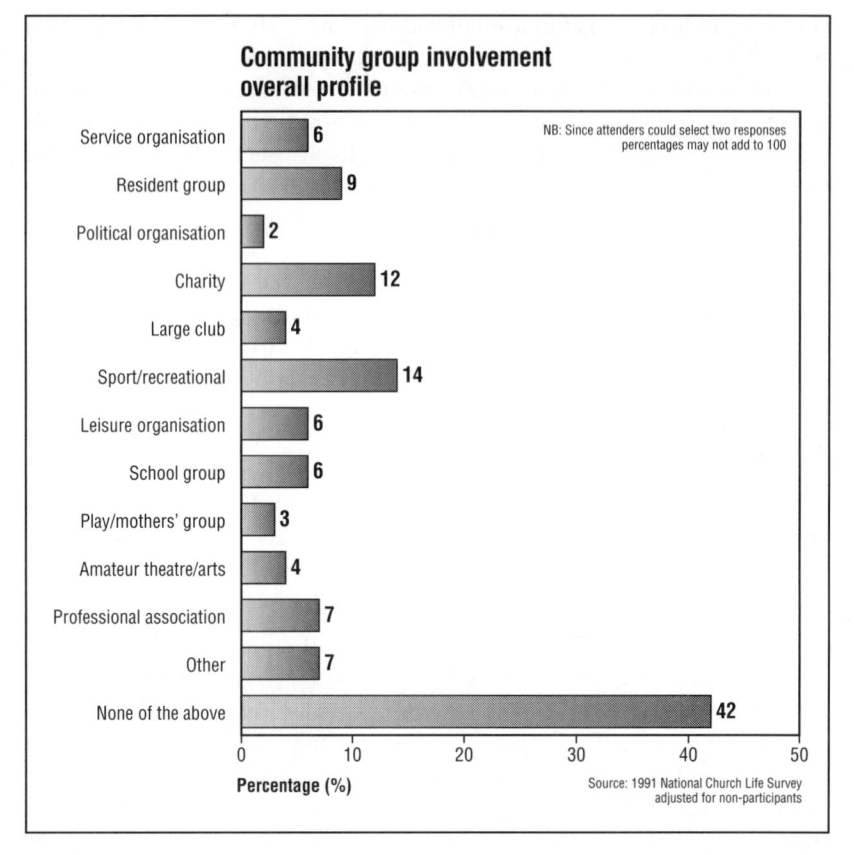

**Community group involvement overall profile**

NB: Since attenders could select two responses percentages may not add to 100

| Category | Percentage |
|---|---|
| Service organisation | 6 |
| Resident group | 9 |
| Political organisation | 2 |
| Charity | 12 |
| Large club | 4 |
| Sport/recreational | 14 |
| Leisure organisation | 6 |
| School group | 6 |
| Play/mothers' group | 3 |
| Amateur theatre/arts | 4 |
| Professional association | 7 |
| Other | 7 |
| None of the above | 42 |

Percentage (%)

Source: 1991 National Church Life Survey adjusted for non-participants

### A window of trust

Anne, who attends a mainstream congregation in a multicultural suburb in Sydney, is involved in the Home Tutor Scheme, a branch of the Adult Migrant Education Service. She says the scheme has not only provided her with an avenue of service; it has given her more than she had expected.

The scheme seeks to provide people from a non-English-speaking background with an informal opportunity to develop conversational English skills. This is done by linking them, one to one, with trained English-speaking volunteers. Students and tutors meet for two hours each week.

Over time, Anne's relationship with the young Afghani woman with whom she was paired has developed into a warm friendship, and she now thinks of her almost as a daughter. Recently, the Afghani woman extended an invitation to the family celebration of the birth of her first child.

'I felt very privileged, not to mention fascinated, to have the chance to experience a different culture so intimately. The food was exotic. The extended family was so excited about the new baby', Anne commented.

'I invited her to come to our church for Christmas celebrations of the birth of the most significant person in our culture, which she didn't refuse. The invitation was able to come naturally, as part of the sharing, the friendship and the education.'

Almost six out of 10 attenders (58%) are involved in community organisations generally. Further, attenders are involved in each of the 11 types of organisation listed in the question. The results confirm Australia's image as a sporting and fun-loving nation – the most common type of involvement is in sporting and recreational organisations (14%).

However, charities (12%), professional associations (7%), school groups (6%), leisure groups (6%) and service organisations (6%) are also popular. By and large, church attenders aren't politically active; only 2% nominate involvement in a political organisation.

*Six in 10 attenders are involved in community organisations*

## WELFARE, SERVICE AND ACTION GROUPS

The NCLS also included the following question, focusing on community service, social action and welfare organisations.

> **Are you involved in any community service/social action/welfare groups not connected to this church?**
> a. No, not really
> b. Yes, with community care/welfare groups
> c. Yes, with community action, justice or lobby groups
> d. Both b and c above

Such a broad question has some shortcomings. No attempt has been made, for instance, to define involvement or the frequency of involvement. Some attenders may feel involved by being a financial supporter of an organisation while, for others, involvement means frequent attendance and taking a leading role. Despite these limitations, the responses still provide some indication of the extent of attender contact with community organisations.

Just over a quarter of all attenders are involved in a service/social action/welfare group. Some 21% are involved in care/welfare groups, 3% in social action/justice/lobby groups and 3% in both types.

**Social action/welfare group involvement overall profile**

| | Percentage (%) |
|---|---|
| No | 73 |
| Yes, welfare groups | 21 |
| Yes, action groups | 3 |
| Both types | 3 |

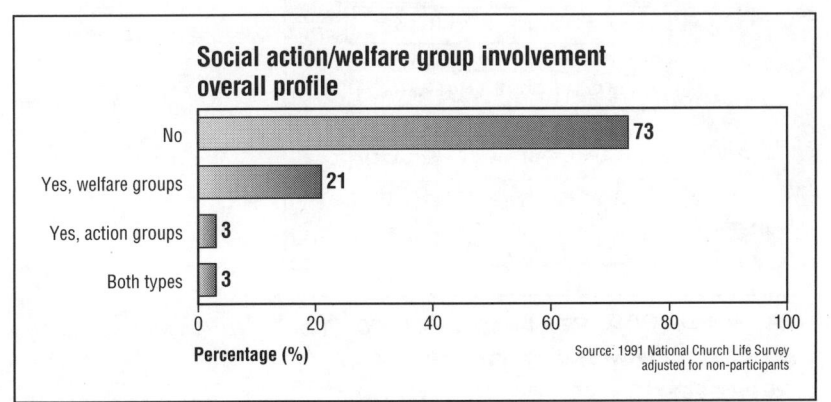

Source: 1991 National Church Life Survey adjusted for non-participants

Figure 2.2

## HOW INVOLVED ARE ATTENDERS?

These results will be encouraging for those who are concerned about Christian values being represented in all arenas of life. In being the salt of the earth, attenders are sprinkled far and wide, mixing with the wider community at work and play.

It is interesting to compare the levels of involvement of attenders with the community in general. In 1983, the Australian Values Study Survey (AVSS) asked Australians to which community organisations they belonged. Religious organisations (27%) and sporting groups (26%) were the most frequently nominated organisations, followed by trade unions (18%), education or arts groups (13%), charities concerned with welfare (13%) and professional associations (12%). Political parties (4%), conservation groups (3%), human rights groups (2%) and consumer groups (2%) were organisations to which Australians were least likely to belong at that time (AVSS, 1984).

The AVSS also asked Australians how they would use extra time if it were available to them. Some 27% of people who described themselves as highly religious said they would use the additional time doing voluntary community work, twice the proportion of the least religious people. The more religious people were more involved in charities, human rights organisations, scouts, guides and other youth organisations (Hughes, undated, 3).

Some may be concerned that, like Australians generally, so few attenders are involved in social action groups – especially considering the important issues facing Australian society. Attender attitudes to particular social action groups are discussed in detail in the next chapter.

RAYMOND HAD REALLY WANTED TO JOIN A COMMUNITY GROUP AS A REPRESENTATIVE OF HIS CHURCH....

Some of the most significant contributions to social justice have required Christians to be heavily involved in community life – sometimes at great cost. By mostly staying out of politics and action groups, attenders may miss the opportunity to shape the values of society and leave power in the hands of other vocal groups.

Others may question the priority of such involvement in the light of demands facing the church, or may question whether it is appropriate for Christians to be involved. Church leaders may want to reflect on the direction of society and community values, and consider whether the church is doing all it should do in this area.

## GENDER AND STAGE IN LIFE

Involvement in community groups increases with age. Only 47% of teenagers are involved in community groups generally, compared to 60% of attenders aged 60 to 69 years. This trend is even more marked for social action/welfare groups. Only 8% of 15 to 19 year olds are involved in such groups, compared to 41% of those in their 60s.

Not surprisingly, the type of group attenders get involved with depends largely on their stage in life. Attenders in their teens and 20s are most likely to be involved in sporting and recreational groups. The focus changes for attenders in their 30s and 40s to include school organisations, mothers' groups and professional associations as well as sporting groups. Attenders over 60 years opt more for charities, resident groups and leisure groups.

Males are slightly more likely to be involved in social action groups: 7% of male attenders are involved compared to 5% of female attenders. In

*The type of group that attenders get involved with depends largely on their stage in life*

**Community group involvement by age group**

NB: since attenders could select two responses, percentages may not add to 100

| | 15–19 yrs % | 20–29 yrs % | 30–39 yrs % | 40–49 yrs % | 50–59 yrs % | 60–69 yrs % | 70+ yrs % |
|---|---|---|---|---|---|---|---|
| Service organisation | 1 | 3 | 4 | 5 | 8 | 8 | 8 |
| Resident group | 5 | 4 | 9 | 6 | 9 | 13 | 11 |
| Political organisation | 0 | 1 | 1 | 3 | 3 | 4 | 2 |
| Charity | 2 | 6 | 5 | 8 | 13 | 14 | 25 |
| Large club | 1 | 1 | 1 | 2 | 2 | 8 | 6 |
| Sporting/recreational | 29 | 24 | 13 | 14 | 14 | 10 | 9 |
| Leisure organisation | 1 | 4 | 2 | 3 | 3 | 10 | 14 |
| School group | 0 | 3 | 13 | 16 | 5 | 0 | 0 |
| Play/mothers' group | 0 | 7 | 13 | 1 | 0 | 1 | 0 |
| Amateur theatre/arts | 8 | 2 | 2 | 3 | 8 | 5 | 1 |
| Professional association | 0 | 9 | 12 | 11 | 13 | 4 | 1 |
| Other | 9 | 6 | 9 | 8 | 7 | 8 | 5 |
| None of the above | 53 | 43 | 42 | 45 | 40 | 40 | 38 |
| Total | 100 | 100 | 100 | 100 | 100 | 100 | 100 |

Source: 1991 National Church Life Survey attender data adjusted for non participants

Figure 2.3

contrast, female attenders (27%) are more likely to be involved in welfare groups than males (19%). This is partly explained by the involvement of older attenders with such groups; there is a higher proportion of older women than men in the church.

## DOES EDUCATION MAKE A DIFFERENCE?

Tertiary-educated attenders and those from professional and managerial households are more likely to be involved in community organisations than attenders from other socio-economic backgrounds. Only half of attenders in blue-collar households are involved in community groups, compared to 63% of attenders from professional/managerial households.

Similarly, 51% of attenders educated to primary school only are involved in community groups, compared to 70% of attenders with university qualifications. This difference is also apparent for involvement in social action groups, where attenders with university degrees (9%) are twice as likely to be involved than attenders educated as far as secondary school only (4%). These differences still exist after accounting for the effects of age.

Various studies have found that there is a relationship between socio-economic status and joining community organisations, including the church itself (eg Demerath, 1965; Willmott and Young, 1960; Goode, 1966). Some of the reasons suggested for this in the Australian context centre on the formal aspects of involvement in a community organisation and the communication skills required to participate (Kaldor, 1987, 138–143).

The NCLS suggests such factors may be operating. Attenders from blue-collar backgrounds are just as likely to be involved in sporting and recreational groups as other attenders, but less likely to be involved in charities, service organisations, school groups, and amateur theatre/arts groups. Participation in these groups may require familiarity with business procedures or particular types of communication skill.

Congregations should examine their own practices and procedures to ensure they don't alienate attenders from blue-collar backgrounds. Do some attenders find congregational meetings or processes threatening, thereby preventing them from making valuable contributions to church ministry and administration? Congregations that encourage people from blue-collar backgrounds to be involved in all aspects of congregational life may also empower them to take a fuller role in the community.

*Only 38% of Pentecostal attenders are involved in a community group, compared to 67% of mainstream attenders*

## DO DENOMINATIONS DIFFER?

There are distinct differences in levels of involvement between denominations and between attenders with differing views of the Bible. Attenders in Pentecostal denominations tend to be less involved in community organisations. Only 38% are actively involved, compared to 51% of attenders in large Protestant denominations and 67% of mainstream attenders.

## Social action/welfare group involvement by denomination

Figure 2.4

| | No % | Yes – welfare groups % | Yes – action groups % | Both types % | Total % |
|---|---|---|---|---|---|
| **Overall** | **73** | **21** | **3** | **3** | **100** |
| Anglican | 68 | 24 | 4 | 4 | 100 |
| Apostolic | 83 | 13 | 2 | 2 | 100 |
| Assemblies of God | 85 | 12 | 2 | 2 | 100 |
| Baptist | 78 | 18 | 3 | 2 | 100 |
| Christian & Missionary Alliance | 83 | 12 | 2 | 2 | 100 |
| Christian Revival Crusade | 85 | 12 | 2 | 1 | 100 |
| Church of the Nazarene | 85 | 10 | 3 | 3 | 100 |
| Churches of Christ | 77 | 18 | 2 | 2 | 100 |
| Congregational | 82 | 14 | 2 | 2 | 100 |
| Foursquare Gospel | 87 | 10 | 1 | 2 | 100 |
| Lutheran | 77 | 17 | 3 | 2 | 100 |
| NZ Presbyterian | 60 | 30 | 5 | 5 | 100 |
| Presbyterian | 71 | 23 | 3 | 3 | 100 |
| Reformed | 84 | 13 | 2 | 1 | 100 |
| Salvation Army | 77 | 18 | 2 | 3 | 100 |
| Seventh-day Adventist | 74 | 22 | 2 | 3 | 100 |
| Uniting | 64 | 29 | 4 | 4 | 100 |
| Wesleyan Methodist | 82 | 14 | 3 | 1 | 100 |
| Westminster Presbyterian | 88 | 8 | 2 | 1 | 100 |
| House Churches | 60 | 17 | 10 | 13 | 100 |
| **Type of denomination** | | | | | |
| Mainstream | 68 | 25 | 4 | 4 | 100 |
| Pentecostal | 85 | 12 | 2 | 2 | 100 |
| Large Protestant | 77 | 19 | 2 | 2 | 100 |
| Small Protestant | 83 | 13 | 2 | 2 | 100 |

Source: 1991 National Church Life Survey attender data adjusted for non participants

A similar picture emerges for the question on involvement with social action/welfare groups. Some 32% of mainstream attenders are involved, compared to 23% of attenders in large Protestant, 17% in small Protestant and 15% in Pentecostal denominations.

Denominational differences depend partly on age. For attenders aged under 30 years, there is little difference in levels of involvement in social action/welfare groups irrespective of denominational background. It is only among attenders aged over 30 years that denominational differences start to emerge.

Another possible explanation for the denominational pattern is that there are more mainstream congregations in rural areas, and rural people are more community minded. Farm families (66%) are more likely to be involved in community organisations generally than attenders overall (58%). However, differences between urban and rural attenders are slight. The denominational differences exist even in urban areas.

A more important factor appears to be the theological orientation of attenders. Some 43% of attenders who believe the Bible is God's word to be taken literally *(literalists)* are involved in community groups, compared to 63% of those who believe the Bible is God's word to be read in the context of the times *(contextualists)* and 63% of those who consider it to be a valuable book *(valuists)*. However, this general trend does not apply to all types of community organisation.

Literalists are less likely to be involved in service organisations, recreational and sporting or leisure organisations than contextualists and valuists. They are just as likely to be involved in resident groups, political parties, school groups and mothers' groups.

Similarly, literalists (22%) are less involved in social action/welfare groups than either contextualists (29%) or valuists (29%).

Attenders who have been influenced by Catholic/Anglo-Catholic tradition (34%) tend to be more involved in social action/welfare groups than those influenced by evangelical (29%) or charismatic (23%) theological traditions.

These denominational and theological differences may be the result of different orientations to the world. In *Winds of Change* (p 70), the relationship between types of faith and patterns of congregational involvement was examined. As was noted there, literalists are more likely to get involved in congregational activities or outreach, or to have a focus on evangelism. Those who are more valuist in orientation have lower levels of involvement in congregational life, but high levels of involvement in community activities.

There are echoes here of classic sociological distinctions between 'church-like' and 'sect-like' groups (eg Troeltsch, 1960). 'Church-like' groups have an open orientation to the world, seeing it essentially as a good place, while 'sect-like' groups treat the world with caution. Although value laden in common usage, the terms are used in a sociological sense with no other values or emotions intended (*Winds of Change*, pp 70–73).

Many congregations provide recreational and service activities which they encourage attenders to join. This approach is common in, but not confined to, Pentecostal congregations. Many mainstream and large Protestant congregations also adopt this approach, which is currently producing a plethora of Christian schools, other organisations and activities. Attenders in congregations with this orientation may be less involved in community groups because they feel less comfortable about being so or because they feel less need since their congregations offer similar activities.

## CONGREGATIONAL SIZE

The larger a congregation, the less likely people are to be involved in community groups. Some 36% of attenders in congregations with fewer than 25 attenders are involved in social action/welfare groups, compared to only 16% of attenders in congregations with more than 500 attenders.

Further analysis shows that this was partly a result of the age of attenders, since younger attenders are more often found in large congregations. However, denominational background or whether the congregation was urban or rural appeared to make little difference to this relationship.

Part of the reason could be that larger congregations are more likely to run their own social action or welfare activities. Larger congregations are more able to organise their own activities and programs; smaller ones may sometimes find it more profitable to encourage attenders to get directly involved in community-based groups.

## CHURCH AND COMMUNITY GROUPS

Are those involved in community groups likely to be less involved in congregational life? The answer appears to be no. There appears to be no relationship between social action/welfare group involvement and the level of involvement in church life. Those who are infrequent church attenders (26%) are just as likely to be involved in social action/welfare groups as those who are highly involved attenders (26%).

Perhaps the old saying holds here: If you need something done, ask a busy person! Clearly, many attenders who make time to be involved in one, make time for both. Congregations should not fear that encouraging attenders to be involved in such organisations will necessarily cause them to reduce their involvement in congregational life.

As will be seen in Chapter 4, a different relationship exists when it comes to congregational mission activities. Attenders involved in such activities are more likely to also be very involved in church life.

... AND PLEASE WELCOME OUR NEW MEMBERS, A COUPLE OF WHOM COME FROM OUR VERY OWN LOCAL CHURCH.....

# WHAT DIFFERENCE DOES IT MAKE?

The previous chapter indicated that attenders involved in community groups had higher levels of overall contact with those in the wider community. This suggests that such involvement may be a useful bridge between congregations and the community.

While a survey of attenders cannot measure their impact in community welfare or social action groups, the NCLS can explore the relationship between such involvement and attenders' perceived growth in faith and patterns of sharing faith. The NCLS examined whether attenders who are involved in community welfare/social action groups are more likely to:

- feel they exert a Christian influence;
- be comfortable in talking about their faith;
- have invited someone to church activities;
- feel they are growing in faith.

### *Sense of influence*

Involvement in social action or welfare groups is slightly related to the sense of Christian influence that attenders believe they have on those around them. Some 61% of attenders who are involved in a social action/welfare group feel they exert great or some influence on those around them, compared to 54% who are not so involved. This pattern generally holds for various age groups, denominational groups, faith types and levels of church involvement.

### *Sharing faith*

Attenders who are involved in social action or welfare groups (61%) are more likely to feel at ease about sharing their faith than attenders who are not involved in community groups (55%). Attenders involved in both kinds of groups are most likely to be at ease in sharing their faith (67%).

Again, this pattern generally holds for various age groups, denominational groups, faith types and levels of church involvement.

### *Inviting others to church*

Attenders who are involved in social action/welfare groups are more likely to have tried to encourage someone to a church activity in the past year. Some 43% who are involved in social action/welfare groups tried to encourage someone to church, compared to 39% who are not involved. Attenders involved in both kinds of group are most likely to have tried to encourage someone to church activities (51%).

### *Growth in faith*

On average, involvement in social action or welfare groups does not appear to affect the extent to which attenders feel they are growing in their faith. Nor is there any relationship between the patterns of prayer of attenders and their involvement in such groups.

\* \* \* \*

## A USEFUL AVENUE FOR MISSION

In the introduction to *Mission under the Microscope*, three broad avenues for contact were described: contacts in everyday life, attender involvement in community groups and congregationally sponsored mission activities.

Involvement in community groups is a useful way for attenders to increase their contact with others outside of church life. This may be a significant avenue of contact for all attenders, but particularly for those in smaller congregations where congregational-based service or mission activities are beyond their resources.

Church attenders appear highly involved in community social action/welfare groups and community organisations in general. Commentators often underestimate the significance of the churches in Australian life. By participating in community groups, attenders at a grass roots level can play a significant role in the wider community. They can meet others with common interests or concerns, form relationships on an equal footing and, possibly, help to shape the future directions of society at large.

Congregations should be aware that the type of community groups with which attenders become involved changes with their stage in life. Recognising this, congregations may be able to build some bridges that help to reach different sections of the wider community. For example, if parents become involved in Parents' and Citizens' groups and youth in sporting clubs and so on, the way may be opened for whole networks of people to make contact with the congregation.

When a congregation helps its members to see that their involvement in such groups can be significant for mission, the congregation may begin to move from being a closed system to one that is more open. Such help may encourage attenders to take their involvement and relationships more seriously, or to feel they are exerting a Christian influence and impact. This may open up possibilities for discussing faith or inviting newcomers into congregational life. In this way, it can be a significant entry point for the gospel into wider community life.

> **Community groups can be a useful avenue for attenders to get involved in wider community life. The types of group chosen by attenders at different stages in their lives provide congregations with a range of mission opportunities.**
>
> - Church attenders have high levels of involvement in charities and welfare groups, an involvement that increases with age.
> - Interest in different groups changes with age; each stage of life provides attenders with contact with different types of people.
> - Those who have completed higher levels of formal education are more likely to get involved with charities, service organisations and school groups.
> - Attenders in Pentecostal denominations or who see the Bible as God's word to be taken literally are less likely to be involved in community groups than other attenders.
> - Attenders with high levels of church involvement are not necessarily less involved in community groups. Attenders who make time for one make time for both.
> - Attenders who are involved in community groups are a little more likely to feel they exert a Christian influence or to have successfully invited someone to church in the past year.

CHAPTER 3

# TAKING A STAND

## Involvement in social action groups

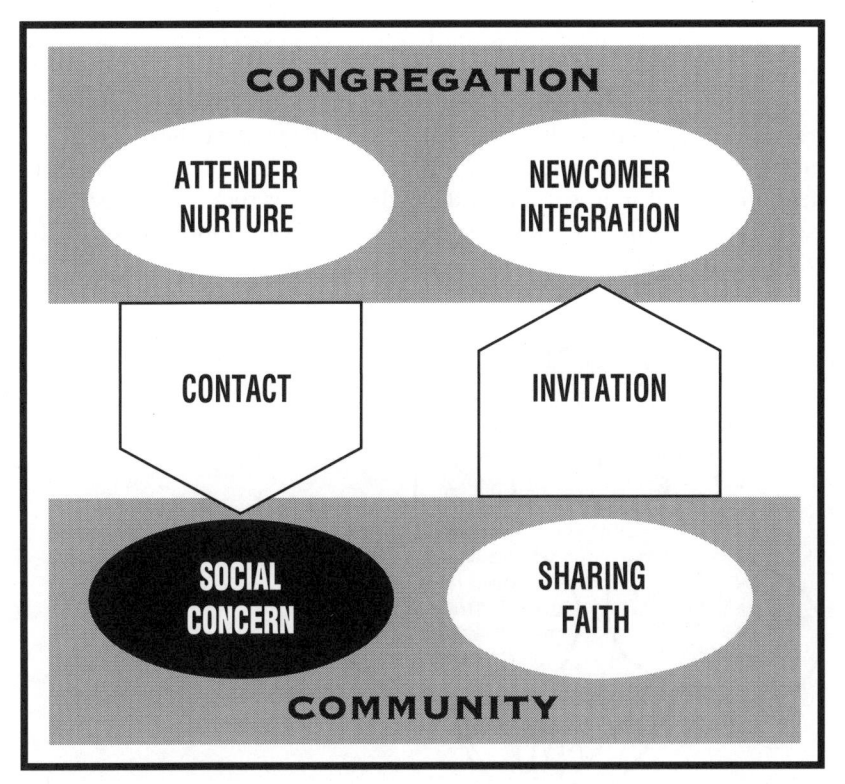

**CONGREGATION**

ATTENDER NURTURE

NEWCOMER INTEGRATION

CONTACT

INVITATION

SOCIAL CONCERN

SHARING FAITH

**COMMUNITY**

Denominations and attenders have clear preferences for the type of action groups they support. In developing a vision for future directions of the wider community, congregations need to consider many different issues.

In the last decade of this century, Australians are confronted by many issues. What should society's values be? How should the community care for the weak, poor or marginalised? For church attenders there is an additional question: Does the Christian faith provide distinctive answers to these questions?

Attender support for and involvement in social action is the focus of this chapter. Christian service doesn't start and end with welfare, significant though the church's contribution in this area is. For centuries the church has also made an impact on matters of social justice and ethics. Christians with a positive vision for the future of society have often made a major difference to its direction.

In the United States, some Christians were a key voice for equality for black Americans. In Britain, members of the Methodist Church and the Salvation Army sought better working conditions for workers trapped in poverty by the industrial revolution. Today, some Christian organisations not only meet immediate needs for food and health services; they also seek solutions to the factors that create poverty.

Some denominations and organisations, such as the World Council of Churches, have a recognised agenda of social action, including the liberation of oppressed peoples. Others, such as the Lausanne Conference for Evangelism, have moved towards a balanced evangelism-social action agenda.

The church has also often taken strong stands on ethical issues. While not always speaking with one voice, Christians have been vocal on matters of morals and appropriate sexual conduct. Apart from denominational spokespeople, independent groups such as the Festival of Light have become well known for their stands on moral issues in the wider community.

While some are not as convinced of the importance of a voice to the wider community as others, the NCLS results reported in *Winds of Change* (p 61) show that only a minority of attenders believe that either evangelism or social action should be the sole focus of their congregation. The majority believe each has a place in church life.

To explore attenders' involvement in social action, the NCLS included several questions. Three questions, with the same response options, covered involvement in environmental groups, peace and justice groups, and the Festival of Light or similar groups. A fourth question asked about involvement in overseas aid and mission.

*Only a minority of attenders believes that evangelism or social action should be the sole focus*

**Are you involved with any environmental groups? (The same question was also asked for peace/justice groups or activities and for the Festival of Light or similar groups.)**
 a. Yes, actively with one or more such groups as an expression of my Christian commitment
 b. I am not involved but strongly support their activities
 c. No, I do not have any strong views on these groups
 d. I believe such groups are misguided

**Are you involved in any activities which mean you have a caring link with people in a developing country in the Pacific, Asia, Latin America or Africa?**
 a. Yes, I have a link with individuals in such places
 b. Yes, I have a link with a community group
 c. Yes, I have a link with a church
 d. Yes, I have another kind of link
 e. More than one of the above
 f. No, I do not have any links of this kind

## ENVIRONMENTAL GROUPS

Environmental issues have loomed large on the political and societal agenda in recent years. Some aspects of the environmental debate, such as forest logging, create heated argument. Others have been willingly embraced by consumers who now recycle glass, aluminium and paper, read energy labels on appliances and opt for environmentally friendly products in the supermarket.

But to what extent do attenders support the activities of environmental groups? Overall, 44% of attenders support such groups, comprising 39% who are supportive but not involved and 5% who are actively involved. Another 47% have no strong views on these groups, while 9% think they are misguided.

Half of all attenders in mainstream denominations support environmental groups, compared to 44% in large Protestant and just 21% in Pentecostal denominations.

Figure 3.1

### Attitude to social action groups by denomination

|  | Environment groups | | Peace/justice groups | | Morals groups | |
|---|---|---|---|---|---|---|
|  | Support/ involved % | See as misguided % | Support/ involved % | See as misguided % | Support/ involved % | See as misguided % |
| **Overall** | **44** | **9** | **36** | **7** | **30** | **13** |
| Anglican | 55 | 8 | 42 | 6 | 22 | 17 |
| Assemblies of God | 20 | 15 | 19 | 13 | 35 | 5 |
| Baptist | 39 | 6 | 34 | 8 | 39 | 10 |
| Churches of Christ | 44 | 7 | 41 | 2 | 29 | 13 |
| Lutheran | 46 | 8 | 30 | 3 | 31 | 7 |
| Presbyterian | 33 | 14 | 27 | 13 | 31 | 11 |
| Salvation Army | 38 | 9 | 36 | 3 | 26 | 8 |
| Uniting | 50 | 9 | 40 | 8 | 19 | 18 |
| **Type of denomination** | | | | | | |
| Mainstream | 50 | 9 | 39 | 7 | 23 | 16 |
| Pentecostal | 21 | 15 | 19 | 12 | 39 | 4 |
| Large Protestant | 44 | 6 | 38 | 5 | 39 | 11 |
| Small Protestant | n.a. | n.a. | n.a. | n.a. | n.a. | n.a. |

Source: 1991 National Church Life Survey attender data adjusted for non-participants

Some 55% of attenders with university degrees support environmental groups, compared to 38% of people who did not go beyond secondary school. Similarly, attenders from white-collar backgrounds are much more likely to support such groups than attenders from blue-collar backgrounds. These different levels of support may be because tertiary-educated attenders have more access to environmental information than others or because their jobs are less threatened by environmental concerns.

Attenders from farm families are the most polarised about environmental groups. On the one hand, 9% of attenders from farm families are actively involved in environmental groups, almost double the proportion of attenders generally. This would reflect the formation of Landcare groups and involvement in tree planting and soil conservation programs. On the other hand, some 21% of attenders from farm families think environmental groups are misguided, which may reflect their attitudes to some of the more controversial aspects of the environmental debate.

The environment is, and will remain, firmly on the world agenda. Crises such as the Chernobyl nuclear accident, the Bhopal chemical accident in India, acid rain in Germany and Canada, and the destruction of tropical rainforests in Brazil and South East Asia have put environmental issues into people's backyards.

To some extent, Australia has been isolated from these crises. However, emerging global problems, such as climatic changes associated with the greenhouse effect, are bringing an end to this isolation. At the same time, the need to protect natural areas and arable land suggests that the environment will remain an important issue in Australian society into the future.

## PEACE AND JUSTICE GROUPS

Peace and justice groups operate in a number of ways, including providing practical support for refugees or political activists and lobbying Australian and foreign governments.

Some 36% of attenders support such groups; 4% are actively involved and 32% are supportive but not involved. Some 57% of attenders have no strong views on peace and justice groups, while 7% see them as misguided.

There are differences between denominations and between attenders from different socio-economic backgrounds. Twice as many attenders in mainstream and large Protestant denominations support peace and justice groups as in Pentecostal denominations.

There is little relationship by educational background of attenders, although university-qualified attenders in mainstream denominations are more likely to support peace and justice groups. Similarly, attenders from white-collar backgrounds are more likely to support such groups than attenders from blue-collar backgrounds.

## MORALS GROUPS

The church has been, at different times, a leading voice and influence on community morality. At the turn of the century, for instance, Protestant clergy were key activists in the movement to reduce alcohol consumption (Hogan, 1987, 152–153). Today there are a number of groups in Australia that promote particular standards on moral and social issues. Many of these groups lobby predominantly on one issue, such as alcohol consumption or abortion. One of the better known groups, the Festival of Light, is involved in a range of issues under the umbrella of family values.

What proportion of church attenders actively supports their work? Around 30% of attenders support morals groups, made up of 27% who are supportive but not involved and 3% who are actively involved. Some 57% have no strong views, and 13% see them as misguided.

Attenders in Pentecostal (39%) and large Protestant denominations, such as the Baptist Church (39%), are much more supportive of morals groups than attenders in mainstream denominations (23%). Uniting Church attenders have the strongest orientation to social action of all denominations, yet the lowest level of support (19%) for morals groups such as the Festival of Light.

Attenders of all ages support and are involved in morals groups. Support is highest among attenders aged 40 to 60 years. There is no relationship by educational background, except that university-qualified attenders in mainstream denominations are more likely to see morals groups as misguided.

Two issues are of particular interest. First, many more attenders oppose such groups (13%) than are actively involved in them (3%). Is this a rejection of morals groups in principle, or the way existing groups operate?

Second, the majority of attenders do not have a view on morals groups. Does this mean they have no opinion on moral issues, or are they simply

*Many more attenders oppose morals groups than are actively involved in them*

Figure 3.2

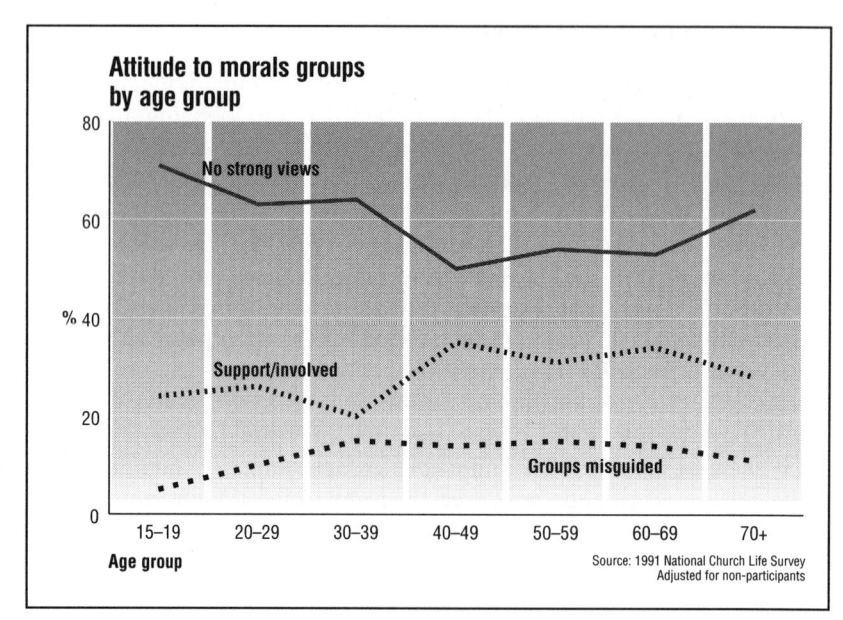

**Attitude to morals groups by age group**

[Line graph showing three lines across age groups 15-19, 20-29, 30-39, 40-49, 50-59, 60-69, 70+ on x-axis, with % from 0 to 80 on y-axis. "No strong views" line starts around 70 and declines to about 50 then rises slightly. "Support/involved" line rises from about 25 to about 35. "Groups misguided" line stays around 10-15.]

Source: 1991 National Church Life Survey
Adjusted for non-participants

not convinced about the way these issues are being raised by morals groups in the community? These questions are food for thought for both morals groups and church leaders alike.

Opinion on moral issues within the church is diverse, and for some issues it may never be possible for the church to speak as one voice to Australian society. The extent of this diversity is revealed in the NCLS publication, *Views from the Pews* (Kaldor et al, 1995).

## CARING LINKS OVERSEAS

In 1990, the Australian International Development Assistance Bureau estimated that one billion people live in poverty (AIDAB, 1990, 3). The church supports overseas aid and missionary work in a range of ways. At the micro level, individual attenders sponsor children in developing countries to provide food, clothing, education and health services. At a macro level, denominations support community development projects and missionary teams.

Almost half of all attenders have a caring link with a developing country in the Pacific, Asia, Latin America or Africa (49%). The most common type of link is with individuals (19%); some of these links are through sponsorship of another person and some with a missionary or missionary team. A further question explored the focus of such links between attenders and people overseas. Activities which focus on Christian ministry are the best supported by attenders, followed by sponsorship of needy people and aid projects.

Overall, attenders in large Protestant denominations are the most likely to have caring links overseas (59%), followed by Pentecostal attenders (54%). Mainstream denominations are less involved; 44% of Anglicans,

**Overseas caring links by denomination**

| | With individuals % | With community groups % | With a church % | Other links % | More than one link % | No links % | Total % |
|---|---|---|---|---|---|---|---|
| **Overall** | 19 | 5 | 13 | 9 | 3 | 51 | 100 |
| Anglican | 14 | 7 | 10 | 9 | 3 | 56 | 100 |
| Assemblies of God | 19 | 1 | 17 | 9 | 4 | 49 | 100 |
| Baptist | 32 | 7 | 9 | 8 | 2 | 41 | 100 |
| Churches of Christ | 22 | 3 | 14 | 15 | 3 | 43 | 100 |
| Lutheran | 13 | 3 | 14 | 4 | 2 | 65 | 100 |
| Presbyterian | 13 | 5 | 17 | 11 | 1 | 52 | 100 |
| Salvation Army | 24 | 5 | 12 | 9 | 5 | 44 | 100 |
| Uniting | 14 | 6 | 11 | 9 | 2 | 57 | 100 |
| **Type of denomination** | | | | | | | |
| Mainstream | 14 | 6 | 12 | 9 | 2 | 57 | 100 |
| Pentecostal | 19 | 3 | 19 | 8 | 5 | 46 | 100 |
| Large Protestant | 27 | 5 | 14 | 10 | 3 | 41 | 100 |
| Small Protestant | n.a. | n.a. | n.a. | n.a. | n.a. | n.a. | n.a. |

Source: 1991 National Church Life Survey attender data adjusted for non-participants

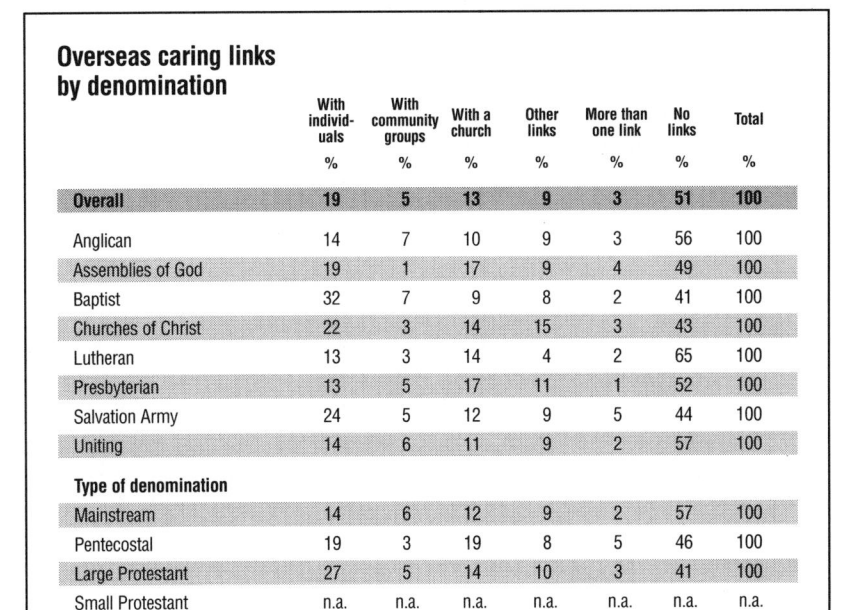

Figure 3.3

43% of Uniting Church attenders and 35% of Lutherans have caring links overseas.

The nature of involvement differs between denominational groups. Pentecostal attenders are more likely to focus on Christian ministry activities than mainstream attenders, who are more likely to have an aid link. More than 50% of Anglican and Uniting Church attenders who have an overseas caring link have an aid or sponsorship link, compared to 36% of Pentecostal attenders.

These differences are not surprising, since Pentecostal missionary organisations are among the fastest growing in the world (Pettifer and Bradley, 1990, 15). Some large Pentecostal congregations support their own missionary teams in developing countries. Attenders in large Protestant denominations support both ministry and aid activities overseas.

Holding the tension between building the church in other countries and providing aid will always be delicate. Attenders in all denominations need to reflect on whether their support of overseas communities holds these two in an appropriate balance.

## DIFFERING DENOMINATIONAL AGENDAS

While attenders in all denominations support social action groups, there are distinct differences in the type of group supported. Attenders in Pentecostal denominations are more likely to support morals groups and Christian ministry overseas, while attenders in mainstream denominations are more likely to support environmental, peace and justice groups and aid in developing countries. Attenders in large Protestant denominations tend to be supportive across the spectrum of these activities.

These differences are also reflected in attenders' views of the Bible. Attenders who view the Bible as the word of God to be taken literally (*literalists*) tend to more supportive of morals groups (42%) than of environmental (28%) or peace and justice groups (27%). In contrast, attenders who think the Bible is a valuable book (*valuists*) tend to be more supportive of environmental groups (43%) than of peace and justice groups (31%) or morals groups (22%). Literalists are nearly twice as likely to have a caring link with someone overseas than valuists.

Interestingly, attenders who think the Bible is God's word to be read in the context of the times (*contextualists*) are more likely to support environmental groups (53%) and peace and justice groups (43%) than either literalists or valuists.

Internationally, social action has become increasingly important to the evangelical wing of the church. Yet many attenders in Australia, particularly from Pentecostal and literalist backgrounds, appear to have adopted the agenda in a selective way, primarily supporting morals groups and overseas ministry. Is this emphasis really justified?

In the same way, many mainstream attenders prefer particular forms of social action over others. Again, the question can be asked as to whether this emphasis is appropriate.

*Many attenders have adopted a social action agenda in a selective way*

\* \* \* \*

## CONNECTING FAITH WITH LIFE ISSUES

The changing shape of contemporary society presents many questions and challenges for decision makers and the society at large. There is much questioning about what values and priorities Australia should have as a nation. These questions are often no easier for attenders to resolve. As the results in this chapter demonstrate, attenders have a wide range of views.

Congregations often help attenders to grapple with the connections between faith and life. Teaching and study groups provide attenders with guidelines for living and forums for discussion. Should congregations also help attenders to develop perspectives on social issues and future directions of society? Some would see it as vital that Christians have clear perspectives in the midst of debate and confusion about future directions.

Australians have probably found it easier to overlook social issues than people in many other countries. Australia is a comparatively clean, spacious, prosperous and democratic country. Many Australians lead comfortable lives. However, while the issues may not be as confronting, they are there – the poor health of Aboriginal people, domestic violence, the plight of the long-term unemployed, the widening gap between the rich and poor, soil conservation, air and water pollution, the development of coastal areas and the debate on the constitution, to name a few.

While many church-based groups parallel community groups in the area of welfare, this isn't necessarily so with social action. And as the survey results presented here show, many attenders do not have strong views on the activities of social action groups. Fewer still are involved.

The low proportion of attenders who are actively involved in social action groups demands further thought. It should be noted, however, that these levels of involvement are probably not much different from the community at large. For instance, the 1983 Australian Values Study Survey found that only 3% of Australians belonged to a conservation, environment or animal welfare group, and 2% belonged to organisations concerned with human rights (AVSS, 1984).

Of course, some attenders may want to be involved, but don't have the confidence to act, feeling they lack skills or are uninformed on the issues. Congregations could have a role in helping attenders to connect their faith to these issues.

Having clear perspectives on social issues may also be important for attenders in sharing their faith. As will be discovered in Chapter 5, many attenders find that discussion about the Christian faith more often involves having a Christian viewpoint on a particular subject than presenting a gospel outline. Having well-developed perspectives on various issues will be helpful for such conversations.

### Growing and giving

Richard, from Brisbane, lived in an Aboriginal community in Queensland for 10 days as part of a faith and culture exchange organised by the churches. The inequality he discovered on his back doorstep came as a shock.

'In response to God's call for us to seek justice, I believe that if we do not take steps to rectify the injustices of the past and bring justice into the present then we will be responsible for injustices in the future', he says. 'While it may be too late to help some Aboriginal people, we can give some hope to the next generation.'

Along with a deeper understanding of the issues concerning this Aboriginal community, Richard's horizons were broadened about the meaning of faith beyond the limitations of the Anglo-Celtic church culture.

Fuelled by these experiences, Richard was incensed when he heard that transfer of some untied grant moneys from his denomination to its Aboriginal work was under threat. He researched the issue, gathered together other concerned people and is preparing to advocate strongly should the funding be withdrawn. 'Praying with others, for people from such a different background, has reminded me of what a loving God we have', he says.

'The need for pleading the case of the poor, the needy and the oppressed occurs inside and outside the church. How can we challenge the action of the government if we don't treat our own people better? Our love of those who are struggling is not only a good witness; it also equips us and challenges us to act similarly in the wider community.'

**Denominations and attenders have clear preferences for the type of action groups they support. In developing a vision for future directions of the wider community, congregations need to consider many different issues.**

- A small minority of attenders are actively involved in environmental, peace and justice, and morals groups, though many more support their activities.
- Around half of all attenders have no strong opinions on the activities of social action groups. Congregations may need to help attenders work through such issues and develop perspectives.
- Denominations have different emphases. Attenders from Pentecostal denominations are more likely to support overseas ministry and morals groups. Mainstream denominations place greater priority on overseas aid, peace and justice and environmental groups. All denominations need to reflect on whether they have developed appropriate balances in this area.

CHAPTER 4

# INVOLVED TOGETHER

**Congregational mission activities**

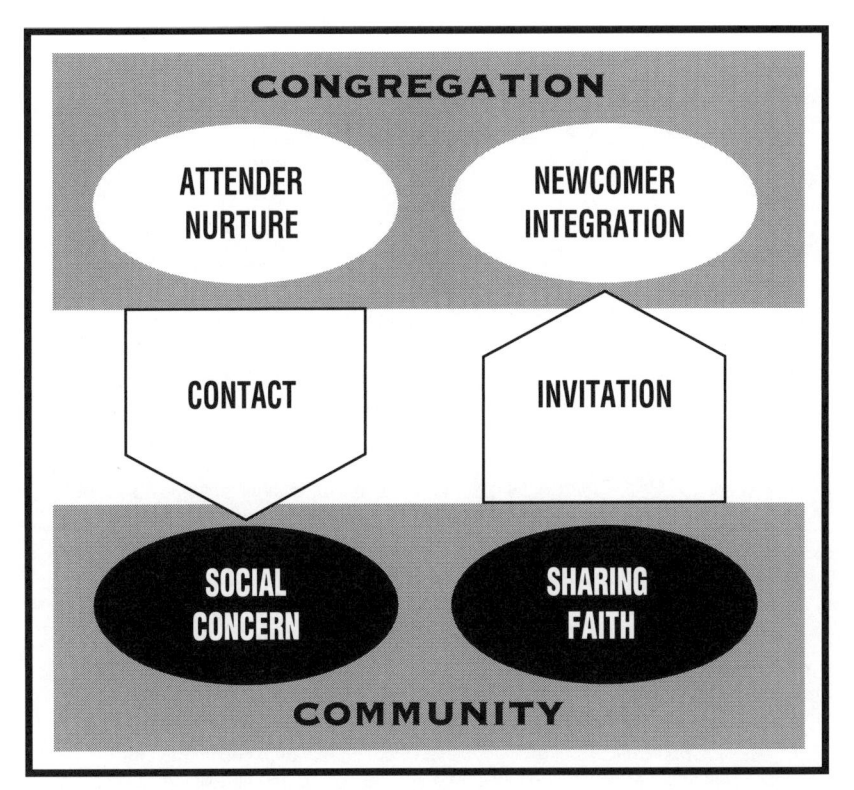

```
┌─────────────────────────────────────────┐
│           CONGREGATION                   │
│                                          │
│    ATTENDER          NEWCOMER            │
│    NURTURE           INTEGRATION         │
│                                          │
│                                          │
│    CONTACT           INVITATION          │
│                                          │
│                                          │
│    SOCIAL            SHARING             │
│    CONCERN           FAITH               │
│                                          │
│           COMMUNITY                      │
└─────────────────────────────────────────┘
```

Corporate mission activities can be an important part of a congregation's involvement with the wider community and provide attenders with a secure environment for living out and sharing their faith.

The church is involved in the wider community through the activities of congregations, as well as individual attenders. Apart from value to the community, corporate mission activity may help a congregation gain a higher profile, help it develop its identity or help attenders grow in their understanding of faith and its implications in everyday life.

To what extent are congregations involved in corporate mission activities? As well as surveying attenders, the NCLS asked the leadership of congregations for details of their corporate life and activities.

Congregations are involved in literally hundreds of different mission activities. Evangelistic activities range from coffee shops and children's holiday programs through to men's breakfasts, church open days and open air worship services. Social action and welfare activities include advocacy groups, opportunity shops and day respite care for the elderly.

### The gentle art of bridge building

Congregations are involved in their communities in a variety of ways. Here are some of them:

- *Courthouse ministry:* Waiting to be called at court can involve many hours with few comforts. Members of one congregation spend time with people in this situation.
- *Christian videos:* One congregation broadened the range of videos at the local video store through the placement of videos with a gospel message.
- *Baptism interviews:* It is now common for clergy to spend time with parents bringing their infants for baptism, doing studies together on the meaning of faith and baptism.
- *Stand against racism:* One city congregation made a stand against racism, which drew opposition, including vandalism and the daubing of graffiti on the church building.
- *Playgroups and kindergartens:* Many congregations have helped to develop playgroups and kindergartens and, in the process, have formed contacts with local families.
- *Behind the bar:* One congregation sought to build bridges to the pub culture by meeting in the local hotel and serving behind the counter. Sometimes the bar can become a confessional!
- *Bus service for the aged:* Activities such as a visit to the shops can be a struggle for some older people. One congregation sought to be of assistance by providing a weekday bus service for the aged.
- *Discussion on university campuses:* To supplement the work of chaplaincies, Christian students have been equipped to share their faith in the marketplace of ideas that is the modern university campus.
- *Streetwork among the homeless:* Through a campaign with other youth workers, involving representations to politicians and appearances in the media, one church-based youth worker helped to establish long-term housing for homeless youth.
- *Teaching English as a second language:* One denomination encouraged its congregations to become involved in programs for teaching English as a second language, to meet a need of many migrants from non-English speaking countries.

A list of activities carried out by congregations is in Appendix 3.

Some activities, such as carols by candlelight, are held at particular times, while others, such as counselling services, are offered continuously throughout the year. A full list of activities is included in Appendix 3. This will be a useful resource for congregations thinking about mission strategies.

Congregational mission includes both evangelistic and social care/justice activities. In many cases, the distinction between the two is blurred. While some activities, such as special worship services for visitors, may be identifiably evangelistic, others such as providing meals to people in crisis, offer much needed support as well as positive contact with the church and Christian people.

## SOCIAL ACTION AND CARE ACTIVITIES

The churches are a major contributor to the welfare effort in Australia and are responsible for administering large amounts of government welfare funding as well as their own funds. In 1993, Anglican and Protestant churches in Australia spent about one billion dollars on social services, including aged care, welfare and community services. Spending by some individual denominations was enormous. While exact figures are hard to estimate, the Anglican Church spent approximately $250 million, the Uniting Church spent about $400 million nationally on aged care and the Salvation Army's income for charitable purposes was about $260 million (Cole, 1994).

This figure accounts only for spending at a denominational level. Although an exact figure isn't available, it is much larger when services provided by individual congregations are taken into account as well.

Services sponsored by congregations vary widely. Some congregations are large enough to run welfare services of their own. Others provide services on a much smaller scale or work with other congregations or recognised community charities. For example, one large congregation from a wealthy suburb travels across the city to staff the meal program of a smaller congregation in a poor area. Similarly, one small inner-city congregation cooperated with the Smith Family to trial a literacy program providing special tutoring to disadvantaged teenagers.

According to the NCLS, almost half of all congregations (46%) allow community groups such as aerobics groups or Alcoholics Anonymous to use the congregational property. It makes sense for buildings which may otherwise stand vacant during the week to be used on a regular basis.

Allowing community groups to use church property doesn't have to be a passive activity; some congregations are actively involved in the community group that uses the property. Other congregations are involved in community groups not meeting at church. Indeed, 45% of all congregations have representatives in community groups or on management committees.

About 35% of congregations are directly involved in providing welfare services such as counselling or opportunity shops, 32% run mothers' groups, play groups, craft groups and so on, and 27% participate in special community activities such as peace marches and community fairs.

Given the older age profile of most denominations, it is surprising that only 11% of congregations provide aged care activities. While most denominations are aware of the need to reach out to younger people and those from blue-collar groups, mission to older people should not be neglected. Congregations with a large proportion of older attenders may find they have both the resources and the empathy to reach out successfully to older people in the community.

A sizeable group of congregations nominated children's clubs as a key contact with the community. Many congregations consider these activities to have both an evangelistic and community care function.

*Most community contact activities focus on people who spend their day in the local area*

Many of the community contact activities listed by congregational leaders focus on reaching people who spend most of their day in the local area, including children, retired people, young people and women who aren't in paid employment. This model of ministry is suitable for congregations that want to serve their local geographic area, but may be inappropriate for such people as working men and women who spend a good part of their time at their place of employment (Jensen and Payne, 1989, 48).

Congregations list a wide range of community care activities (see Appendix 3), which suggests that many congregations are responding creatively to the specific needs in their local area. However, in developing strategies, congregations need to consider not only local needs, but also the existing activities of other congregations and community service agencies. Ideally, activities across a region should complement rather than compete with one another. Congregations also need to consider the nature of their community and the stage in life of most of the population, so that they can develop appropriate responses. Some denominations have trained community workers who can advise congregations on needs and existing services in the wider community. They may also be able to help congregations move through the steps from planning a project to putting it into effect.

> **Developing effective social concern strategies**
> - Carry out a survey among residents and consult with welfare agencies and the local council to discern needs.
> - Identify existing activities and services of neighbouring congregations and community groups.
> - Identify the resources of the congregation. Questions to consider include:
>   - Will volunteers need special skills? If so, is training available?
>   - How many people will be available to staff the service?
>   - How much time can volunteers commit to the service?
>   - What physical resources such as buildings, equipment and vehicles are required?
>   - What financial resources are required? Will ongoing funding need to be raised?
> - Select a program that matches congregational strengths to needs within the area. However, sometimes congregations feel called to ministries which seem beyond their capacity. Logic and planning should not necessarily replace obedience to such a calling.
> - Monitor the effectiveness of the program. At different times, the program may need to be modified, expanded or even closed.
> - Provide regular support, training and evaluation meetings to encourage volunteers and maintain the ministry. Pray together before expansion or change.
> - Expect to make mistakes and learn from them. Ministry is not a pass/fail exercise.
>
> Source: Ruth Smitherman, Anglican Home Mission Society

## EVANGELISTIC ACTIVITIES

The most popular evangelistic activities run by congregations are Bible studies for the wider community, such as *Christianity Explained* (26%), and services and crusades (23%). Only 13% of congregations say they currently hold mission activities in schools. This figure is quite low; however, some congregations may not have considered religious education in schools to be a mission activity.

A significant proportion of congregations conduct visitation programs (9%), street evangelism (8%) and drop-in centres (6%). Other common activities noted by congregations include letterbox drops, children's programs, school holiday programs, special Easter and Christmas services and door knocks.

When planning mission initiatives, congregations need to consider who will come to the activities and who will invite them. The NCLS shows that the majority of newcomers to church join because of a personal invitation (*Winds of Change*, p 161).

Congregations may also want to experiment with activities on 'neutral territory' such as community halls and restaurants. While more difficult to arrange than those at the congregational centre, they may be less threatening to non-churchgoers and therefore more accessible to them.

Another approach to consider is running joint activities with other congregations. Together, congregations may have a much greater impact than one congregation alone. A joint approach may overcome the distrust Australians seem to have of organisations that cannot work in harmony. One notable example of joint activities is the annual Reclaim Easter festival. Many successful ecumenical festivals are now being held throughout Australia each year.

## INVOLVEMENT IN MISSION ACTIVITIES

To identify attenders' involvement in congregational mission activities, the NCLS included the following question.

**Q** Do you regularly take part in any mission activities of this church? (eg visitation, evangelism, community service/social justice/welfare)
  a. No, we don't have such activities
  b. No, I am not regularly involved
  c. Yes, in evangelistic activities
  d. Yes, in social care/social justice activities
  e. Yes, both c and d above

The results support the evidence from leaders that there are many congregational mission activities going on. Only 9% of all attenders say their congregation does not have evangelistic or social care/justice activities.

However, a minority of attenders carries out these activities. Overall, 34% of attenders are regularly involved in congregationally based mission: 10% in evangelistic activities, 13% in social care/social justice activities and 11% in both types. Two-thirds of all attenders are not regularly involved or their congregation has no mission activities.

Figure 4.1

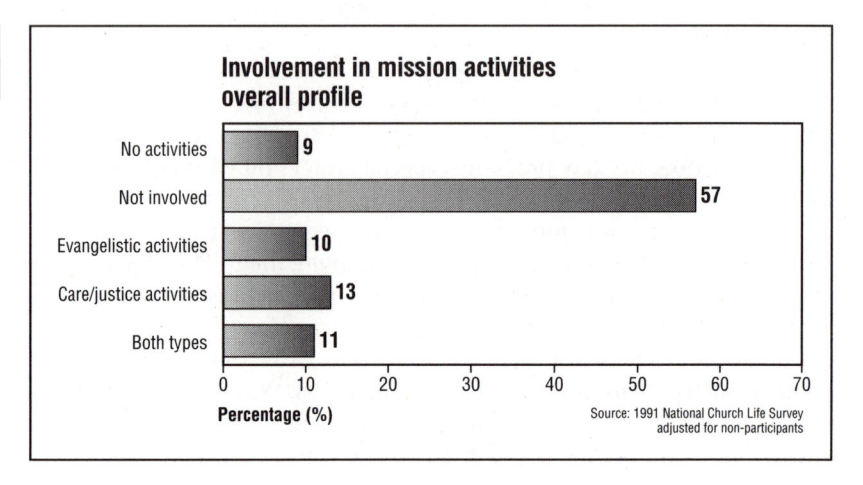

**Involvement in mission activities overall profile**

| Category | Percentage (%) |
|---|---|
| No activities | 9 |
| Not involved | 57 |
| Evangelistic activities | 10 |
| Care/justice activities | 13 |
| Both types | 11 |

Source: 1991 National Church Life Survey adjusted for non-participants

42  Mission under the Microscope

It should be noted that regular attenders will be over-represented in a 'slice in time' survey such as the NCLS, compared to one which surveys all those who ever attend church. When all attenders are considered, the percentage involved in mission activities would be lower.

Nevertheless, it is encouraging that a third of attenders have some kind of involvement in activities with an outward focus. When asked what aspect of congregational life they most value, only 13% of attenders nominate their congregation's outward focus (*Winds of Change*, p 186). While attenders may not value it most, many are involved in mission activities as a consequence of their faith and because they are part of the congregation.

## WHO IS INVOLVED?

Older attenders are much more likely to be involved in church-based mission activities than younger attenders. Only 15% of 15 to 19 year olds are involved, compared to 42% of attenders in their 60s. Figure 4.2 shows the type of involvement in each age group.

**Involvement in mission activities by age group**

| Age group | % |
|---|---|
| 15–19 | 15 |
| 20–29 | 27 |
| 30–39 | 31 |
| 40–49 | 36 |
| 50–59 | 41 |
| 60–69 | 42 |
| 70+ | 36 |

Legend: Evangelistic, Care/justice, Both types

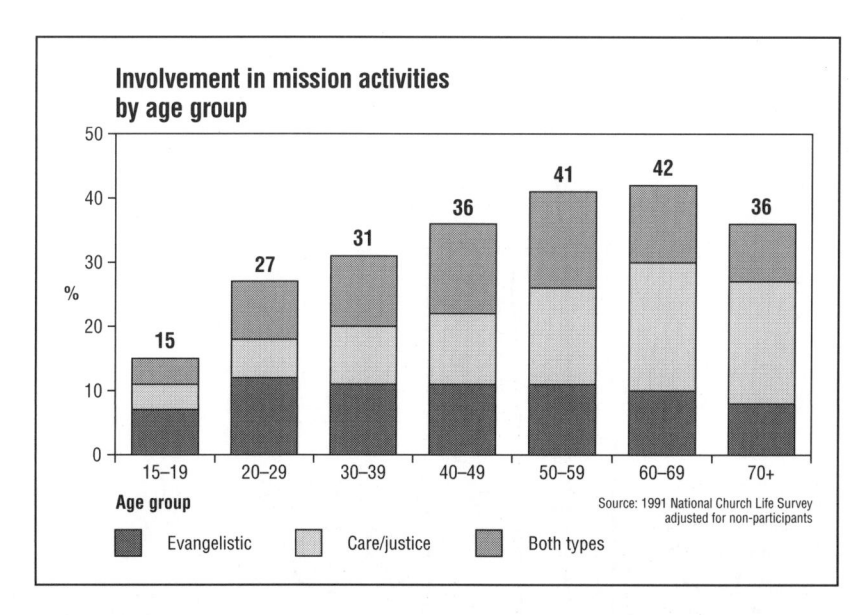

Source: 1991 National Church Life Survey adjusted for non-participants

Figure 4.2

As will be seen in Chapter 5, older attenders are less comfortable talking about their faith than younger attenders. However, they are just as likely to be involved in evangelistic activities based in the congregation. Older attenders appear to be no less committed to the concept of evangelism than younger attenders; possibly they are more comfortable with a formalised church activity than informal, one-to-one discussions in everyday life. The fact that older attenders have fewer contacts in everyday life than younger attenders may also be a factor.

Older attenders are, however, more likely to be involved in social care or social justice activities than younger attenders. This is probably due, in

> **Older attenders are more likely to be involved in social care issues than younger attenders**

part, to attenders being in different life stages. Older attenders, many of whom have retired and no longer have a continual responsibility for children, may have more time for such activities.

However, if life stage were the only factor, attenders in their 60s, who have even more time when they retire, would be much more involved. In fact, attenders in their 60s are only slightly more involved than attenders in their 50s.

Another possible contributing factor is a generational shift. *Winds of Change* (p 285) suggested that there are significant generational differences in many areas of church life, including patterns of faith, levels of participation and attitudes to congregational life. Social changes, such as more women in the workforce, may also lead to a decline in voluntary church activity among the younger generations of church attenders.

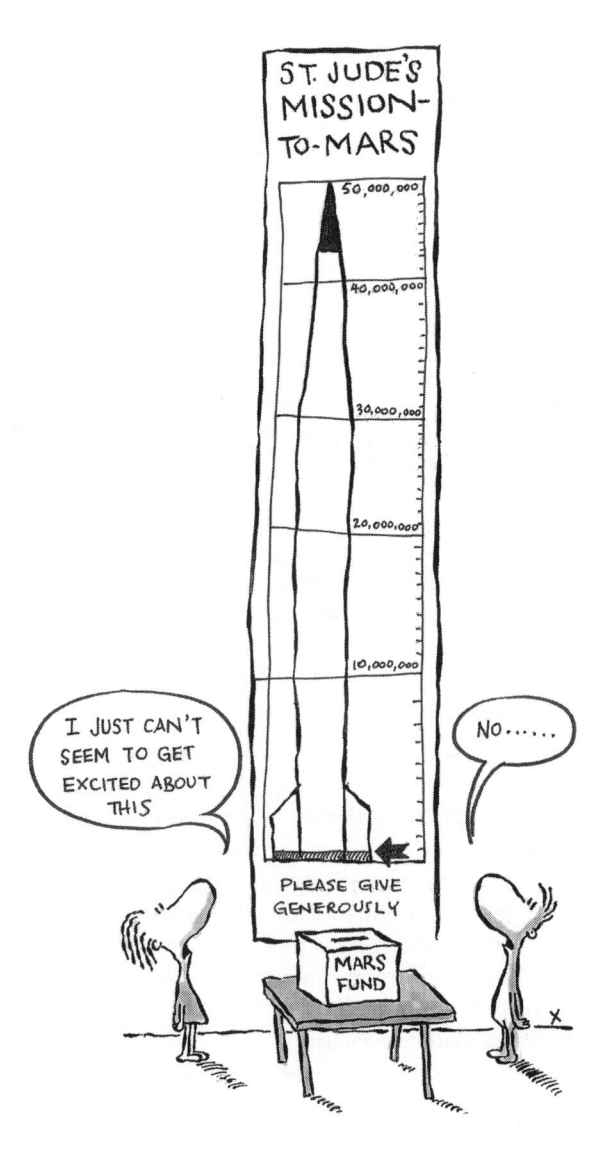

If the trend away from involvement in welfare and social justice activities is due to a generational shift, it may have a long-term effect on both denominational and congregational social concern activities. Older attenders currently form a large part of the voluntary workforce for social care. Who will do the work when they are no longer able to continue? Denominations will need to do further research in this area.

## DENOMINATIONAL DIFFERENCES

Attenders in most denominations are about equally likely to be involved in congregational mission activities. Attenders from the Seventh-day Adventist Church (55%) and Salvation Army (46%) have the highest levels of involvement, compared to an average of 34% overall.

There are few regional differences within the largest denominations. For instance, Anglican attenders in the Sydney, Melbourne, Brisbane and

**Involvement in mission activities by denomination**

| | No activities % | Not involved % | Evangelistic activities % | Care/justice activities % | Both types % | Total % |
|---|---|---|---|---|---|---|
| **Overall** | 9 | 57 | 10 | 13 | 11 | 100 |
| Anglican | 12 | 60 | 9 | 12 | 8 | 100 |
| Apostolic | 6 | 56 | 15 | 8 | 15 | 100 |
| Assemblies of God | 7 | 57 | 15 | 8 | 13 | 100 |
| Baptist | 6 | 59 | 12 | 11 | 11 | 100 |
| Christian & Missionary Alliance | 8 | 54 | 20 | 5 | 13 | 100 |
| Christian Revival Crusade | 7 | 57 | 11 | 9 | 14 | 100 |
| Church of the Nazarene | 11 | 53 | 19 | 4 | 12 | 100 |
| Churches of Christ | 8 | 59 | 10 | 12 | 11 | 100 |
| Congregational | 10 | 59 | 11 | 9 | 11 | 100 |
| Foursquare Gospel | 10 | 53 | 16 | 8 | 14 | 100 |
| Lutheran | 12 | 59 | 9 | 10 | 9 | 100 |
| NZ Presbyterian | 8 | 56 | 6 | 21 | 9 | 100 |
| Presbyterian | 13 | 57 | 9 | 12 | 8 | 100 |
| Reformed | 6 | 61 | 11 | 11 | 10 | 100 |
| Salvation Army | 6 | 48 | 18 | 12 | 16 | 100 |
| Seventh-day Adventist | 3 | 43 | 14 | 16 | 25 | 100 |
| Uniting | 10 | 56 | 6 | 18 | 10 | 100 |
| Wesleyan Methodist | 7 | 59 | 16 | 6 | 12 | 100 |
| Westminster Presbyterian | 6 | 63 | 13 | 7 | 11 | 100 |
| House Churches | 35 | 21 | 2 | 27 | 15 | 100 |
| **Type of denomination** | | | | | | |
| Mainstream | 11 | 58 | 8 | 14 | 9 | 100 |
| Pentecostal | 7 | 57 | 15 | 8 | 13 | 100 |
| Large Protestant | 6 | 55 | 12 | 12 | 14 | 100 |
| Small Protestant | 7 | 59 | 14 | 8 | 11 | 100 |

Source: 1991 National Church Life Survey attender data adjusted for non-participants

Figure 4.3

Perth dioceses have similar levels of involvment in mission activities. Uniting attenders in New South Wales, Queensland and South Australia have similar levels of involvement, though attenders in Victoria are more highly involved in social concern activities.

Chapter 2 indicated that attenders in Pentecostal and small Protestant denominations are the least likely to be involved in community-based social action/welfare activities. However, their levels of involvement are higher when activities are sponsored by the congregation. This suggests that these variations are partly explained by differing orientations to the world as well as differing views on the place of social action/welfare activities.

Different theological orientations show different levels of involvement. Those who have been influenced by Anglo-Catholic or Catholic traditions (32%) are less likely to be involved in congregational mission activities than those influenced by evangelical (44%) or charismatic (42%) traditions.

There are clear differences according to an attender's view of the Bible. Those who view the Bible as God's word to be taken literally are more likely to be involved in congregational mission activities (42%) than attenders who think the Bible is God's word to be read in the context of the times (35%) or attenders who view it as a valuable book (27%).

These differences are due mainly to variations in involvement in evangelistic activities; however, it is interesting to note that literalists (25%) and contextualists (26%) have slightly higher levels of involvement in congregationally based social concern activities than valuists (20%). Literalists and contextualists are more involved in congregational mission activities, both social concern and evangelistic. However, as Chapter 2 showed, valuists tend to have higher levels of involvement in community-based groups than literalists. Again this suggests that the differences between these groups are related to orientation to the world, apart from considerations about the importance of social concern.

Figure 4.4

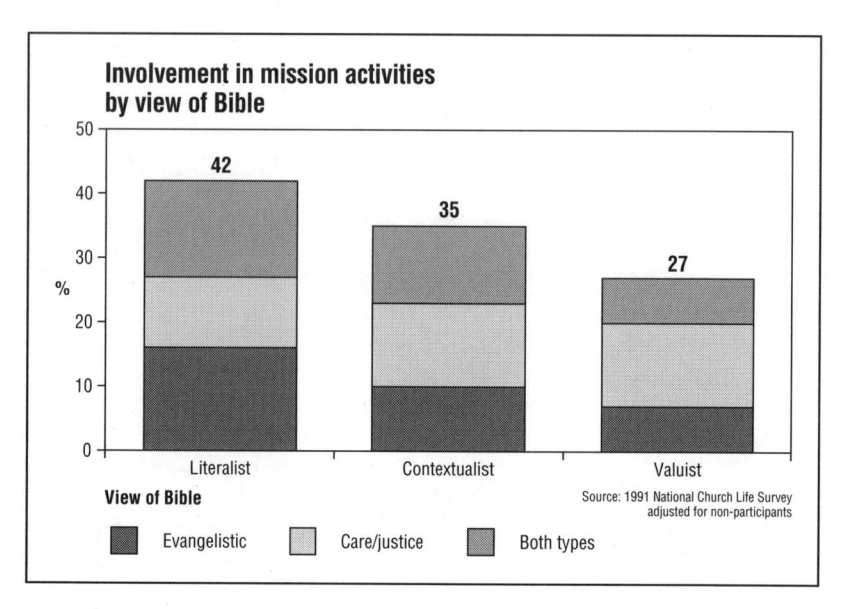

**Involvement in mission activities by view of Bible**

Source: 1991 National Church Life Survey adjusted for non-participants

Legend: Evangelistic, Care/justice, Both types

Literalist: 42
Contextualist: 35
Valuist: 27

> **Housing and health in poorer areas**
>
> In the early 1980s, members of a Baptist congregation in Melbourne began offering their spare rooms to people in crisis. As demand for emergency accommodation grew, the congregation recognised that what they really needed was a house. Immediately after the meeting at which this was agreed, the pastor received a phone call from a local businessman offering a five-bedroom house and attached bungalow. So began a housing project which today has more than 20 housing units, employs five staff and receives government funding.
>
> The housing group is just one of the social service projects operating under the wing of the congregation. Other projects are a health services cooperative and a community initiatives group which provides training for disadvantaged and long-term unemployed people.
>
> 'A summary doesn't do justice to the true history', says a member of the congregation. 'These projects didn't happen overnight. They grew from small beginnings. The health cooperative started with just one doctor who was employed because there was no doctor in the area who would bulk bill, even though this is quite a poor area. A summary also doesn't mention the failures and tensions along the way. For example, we began the employment project as a delivery service, which proved to be a costly mistake!'
>
> The projects have raised the profile of the congregation, especially among local community leaders. While recognising the value of the projects, the congregation is wary of becoming just project managers, with no personal link to people in the area. 'We want to live out the good news. We're looking at how to develop our role as a local church as well as a provider of community services.'

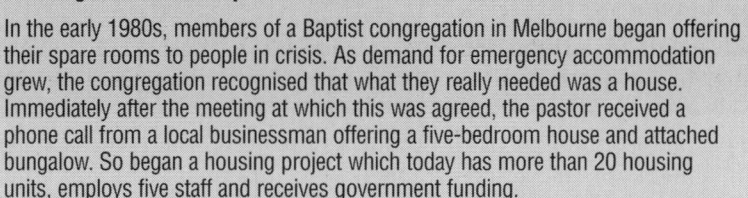

## CHURCH INVOLVEMENT

Attenders who are most involved in congregational life are also most involved in mission activities. Some 63% of highly involved attenders are also involved in congregationally based mission activities, compared to just 10% of infrequent worshippers.

Many leaders will not be surprised by these results. Congregations of all sizes appear to be dependent on a core of attenders who are highly involved in their activities. Such attenders may more easily catch and own the vision for mission activities through their small groups and other activities. In addition, their regular attendance at worship and in small groups may give them a better understanding of the church's call to mission.

Congregations need to help attenders to see more clearly the importance of mission activities. This applies especially to first-time newcomers and attenders who have returned to church after an absence of years. Only 16% of these attenders are involved in mission activities, compared to 26% of attenders who have recently switched denominations and 34% who have transferred congregations within a denomination. However, newcomers may be tentative about mission because they need time to adjust to church life.

# WHAT DIFFERENCE DOES IT MAKE?

*Sense of influence*

Involvement in mission activities, particularly evangelistic activities, is related to having a sense of Christian influence. Some 73% of those involved in mission activities feel they exert a great or some influence, compared to only 47% of those not so involved. The level of church involvement of respondents, their age or their denominational background do not account for this trend.

*Sharing faith*

Those involved in congregational mission activities are more comfortable discussing their faith than other attenders. While 29% of attenders not involved in mission activities feel they have difficulty discussing their faith, only 18% of those involved in mission activities feel this way. Clearly, such mission activities are more likely to attract attenders who are comfortable discussing their faith or who look for opportunities to do so.

At the same time, there is a substantial number of attenders involved in mission activities who have difficulty discussing their faith. Possibly congregationally based mission activities give some attenders who find it hard to discuss their faith an avenue for mission in a structured, supportive environment.

*Inviting others to church*

> **Attenders involved in mission activities are more likely to have invited someone to church in the past year**

Those involved in mission activities are more likely to have tried to encourage someone to church in the past year than those not so involved (53% compared to 33%). This relationship is stronger for those involved in evangelistic activities.

*Growth in faith*

Attenders involved in mission activities generally report higher levels of growth in their faith, irrespective of their age or denominational background. For instance, 61% of attenders involved in mission activities feel they have experienced much growth in their understanding of their faith in the past year, compared to 42% of other attenders.

Closer examination of the data suggests that the relationship is strongest among those who have lower levels of involvement in congregational life, such as infrequent worshippers. The highly involved have many forums for growth in faith; mission activities may be but one.

Attenders involved in mission activities are likely to pray more frequently than other attenders. Of those involved in mission activities, 29% have both a set time for prayer each day and also pray informally during the day, compared to 16% of other attenders. Among those involved in evangelistic activities the figure is still higher.

There are clear links between involvement in mission activities and discussing faith, inviting others to church, personal growth in faith and a sense of influence. It is not clear which factor causes which. It may well be that involvement in mission activities not only promotes these, but is also the result of them. What is important for leaders to note is that mission activities may have an important role, alongside other aspects of congregational life, in encouraging growth in faith among attenders.

## COMMUNITY-BASED OR CHURCH-BASED?

Should congregations place a greater priority on developing mission activities in their own name or on encouraging attenders to get involved in existing community groups? The NCLS cannot evaluate which avenue has the greater impact. No doubt different approaches are more appropriate in different contexts; the background and resources of a congregation, the hopes and passions of its attenders, and the needs of the community all need to be considered.

However, a comparison can be made of the profiles of attenders involved in each avenue of contact. For those involved in each avenue, are there differences in reported levels of growth in faith, patterns of sharing faith, inviting others to church, or having a sense of Christian influence?

In the following discussion, those involved in congregationally based social action/welfare activities are compared with those involved in community-based social action/welfare activities. Congregational evangelistic activities have been excluded from consideration.

Generally, attenders involved in congregationally based social action/welfare activities report higher levels of growth in faith, invitations to join congregational life and so on. However, closer inspection reveals that these differences largely reflect the level of church involvement of the respondents.

For instance, people who are much involved in church are just as likely to be growing in their faith, irrespective of their preferred avenue of social action/welfare activity. Some 63% of highly involved attenders who are also in congregationally based social concern activities grew much in their faith in the past year, compared to 61% among those in community-based activities.

Similar results are found for the readiness of attenders to share their faith, invite others to church and the sense of influence they feel that they have. This suggests that those who are involved in church life are not necessarily distracted from growth in faith or evangelism by being involved in a community group rather than a congregational mission activity.

Each of the different avenues has a place. Both congregationally sponsored mission activities and attender involvement in community groups provide opportunities for service and growth. There are good reasons for congregationally based activities; there are also good reasons for cooperating with other congregations and community organisations. Congregations may want to examine what attenders are doing and why.

There are some advantages to encouraging attender involvement in community groups, including the fact that attenders meet members of the wider community on their own turf in an environment that may be less threatening. Encouraging attenders to get involved and actively supporting them requires energy and effort, but does not require the same infrastructure and administration that many congregationally sponsored activities require.

On the other hand, congregationally based mission activities can give congregations an identity in the wider community and raise awareness of the congregation. Such activities can help a congregation to live out and model its stated vision, and help attenders to grow in discipleship and to develop a mission outlook. In some instances, congregational mission activities avoid potential conflicts of interest or perceived 'additional agendas' which people may feel that attenders have when they are involved in community groups.

\* \* \* \*

## IN MISSION TOGETHER

A third of attenders are regularly involved in congregationally based mission activities. This suggests that congregations need to reflect on the profile of outreach activities, compared to other congregational activities.

For many attenders, involvement in mission activities flows out a sense of belonging or growth in faith through being involved in a congregation. However, this is not their primary reason for involvement. Congregations may want to examine why attenders value mission as they do.

Congregations may also want to consider whether mission activity needs to be promoted in a different way. Rather than presenting it mainly in terms of a responsibility or a challenge, leaders should seek to present it as a natural outflow of the love and caring experienced within the congregation and of the love of God attenders experience in their daily lives. As was noted in *Winds of Change* (p 192) there is some evidence that many attenders are motivated by a sense of belonging or by compassion, rather than by a challenge or an appeal to commitment in their involvement in their congregation.

In reflecting on the base of support for mission activities, congregations should consider how better to promote such activities among younger attenders. The young may be less involved in social care and justice activities because of their stage in life. However, if these lower levels of involvement are a generational effect, this may have an impact on the future provision of such services by many congregations and denominational agencies.

---

**Corporate mission activities can be an important part of a congregation's involvement with the wider community and provide attenders with a secure environment for living out and sharing their faith.**

- More than three in 10 attenders are regularly involved in congregationally based mission activities.
- Older attenders are more involved in welfare/social justice activities than younger attenders. Congregations and denominations need to reflect on why this is so and how this might affect future patterns of ministry.
- Attenders who see the Bible as God's word are more likely to be involved in congregational mission activities than those who do not. This is true for both evangelistic and social care activities.
- Attenders who are involved in their congregation's mission activities, especially evangelistic activities, are more likely to be growing in their faith, discussing it with others and inviting others to church. Apart from its value in the wider community, such involvement may be of significant benefit to attenders themselves.
- Both congregationally based social care activities and community-based social care activities have a place in providing opportunities for attenders to serve and to grow.

# PART 2

# BEARERS OF THE WORD

Previous chapters examined the extent to which attenders are involved in community groups, social action activities, congregational mission activities and the wider community in everyday life. In this part the focus shifts to the question of discussing matters of faith in these contexts.

Several key issues are dealt with.
- How open and willing are attenders to discuss matters of faith with others? How comfortable do they feel talking about their faith in natural, jargon-free ways?
- What factors may be inhibiting attenders in sharing the faith, and how can congregations support and equip them to move forward in these areas?
- To what extent are attenders actually sharing their faith with others? How are they doing that, and to what extent are they inviting others to join the life of a Christian congregation?

CHAPTER 5

# READINESS TO SHARE FAITH
## An important prerequisite

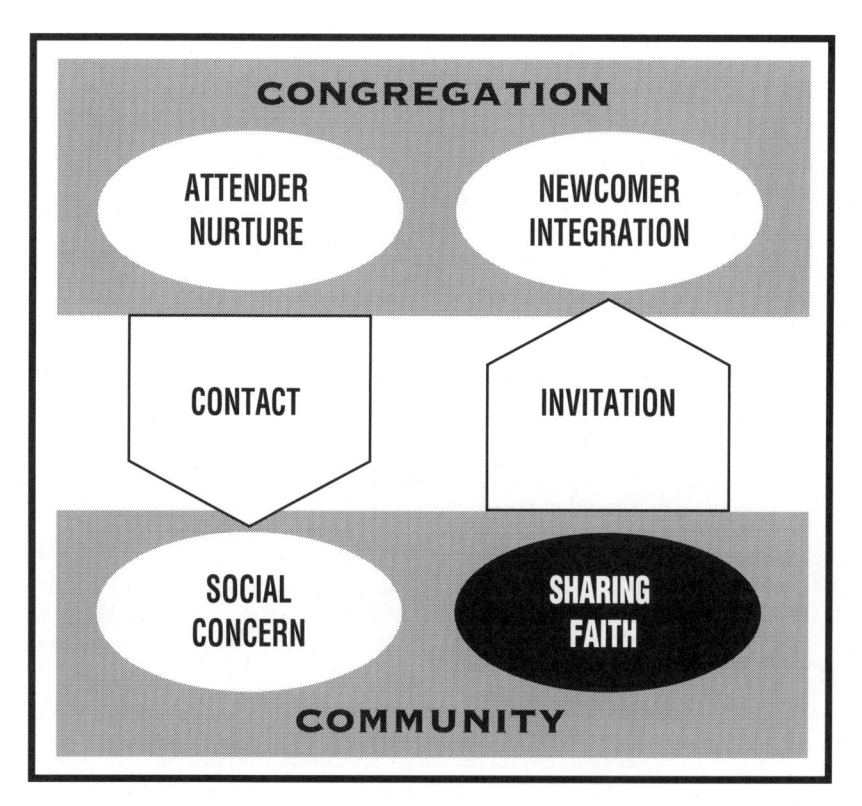

**CONGREGATION**

ATTENDER NURTURE

NEWCOMER INTEGRATION

CONTACT

INVITATION

SOCIAL CONCERN

SHARING FAITH

**COMMUNITY**

A major challenge for the church today is to equip attenders to be comfortable discussing their faith in daily life in natural ways.

Being Christian disciples is not only a matter of actions. Christians are often asked to name the source of their strength, values and beliefs.

For some church attenders, this isn't a problem – they are comfortable talking about their faith. Indeed, some are intentional about it, creating opportunities to share their faith rather than waiting for opportunities to arise.

Other attenders, however, prefer to live out their faith rather than talk about it. Perhaps they believe this is the best way they communicate, that actions can speak louder than words. Still others would like to share their faith, but find it difficult or threatening to do so.

The NCLS confirms that there is a wide range of attitudes among attenders about discussing their faith. However, while attenders may disagree on just how to go about it, almost all attenders believe it is appropriate to talk about their faith under some circumstances. The NCLS included three questions that explore attenders' attitudes to faith sharing.

## WHEN IS IT RIGHT TO SHARE?

The NCLS asked attenders the following question.

**Q**

**When is it right for you to talk about your faith with others in the wider community?**

a. It is best kept to oneself
b. Only if I am asked
c. Only in the context of my ongoing friendships
d. Only if I know the person
e. Any time, anywhere
f. Don't know

Figure 5.1

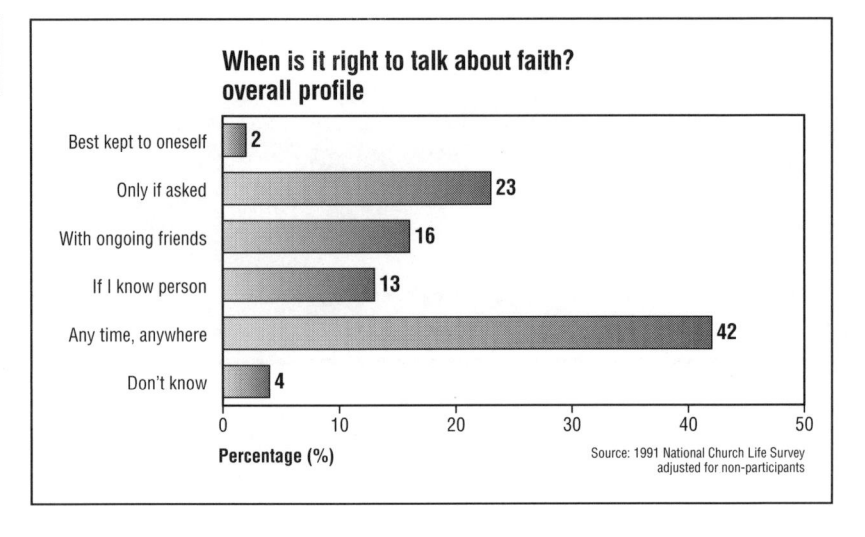

**When is it right to talk about faith? overall profile**

| Response | Percentage (%) |
|---|---|
| Best kept to oneself | 2 |
| Only if asked | 23 |
| With ongoing friends | 16 |
| If I know person | 13 |
| Any time, anywhere | 42 |
| Don't know | 4 |

Source: 1991 National Church Life Survey adjusted for non-participants

The largest proportion of attenders (42%) is prepared to share their faith anywhere, any time. Some 23% share their faith only if asked, 16% in the context of ongoing friendships and 13% if they know the person. Only 2% believe faith is best kept to themselves, and 4% don't know.

Pentecostal attenders are most likely to share their faith anywhere, any time (61%), while mainstream attenders are the least likely (37%). Is this difference related to the numerical growth of congregations rather than denomination? There appears to be little relationship here with numerical growth. Attenders in declining and stable congregations within each denominational grouping are about as likely to share their faith anywhere, any time as those in growing congregations.

## APPROACH TO FAITH SHARING

Christians share their faith in different ways. Stephen Abbott (1994) suggests some key ways:

- proclaiming the claims of Christ, as Peter did in his sermon on the day of Pentecost (Acts 2);
- testifying to the impact of Christ in one's life, as the blind man did after he was healed by Jesus (John 9);
- building bridges of relationship by interacting with others on their own turf, as Paul suggests in becoming all things to all people (1 Corinthians 9).

> LIGHT... Julie just couldn't explain it, measure it, weigh it, understand it, account for it, say why she had it....
>
> So she kept it at home.

The NCLS asked attenders whether they most often share their faith by their life example, giving a Christian viewpoint in discussion, sharing the claims of Christ, or persuading others.

**Q** **Which of the following best describes your usual approach to sharing your faith?**
a. My life and actions are a sufficient example
b. Sharing a Christian viewpoint on various issues
c. Presenting people with the claims of Christ – the decision is theirs
d. Persuading people to become Christians
e. Other

The largest proportion of attenders (42%) usually shares a Christian viewpoint on various issues. A smaller proportion usually shares the claims of Christ (17%) or seeks to persuade others to become Christians (4%). Some 30% feel their life and actions are the usual way their faith is shared.

Figure 5.2

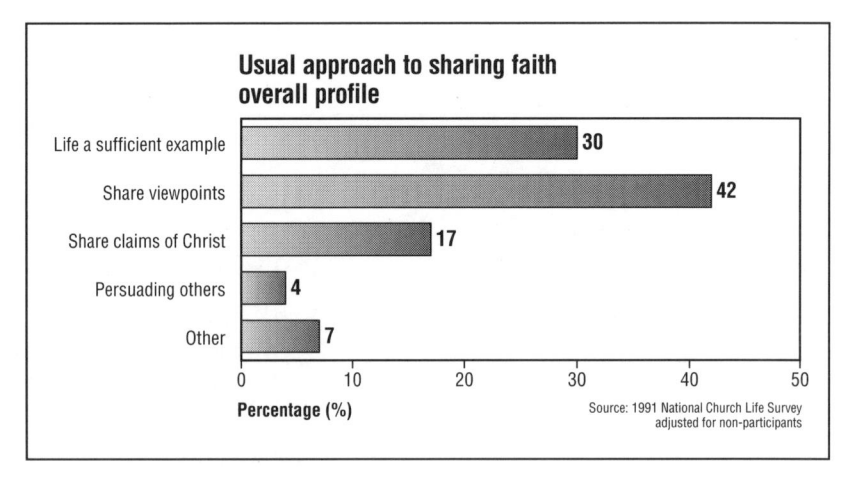

**Usual approach to sharing faith overall profile**

| Approach | Percentage (%) |
|---|---|
| Life a sufficient example | 30 |
| Share viewpoints | 42 |
| Share claims of Christ | 17 |
| Persuading others | 4 |
| Other | 7 |

Source: 1991 National Church Life Survey adjusted for non-participants

Attenders clearly take different approaches to discussing their faith. Some will feel that an approach that simply gives a Christian viewpoint is too casual and undersells the importance of proclaiming the Christian message. Others will be relieved that only a small proportion of attenders seeks to persuade others to make a Christian commitment as their usual approach to sharing their faith. If done insensitively, attempts to persuade others may be perceived as uncaring or downright aggressive.

Yet persuasion is not always a bad thing. A willingness to be candid about Christian faith, combined with behaviour that is consistent with the message, is seen by mission trainers as a powerful combination, particularly in the Australian context (Chapman, 1981, 112–118; Garvin, 1992, 13–15).

## READINESS TO SHARE FAITH

The NCLS asked the following question.

> **Which of the following best describes your readiness to talk to others about your faith?**
> a. I lack faith, so the question is not applicable
> b. I do not like to talk about my faith, I believe my life and actions give sufficient example
> c. I find it hard to express my faith in ordinary language
> d. I mostly feel at ease about expressing my faith and do so if the opportunity comes up
> e. I feel at ease about expressing my faith and seek to find opportunities to do so

More than half of all attenders feel ready to discuss their faith. Some 43% are at ease sharing their faith if the opportunity arises, while another 13% intentionally seek opportunities.

The majority of attenders who share their faith if the opportunity arises usually do so by sharing a Christian viewpoint on any subject that comes up in conversation. In contrast, the majority of attenders who intentionally set out to share their faith usually present the claims of Christ or actively persuade other people to become Christians.

*More than half of all attenders feel ready to discuss their faith*

**Readiness to share faith overall profile**

| Category | Percentage (%) |
|---|---|
| I lack faith | 2 |
| Life a sufficient example | 17 |
| Hard to express | 25 |
| At ease | 43 |
| Look for opportunities | 13 |

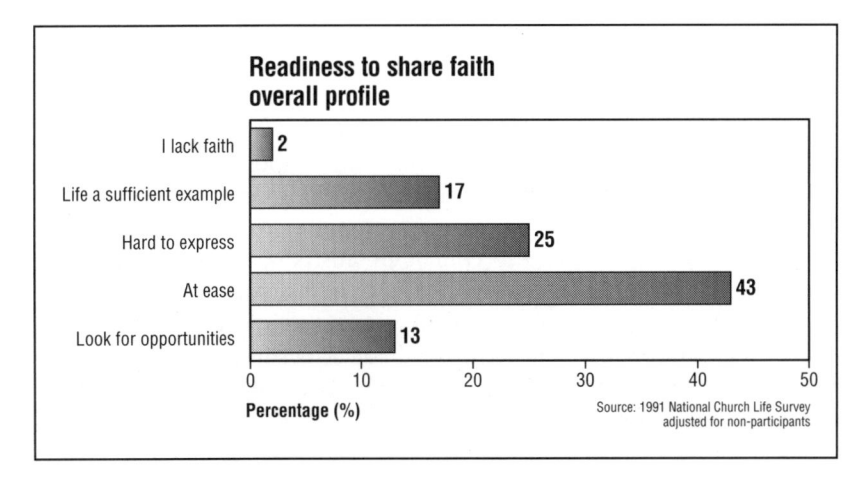

Source: 1991 National Church Life Survey adjusted for non-participants

Figure 5.3

Some 17% of attenders do not like to talk about their faith, but consider their life and actions to be a sufficient example. The size of this group may be of concern to some church leaders, who feel that, while a non-verbal example is critical to credibility, Christians are also called to be ready to give an account of their faith.

However, only a small fraction of this group never talk about their faith, believing faith is 'best kept to oneself'. The vast majority are happy to talk about their faith under certain circumstances, such as when directly asked.

What can be said about the 17% of attenders who don't like to talk about their faith? They may be opposed to proactive evangelism, or see faith as something lived out, which cannot easily be put into words. Alternatively, they may simply lack the confidence to share their faith and need encouragement, support or training to do so.

A quarter of all attenders (25%) find it hard to express their faith in ordinary language. This shouldn't come as a surprise. Over the centuries, the church has developed its own jargon, which appears in everything from songs and prayers to administration.

Discussing issues that touch on the core of a person's identity, that give meaning in life, can sound trite or superficial. Sometimes people misunderstand comments about faith and church because of the perceptions they have of church life. Some attenders may be trying hard to get away from these stereotypes of church life.

While some religious terms may be impossible to replace, congregations need to make a conscious effort to express faith in ways understandable to those in the wider community. What difference would it make to the mission of the church in Australia if another 200 000 attenders felt comfortable sharing their faith in everyday language?

There are many courses and workshops which equip attenders to discuss their faith with their friends and colleagues in an understandable way. These would be helpful to attenders in many congregations. Chapter 6 explores more fully the importance of training.

## THE YOUNG ARE A KEY

*Older attenders are more likely to prefer not to talk about their faith*

Older attenders are more likely than younger attenders to prefer not to talk about their faith, believing that their life example is sufficient. Some 23% of attenders in their 60s do not like to talk about their faith, compared to 9% in their 20s.

This age difference echoes some other aspects of the NCLS research. Older attenders have a more private approach to faith; as *Winds of Change*

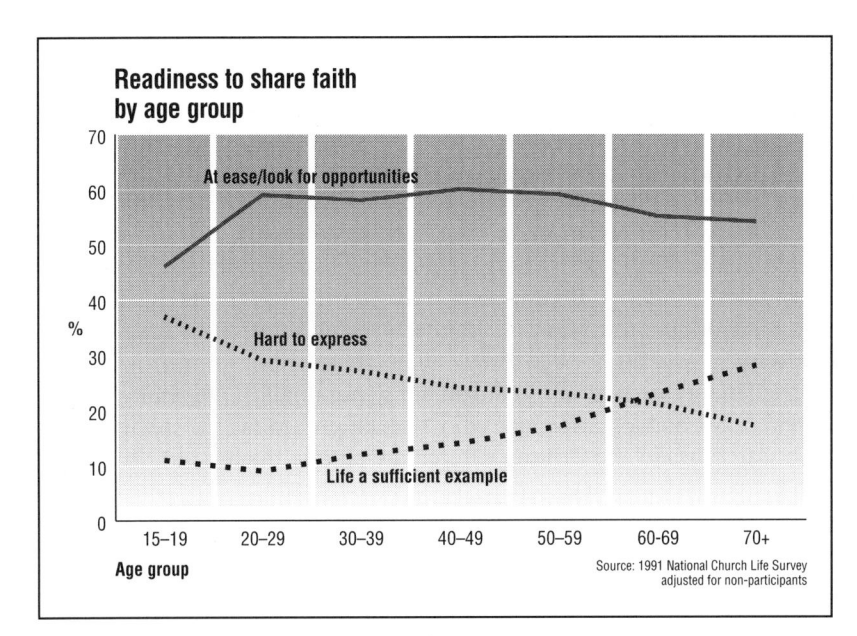

**Figure 5.4**

Readiness to share faith by age group

*(chart showing three lines across age groups 15-19, 20-29, 30-39, 40-49, 50-59, 60-69, 70+: "At ease/look for opportunities" rising from ~47% to ~60% and staying around 55-60%; "Hard to express" declining from ~35% to ~20%; "Life a sufficient example" rising from ~8% to ~28%)*

Source: 1991 National Church Life Survey adjusted for non-participants

(p 143) shows, they are less likely to discuss important daily matters with others in their congregation than younger attenders.

Encouraging older attenders to be more open about their faith will be important in some congregations, while in others, leaders may need to recognise and accept their approach. This does not mean that older attenders cannot support the mission of their congregation; they can, for instance, by supporting new disciples in prayer and other ways.

Younger attenders, on the other hand, are more likely to find it difficult to talk about their faith. Some 29% of those in their 20s find it hard to share their faith in ordinary language, compared to 21% in their 60s. This may, in part, be a reflection of their own growth in faith or the attitudes of those around them. Assisting younger attenders to discuss their faith in natural ways will be very important, given their wider levels of contact with non-churchgoers.

## EDUCATION AND ETHNICITY

Formal education does not make attenders more articulate in sharing their faith. Some 23% of attenders with a university degree find it difficult to express their faith in everyday language, compared to 25% of attenders who did not progress beyond secondary school.

Attenders from non-English-speaking backgrounds are more likely to look for opportunities to share their faith (22%) than attenders born in Australia (12%) or in other English-speaking countries (15%). This is true even when factors such as age and denomination are taken into account.

One explanation for this may be that many attenders from non-English-speaking countries come from other faith backgrounds and are converted to Christianity. As will be seen in Chapter 10, attenders who have had a conversion experience are more likely to seek opportunities to share their faith. The importance of religion in the country of origin and the migration experience may provide other explanations.

## DENOMINATIONAL DIFFERENCES

Attenders who set out to share their faith intentionally are not scattered evenly across all denominations. The Foursquare Gospel, Apostolic and Assemblies of God denominations have the highest levels of attenders who look for opportunities to share the faith and some of the lowest levels of attenders who do not like to talk about their faith.

The large Protestant and mainstream denominations generally have a lower proportion of attenders who seek opportunities to discuss their faith. Attenders in the Uniting Church are among the least likely to look

Figure 5.5

**Readiness to share faith by denomination**

|  | I lack faith % | Life a sufficient example % | Hard to express % | At ease % | Look for opportunities % | Total % |
|---|---|---|---|---|---|---|
| **Overall** | 2 | 17 | 25 | 43 | 13 | 100 |
| Anglican | 2 | 22 | 23 | 43 | 10 | 100 |
| Apostolic | 2 | 5 | 19 | 46 | 27 | 100 |
| Assemblies of God | 2 | 5 | 18 | 48 | 28 | 100 |
| Baptist | 2 | 10 | 29 | 45 | 14 | 100 |
| Christian & Missionary Alliance | 2 | 6 | 26 | 48 | 18 | 100 |
| Christian Revival Crusade | 2 | 7 | 21 | 49 | 21 | 100 |
| Church of the Nazarene | 3 | 10 | 22 | 44 | 21 | 100 |
| Churches of Christ | 2 | 13 | 27 | 44 | 13 | 100 |
| Congregational | 1 | 10 | 25 | 49 | 15 | 100 |
| Foursquare Gospel | 1 | 7 | 15 | 47 | 30 | 100 |
| Lutheran | 2 | 16 | 30 | 43 | 10 | 100 |
| NZ Presbyterian | 3 | 26 | 24 | 39 | 8 | 100 |
| Presbyterian | 2 | 21 | 25 | 42 | 11 | 100 |
| Reformed | 2 | 9 | 34 | 47 | 8 | 100 |
| Salvation Army | 3 | 14 | 23 | 42 | 18 | 100 |
| Seventh-day Adventist | 2 | 10 | 20 | 45 | 23 | 100 |
| Uniting | 2 | 25 | 25 | 40 | 8 | 100 |
| Wesleyan Methodist | 2 | 10 | 29 | 44 | 16 | 100 |
| Westminster Presbyterian | 3 | 6 | 32 | 44 | 15 | 100 |
| House Churches | 1 | 13 | 22 | 53 | 12 | 100 |
| **Type of denomination** |  |  |  |  |  |  |
| Mainstream | 2 | 23 | 25 | 42 | 9 | 100 |
| Pentecostal | 2 | 5 | 18 | 48 | 27 | 100 |
| Large Protestant | 2 | 11 | 26 | 44 | 16 | 100 |
| Small Protestant | 2 | 8 | 30 | 46 | 13 | 100 |

Source: 1991 National Church Life Survey attender data adjusted for non-participants

> **Making the most of opportunities**
>
> Annette, an Adelaide businesswoman, travels extensively to Sydney and Melbourne for her company. She uses the opportunities to talk about her faith with taxi drivers and people she sits next to on the plane.
>
> 'I know this isn't classic friendship evangelism that we hear about all the time, but it is easier to speak frankly to someone you'll never see again than with someone you have to see every day at work or at every family gathering', she says.
>
> 'In fact, I even pray for opportunities to come up with cabbies. They often ask what I did on the weekend, and when I say I went to church, the door is opened with questions such as: Why do you bother with church stuff? What do you think happens when we die?'
>
> Annette recognises that what she says may not convert them, or get them to church. 'I just think about the Bible passage which says that one sows and another reaps', she says. 'I'm sure that what I say will make them think twice next time they come across a Christian or think about God.'

for opportunities and the most likely to believe that their life is a sufficient example. There are few regional differences within the biggest of these denominations (Anglican, Uniting and Baptist).

These patterns are not accounted for by the higher proportion of older attenders in mainstream denominations. Nor are they related to congregational growth or decline. There is a culture in many Pentecostal congregations which is clearly encouraging attenders to be proactive about faith sharing.

Theology also influences attenders' attitudes to discussing their faith. Attenders who view the Bible as God's word to be taken literally are more likely to seek opportunities to share their faith, as are attenders who speak in tongues. More than a quarter of attenders influenced by charismatic theology or who speak in tongues intentionally set out to share their faith, as do 19% of attenders influenced by evangelical theological tradition.

## INVOLVED ATTENDERS SHARE FAITH

There is a clear link between church involvement and readiness to discuss matters of faith. The stereotype of intentional faith sharers as 'lone rangers', operating without the support of a body of believers, appears to be without substance. Attenders who spend more than six hours each week in congregational activities are almost three times more likely to seek opportunities to discuss their faith than those who attend services of worship only. This relationship exists even after denominational differences are taken into account.

Involvement in activities such as small groups or ministry teams may encourage attenders in this area. Leaders who want to nurture a heart for evangelism in their congregation may find they can do this effectively through such group activities.

*There is a clear link between church involvement and readiness to discuss faith*

## WHAT DIFFERENCE DOES IT MAKE?

Is there a link between readiness to share faith and attenders' growth in faith? In examining this issue, it should be noted that a relationship between two aspects of church involvement does not necessarily imply that one factor causes another.

*Sense of influence*

The old adage that success breeds success appears to apply to sharing faith. Or, perhaps it would be better phrased, success breeds confidence. Attenders who believe that what they do makes a difference, maintain their enthusiasm for outreach and look for opportunities to share their faith.

Not surprisingly, virtually all attenders (87%) who look for opportunities to share their faith feel they have great or some influence on others.

*Inviting others to church*

Those who look for opportunities to share their faith (66%) or feel at ease in sharing their faith (45%) are more likely to have tried to invite someone to church in the past year than those who do not like to do so (24%) or who find it hard to talk about their faith in everyday language (30%).

*Growth in faith*

Attenders who look for opportunities to share their faith are more likely to feel they have grown much in their faith (72%) than those who feel at ease in sharing their faith (49%), find it hard to share their faith (32%), or do not like to do so (26%).

Similarly, attenders who look for opportunities to share their faith are five times more likely to have made major changes in their lives as a result of their faith than those who do not like to talk about their faith.

NATHANIEL WAS YET TO MAKE HIS FIRST CONVERT

> **The reluctant faith sharer**
>
> Although Susan had been a member of mission teams during her early 20s, she had little success in drawing others into relationship with God. She stuck at it out of a sense of duty, rather than because she thought it would ever be fruitful. Over the course of a year, she struck up a casual acquaintance with Ian, the gardener at her townhouse complex. The conversation got around to church, and Susan mentioned that her husband Peter was a lay preacher.
>
> 'Ian was instantly interested. He told me he hadn't attended church since he was a child and asked me when Peter would next be preaching since he wouldn't mind hearing him. I was on my way to the shops and said I would let him know when I had returned', recalls Susan.
>
> 'He said he might be gone by then, and asked me if I had time to check before I went. I suddenly realised what I was doing – putting off inviting someone to church when they clearly wanted to come!'
>
> Susan admits with some shame that even though she had been praying for opportunities to share her faith, she hadn't really expected it to happen. 'I'm glad that Ian persisted', she says. 'I almost missed the opportunity altogether. As it is, Ian came to church, enjoyed it, and now brings his kids to Sunday school. I'm still not totally comfortable talking about my faith or inviting others to church, but I'm working on it.'

Does growing in faith result in a desire to share faith or does sharing faith cause it to grow? It is likely that one promotes the other.

Perceived spiritual growth is closely linked to readiness to discuss faith. The relationship between the two underlines the fact that equipping attenders to discuss their faith is not simply a matter of the latest techniques and motivational sermons; motivation is linked to a sense of deepening spirituality and growth in faith of believers.

A link was also found to exist between readiness to discuss matters of faith and patterns of prayer. Among attenders who look for opportunities to share their faith, 90% have a set time for prayer each day or pray informally during the day. This declines to only 48% of those attenders who do not like to share their faith.

It is important to note that these relationships do not depend simply on attenders' denominational background or view of the Bible. Within each denominational group or faith type category, attenders who are growing in their faith or are active in prayer are more likely to be comfortable discussing their faith.

\* \* \* \*

## A PREREQUISITE FOR FAITH SHARING

While some attenders are eager to share their faith, others are reluctant to do so – perhaps because they see it as a private matter or because they try to avoid the stereotypes of evangelism. Yet leaders, and particularly those with a heart for mission, may be reluctant to leave it at that, since most theological traditions uphold the importance of talking about faith.

While some may never be convinced of the need to share their faith, the vast majority of attenders are willing to do so under certain circumstances. It is important that they feel comfortable talking about their faith in a natural, jargon-free way.

Attenders often need assistance or training to be able to do this. Experience, practice and mentoring may all help attenders to be natural and relaxed when discussing their faith. They need encouragement to share their own faith story, to proclaim the gospel story and to listen to others' stories (Robinson, 1992, 17). Congregational mission activities may also be useful in this regard. Attenders can feel more comfortable discussing their faith in their daily lives if they have had experience doing so supported by other attenders.

Different attenders need different kinds of support. Young adults, who have many non-church contacts and are willing to explore questions of belief, are more likely to find it hard to express their faith in everyday language, while older people are more likely to be reluctant to talk about their faith.

The results in this chapter suggest that discussion of faith with others may more readily flow from attenders who feel they are growing in their faith and pray frequently. Attenders with a faith that is growing are more likely to make the effort to develop their ability to communicate something that is vitally important to them. This supports the idea that a mission mindset is more than techniques and strategies.

Finally, in a chapter on verbal discussion of faith, it is worth noting the importance of holding actions and words together. Australians have a natural cynicism which makes them quick to spot a fraud. As Robyn Claydon puts it, Christians must ensure that 'the good news of message we preach is not limited or denied by the bad news of the life we lead' (Robinson et al, 1991, 85). A verbal message which is not supported by credible actions can amount to little more than hot air.

---

**A major challenge for the church today is to equip attenders to be comfortable discussing their faith in daily life in natural ways.**

- Four in 10 attenders are at ease sharing their faith if the opportunity arises, while another 13% intentionally seek opportunities to do so. A quarter of all attenders find it hard to express their faith in ordinary language and 17% do not like to talk about their faith, believing their life and actions are sufficient example.
- Older attenders are more likely to prefer not to talk about their faith, while younger attenders are more likely to find it difficult to do so.
- Attenders in Pentecostal denominations are three times more likely to share their faith intentionally than attenders in mainstream denominations.
- Attenders who are highly involved in congregational life or who feel they are growing in their faith are more likely to seek opportunities to discuss their faith.

CHAPTER 6

# MOVING BEYOND THE BARRIERS

## Equipping attenders for faith sharing

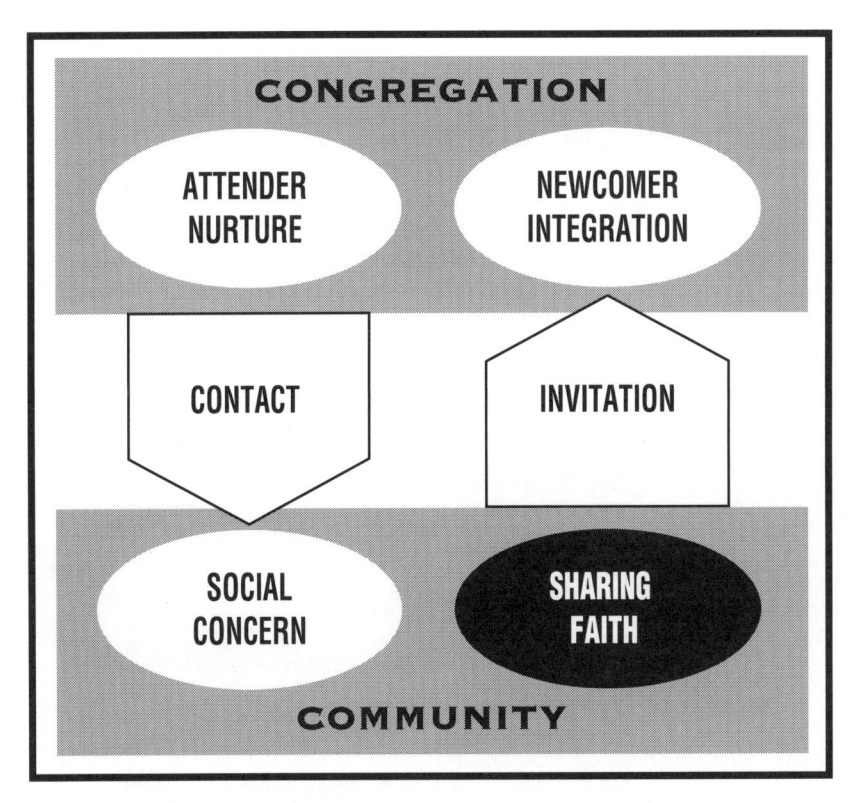

```
┌─────────────────────────────────────────┐
│            CONGREGATION                 │
│   ╭───────────╮      ╭───────────╮      │
│   │ ATTENDER  │      │ NEWCOMER  │      │
│   │  NURTURE  │      │INTEGRATION│      │
│   ╰───────────╯      ╰───────────╯      │
│                                         │
│     ┌───────┐         ┌───────┐         │
│     │CONTACT│         │INVITATION│      │
│     └───────┘         └───────┘         │
│                                         │
│   ╭───────────╮      ╭───────────╮      │
│   │  SOCIAL   │      │  SHARING  │      │
│   │  CONCERN  │      │   FAITH   │      │
│   ╰───────────╯      ╰───────────╯      │
│             COMMUNITY                   │
└─────────────────────────────────────────┘
```

Discussing matters of faith is not easy. Support and training can help attenders to grow beyond the barriers that inhibit them.

During a trip to Russia in its communist days, Rev Sir Alan and Lady Walker took a sightseeing tour which included many splendid churches that had been converted to museums. The guide's explanation that churches were no longer needed in the enlightened USSR didn't wash with Sir Alan, who challenged the statement publicly.

Despite Lady Walker's concern that the itinerary might switch from museums to gaols if he didn't keep quiet, Sir Alan refused to be silenced. Nothing could prevent him defending the faith to which he had committed his life.

While the context may be very different, many Australian Christians face barriers which prevent them sharing their faith with others. Embarrassment, feelings of inadequacy, fear of losing face, hostility . . . all can effectively prevent attenders from discussing their faith with others. To determine the main barriers to faith sharing, the NCLS included the following question.

> **Q** **If you do not feel comfortable talking about your faith, what is the major reason?**
> a. It is not appropriate in our society
> b. I'm fearful of other people's reactions
> c. I'm afraid I cannot answer people's difficult questions
> d. I do not understand my faith enough to talk about it
> e. Other
> f. Not applicable

Seven in 10 attenders can identify reasons for feeling uncomfortable about sharing their faith. The most common reason given is that they feel unable to answer difficult questions (31%), followed by fear of people's reactions (15%), not having enough understanding of the Christian faith to talk about it (9%) and other reasons (11%). Only 3% think it is not appropriate to talk about faith.

Figure 6.1

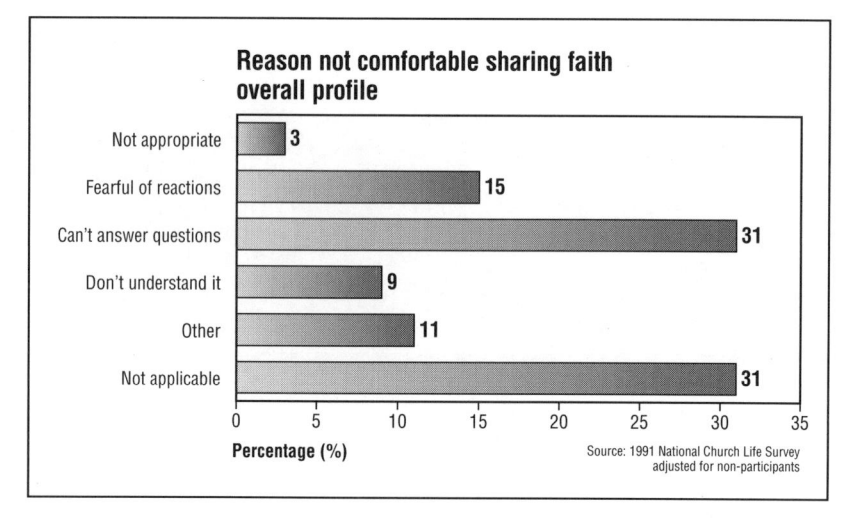

**Reason not comfortable sharing faith overall profile**

| Category | Percentage (%) |
|---|---|
| Not appropriate | 3 |
| Fearful of reactions | 15 |
| Can't answer questions | 31 |
| Don't understand it | 9 |
| Other | 11 |
| Not applicable | 31 |

Source: 1991 National Church Life Survey adjusted for non-participants

Three in 10 attenders consider the question is not applicable. A large proportion of these attenders also say they are at ease sharing their faith or look for opportunities to do so.

However, 35% of attenders who look for opportunities to share their faith and 59% of attenders who are at ease if the opportunity arises do identify barriers to faith sharing. While this group may generally feel at ease talking about their faith, this does not mean that they never have problems doing so.

The majority of attenders can identify barriers to faith sharing, including a sizeable proportion who are committed to outreach. Clearly there is work to be done if Australian attenders are to make the most of the opportunities that arise to discuss their faith with others.

*There is work to be done if attenders are to make the most of faith sharing opportunities that arise*

## LACK OF KNOWLEDGE

Some 9% of attenders say the major reason they feel uncomfortable is that they do not understand their faith well enough to talk about it. Less involved attenders (16%) are more likely to feel they lack knowledge than involved (7%) or highly involved attenders (4%).

Many congregations use small groups as an avenue for teaching, yet attenders on the fringes of congregational life are usually not part of such groups. When speaking to the whole congregation, preachers often assume a base level of knowledge. This result indicates that some attenders, even frequent worshippers, may know less about the basics of Christian faith than supposed. Congregations need to find ways to explain the principles of Christian belief, such as providing simple written material for newcomers to read. They may also need to provide attenders with a comfortable forum for asking questions and developing their understanding.

MARGERY HAD THE EMBARRASSING EXPERIENCE OF HAVING FINALLY BEEN ABLE TO SHARE HER FAITH, ONLY TO FIND THAT SHE DIDN'T ACTUALLY HAVE ANY.

## FEAR

Some 15% of attenders are uncomfortable about sharing their faith because they are afraid of other people's reactions. Christians are often hesitant to state a Christian viewpoint. Many can testify to occasions when they have kept silent, rather than risk being ridiculed or getting into an argument with those outside of church life.

Attenders may stay silent to keep the peace or for the sake of their relationship. They may believe that maintaining friends over the long term is better than possibly alienating them over one issue. Of course, on some occasions, remaining silent may be an appropriate response. However, on other occasions, attenders may be surprised by the open response of others.

Fears also often arise about inviting people to Christian discipleship. Some people can attend church for years without being invited to make a commitment to discipleship. Although some eventually drift into commitment, others move in and out of congregational life without ever facing the issue. The value of public commitment as part of Christian nurture is discussed in Chapter 10.

## TOUGH QUESTIONS

Almost a third of all attenders feel unable to answer difficult questions. In a separate question, the NCLS asked attenders what types of question they commonly hear about Christianity. The results are summarised in Common Questions on page 80. They provide leaders and those with a concern for mission with an idea of some of the issues attenders may want to work through.

It is important that attenders are given an opportunity to discuss difficult questions. Some questions are easier to answer than others. Many attenders may simply need experience in discussing the issues with others. Leaders may want to hold workshops at which attenders can gain experience and work through responses with which they are comfortable.

There are many other types of question that attenders face, including moral, ethical, workplace and other day-to-day issues. No single training course can fully equip attenders to handle all issues. Daily conversations are wide ranging and unlikely to follow a text-book pattern. It is important that attenders are helped in an ongoing way to become more articulate on a range of everyday issues and to provide credible answers to people's questions.

Many workshops and courses cover this issue. For example, *Gossiping the Gospel* encourages participants to look at different responses to issues and take into account the questioner's experience and current situation (Robinson, 1992). Similarly, *Everyday Evangelism* and *Two Ways to Live* identify common objections to Christianity and outline a variety of responses to questions (Abbott, 1994; St Matthias Press, 1989). Information on courses and materials is available from some denominational offices.

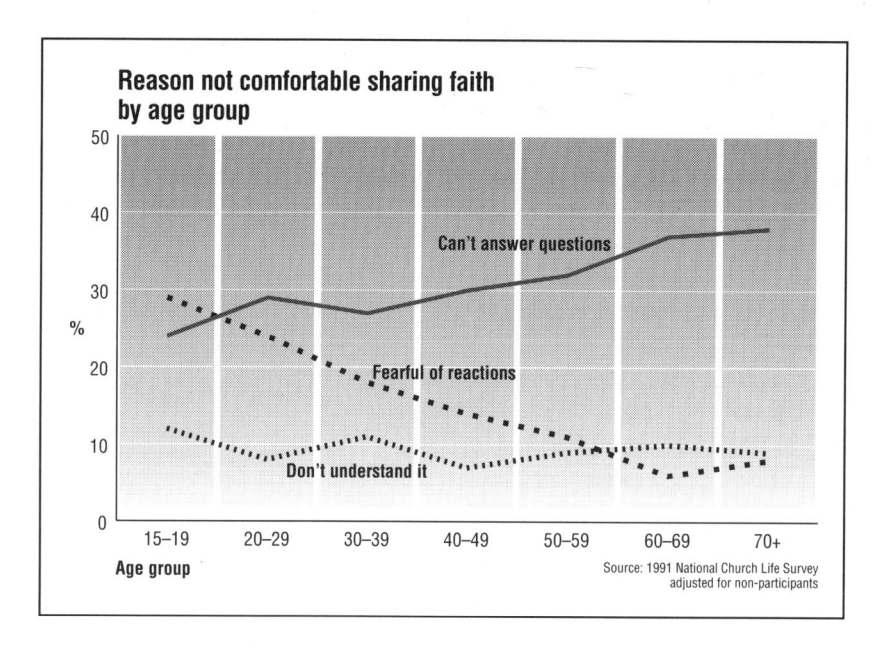

**Reason not comfortable sharing faith by age group**

[Chart showing three lines across age groups 15-19, 20-29, 30-39, 40-49, 50-59, 60-69, 70+:
- Can't answer questions (rising from ~24% to ~38%)
- Fearful of reactions (declining from ~29% to ~8%)
- Don't understand it (around 8-12%)

Source: 1991 National Church Life Survey adjusted for non-participants]

Figure 6.2

## AGE BARRIERS

In Chapter 5 it was noted that while 23% of attenders in their 60s do not like to talk about their faith, only 9% of attenders in their 20s have this view. However, while 21% of attenders in their 60s have trouble expressing their faith in ordinary language, this is an issue for 29% of attenders in their 20s.

Similar differences appear in barriers to faith sharing. While only 6% of attenders in their 60s fear other people's reactions, nearly a quarter of attenders in their 20s mention this as a problem. Attenders over 60 years of age (37%) are more likely to feel they can't answer difficult questions, compared to 29% in their 20s.

## CULTURAL BARRIERS

For many churchgoers, the word 'mission' implies outreach to people who are culturally and geographically distant. Missionaries are people who minister in distant lands . . . to be admired but probably not emulated, especially if the call is to deepest, darkest Africa.

In Australia, Christians no longer need to cross the ocean to mix with people who are culturally different. They are living next door, working at the next desk, standing across the shop counter and sitting in the row in front at the movies or football.

Many of the cultural differences arise from ethnic background. Australia is now home to people from virtually every country and region in the world. However, many subcultures in society can be just as alien as cultures from another country. These subcultures are often identifiable by dress, language or behaviour.

**Only 19% have shared their faith across cultural boundaries with ease**

The NCLS asked attenders if they have ever sought to explain their faith to someone from a very different culture. Only 19% have done so with ease. A further 24% have shared across cultural boundaries, but found it difficult. Another 15% of attenders believe they wouldn't know where to start, while 30% say they generally do not come across people from other cultures. Some 12% do not believe cross-cultural sharing is appropriate.

> **Q** **Have you ever sought to explain your faith to someone from a very different culture?**
> 
> a. No, it would not be appropriate
> b. No, I generally do not mix with such people
> c. No, I wouldn't know where to start
> d. Yes, and I found it rather difficult
> e. Yes, it was really no problem

Attenders in Pentecostal denominations are more likely to have tried to share across cultural boundaries, as have attenders with a university degree. Attenders from non-English-speaking backgrounds are also more likely to be comfortable sharing with people from other cultures. This is not surprising – in migrating to Australia many have already learnt to communicate with those who are culturally different.

Attenders who look for opportunities to share their faith find sharing with people from other cultures much easier than other attenders. This may be because those who intentionally share their faith are more practised or better equipped. Attenders who find it hard to express their faith in ordinary language also find cross-cultural sharing particularly difficult; only 5% do so with ease.

## Training and support

Barriers to faith sharing don't have to be insurmountable. However, arming attenders with more facts and arguments will not necessarily move them beyond the barriers. Along with more knowledge, attenders may need support to feel comfortable talking about their faith.

However, if faith sharing wasn't meant to be easy, it also wasn't meant to be a solo affair. The Bible records that Paul was usually accompanied in his missionary work by other Christians. In writing to the Christian communities, Paul often acknowledged their prayers and support for his ministry.

The NCLS asked attenders whether they feel supported by their congregations in seeking to share their faith.

> **To what extent are you supported by your church in such faith sharing?**
> a. I'm part of a small group or mission team that provides strong support and prayer
> b. I'm part of a small group which is generally supportive
> c. Neither of the above, but the church is generally supportive
> d. The church does not seem to be concerned about faith sharing
> e. Don't know

Attenders who did not help another person to explore faith in the past 12 months have been excluded from the following analysis.

Virtually all attenders who have shared their faith in the past 12 months feel supported by their congregation. Some 19% are actively supported by a small group or mission team.

**Congregational support for sharing faith by denomination**

| | Strong support % | Group supportive % | Church supportive % | Church not supportive % | Don't know % | Total % |
|---|---|---|---|---|---|---|
| **Overall** | 19 | 25 | 44 | 2 | 10 | 100 |
| Anglican | 22 | 30 | 41 | 1 | 6 | 100 |
| Assemblies of God | 26 | 17 | 48 | 1 | 6 | 100 |
| Baptist | 14 | 31 | 42 | 3 | 10 | 100 |
| Churches of Christ | 12 | 33 | 44 | 2 | 10 | 100 |
| Lutheran | 11 | 23 | 54 | 3 | 10 | 100 |
| Presbyterian | 16 | 33 | 35 | 4 | 13 | 100 |
| Salvation Army | 22 | 29 | 41 | 2 | 7 | 100 |
| Uniting | 19 | 27 | 39 | 5 | 10 | 100 |
| **Type of denomination** | | | | | | |
| Mainstream | 19 | 29 | 41 | 3 | 9 | 100 |
| Pentecostal | 26 | 19 | 48 | 2 | 6 | 100 |
| Large Protestant | 15 | 26 | 45 | 2 | 12 | 100 |
| Small Protestant | n.a. | n.a. | n.a. | n.a. | n.a. | n.a. |

Source: 1991 National Church Life Survey attender data adjusted for non-participants

Figure 6.3

The majority feel they receive passive support; 25% from their small group and 44% from the wider congregation. Only 2% believe their congregation doesn't support faith sharing, while 10% don't know.

Attenders in Pentecostal denominations are more likely to receive active support from some kind of group than attenders in other denominations. Highly involved attenders are more likely to be involved in a supportive mission team or group than attenders overall. Some 31% of highly involved attenders feel strongly supported, compared to 19% of attenders overall.

## THE ROLE OF TRAINING

To find out how many attenders have had recent training in discussing their faith, the NCLS included the following question.

**Q**

> **In the last two years have you had any training in sharing your faith? (circle the main one only)**
> a. Yes, in this church
> b. Yes, with another church or mission group
> c. Yes, informal help from others
> d. No, never

More than half of all attenders have received some kind of training in the past two years. Three in 10 attenders have received training within their congregation, and a further 10% with another church or mission group. Informal help has been given to another 16% of attenders.

To some, these figures may be unexpectedly high. Certainly, people involved in running formal mission courses do not think they are training anything like this proportion of attenders.

However, many congregations run their own training in evangelism. When congregational leaders were asked if any training courses in evangelism had been conducted in their congregation in the previous two years, some 29% said their congregation had conducted such courses and a further 18% said that attenders went to courses elsewhere. It should also be noted that the question does not define training specifically. Training can include training at all levels, from formal courses at institutions and short courses conducted by a congregation or external organisation through to teaching from the pulpit and studies in small groups.

## DENOMINATIONAL DIFFERENCES

Seven in 10 attenders in Pentecostal denominations have received training, compared to six in 10 attenders in large Protestant denominations and five in 10 attenders in mainstream denominations. Interestingly, similar proportions of attenders in all denominations receive informal help from others.

**Recent training in sharing faith by denomination**

| | Through this church % | Through another church % | Informal help % | Never % | Total % |
|---|---|---|---|---|---|
| **Overall** | 29 | 10 | 16 | 45 | 100 |
| Anglican | 25 | 9 | 15 | 51 | 100 |
| Assemblies of God | 42 | 13 | 15 | 30 | 100 |
| Baptist | 27 | 11 | 16 | 46 | 100 |
| Churches of Christ | 27 | 9 | 18 | 46 | 100 |
| Lutheran | 26 | 6 | 20 | 48 | 100 |
| Presbyterian | 34 | 9 | 13 | 44 | 100 |
| Salvation Army | 44 | 6 | 14 | 36 | 100 |
| Uniting | 24 | 9 | 16 | 51 | 100 |
| **Type of denomination** | | | | | |
| Mainstream | 25 | 9 | 16 | 50 | 100 |
| Pentecostal | 41 | 14 | 15 | 30 | 100 |
| Large Protestant | 32 | 9 | 17 | 42 | 100 |
| Small Protestant | n.a. | n.a. | n.a. | n.a. | n.a. |

Source: 1991 National Church Life Survey attender data adjusted for non-participants

Figure 6.4

The major difference between denominations is in the level of formal training. Only 34% of attenders in mainstream denominations have received formal training, compared to 55% of Pentecostal attenders.

## WHO IS BEING TRAINED?

Since young attenders are more involved in faith sharing than older attenders, it might be expected that they are having more training. Overall, this is true. However, when it comes to formal training, attenders aged in their 20s are only marginally more likely to have undertaken some formal training than attenders in their 70s.

This suggests that formal training in faith sharing is not just a one-off event, but something that continues throughout a lifetime. Attenders may be pursuing more than just knowledge. They may simply appreciate the motivation and support that comes from mixing with like-minded people, whether this be in formal training courses, small groups or wider church involvement.

Men and women are equally likely to have had training in recent years, as are people from white-collar and blue-collar backgrounds. This is encouraging, since it means that people from all walks and stages of life are being equipped to share their faith.

Highly involved attenders are more likely to have had training than other attenders. Some 81% of attenders who spend at least six hours at congregational activities each week have had recent training, compared to 35% of those who attend worship services only.

Again, this result suggests that, far from their congregational involvement having a cloistering effect, highly involved attenders are outward looking. Since the vast majority of highly involved attenders are receiving training, it also suggests that much of this training takes place during the course of normal church involvement, such as at small groups, rather than at special events.

## WHAT DIFFERENCE DOES IT MAKE?

### Sharing faith

There is a link between training and intentional faith sharing. Some 78% of attenders who look for opportunities to share their faith have had training, compared to 62% who discuss faith if the issue arises, 47% who find it hard to talk about their faith, and 30% who do not like to talk about their faith. Again, this relationship is true across denominational groups.

> *Some 78% of attenders who look for opportunities to share their faith have had training*

### The back fence

Bill and Joan attend a Baptist church in a thriving rural centre, where they belong to a ministry equipping group. After going to the group for a year, without feeling game enough to share their faith or invite others to church, they realised they were going to have to go the next step and put the theory they were learning into practice.

'We had a casual "over the back fence" relationship with our neighbours who were Christmas and Easter churchgoers', recalls Joan. 'We had talked about the kids, the weather, the condition of the fence, town politics, but never religion. With our pastor's reminder ringing in our ears that we are the ministers, and if we don't do it, it won't get done, we took the plunge and invited them to church on a regular Sunday. To our surprise they came and have now joined the church and even a home group.'

The senior pastor is delighted. 'It's great to see people like Bill and Joan taking risks with the folk they know. We aim to lay a foundation for people to minister in the places they spend their daily lives. This is done through the ministry equipping groups, which are 18 months of weekly practical training in worship, prayer, mission and healing.

'We have had many new people join us in the past four months, the majority through word-of-mouth contacts; mainly workmates, friends, family and neighbours. It just goes to show how important the personal touch is, because we have had no special advertising or activities. The challenge now is to keep pace with the demand for home groups. It is my hope that the ministry equipping groups will provide a new breed of home group leadership. It's early days, but it is exciting.'

Although, on the face of it, this looks like fairly compelling evidence for training, the research doesn't prove cause and effect. Attenders may be more intentional about faith sharing because of training, or they may undertake training because they are successfully involved in faith sharing.

Of attenders who find it difficult to talk about their faith, 53% have not had any training. With encouragement and support, these attenders might find it much easier to discuss their faith.

Viewed the other way, this statistic is also cause for concern. Some 47% of attenders who find it hard to talk about their faith have had recent training, and yet are still not at ease sharing their faith. Apparently the training did not increase their confidence.

Perhaps difficulty in discussing faith isn't addressed in some training courses, or there isn't time to work through individual concerns. Major shortcomings in some courses can include failing to help people to recognise how to build friendships and acquire basic interpersonal skills (Bruce Dutton, private communications).

### *Inviting others to church*

Some 49% of attenders who have had training have tried to invite someone to church in the previous year. By comparison, 28% of attenders who did not have training invited someone. This is true across all denominational groups.

*Growth in faith*

Training may not only make attenders more effective faith sharers, but it may also strengthen their faith. More than 52% of attenders who have had training have grown much in their faith, compared to 31% of attenders who have not had training. This relationship is only partly accounted for by level of involvement of attenders in church and their readiness to share faith. As with the question of sharing faith, it isn't possible to prove cause and effect. However, again the link will be good news to leaders and trainers.

\*   \*   \*   \*

## TRAINING AND SUPPORT ARE VITAL

Training and support are vital if attenders are to move beyond the roadblocks that prevent them sharing faith. Attenders need to develop skills to share their faith with confidence.

Clearly, not all training is adequate. A substantial proportion of attenders find it difficult to share their faith even after training. Leaders need to ensure that the training they provide or suggest is appropriate for the particular audience.

Different groups will have different stumbling blocks. Young attenders are keen to share their faith, but struggle to find the right words and are afraid of others' reactions. This group needs skills, mentors, models, practice and support to overcome their fears.

Older attenders, on the other hand, are more reluctant to talk about their faith and are concerned that, if they do, they will not able to answer the questions put to them. As a starting point in any training, this group needs to be motivated to share their faith with others.

Leaders and those concerned for mission need to recognise that one training program is unlikely to meet the needs of all attenders. Congregations also need to consider the issue of crossing cultural barriers. The church is under-represented in many subcultures; if it is to reach all Australians, it will need to learn to share the gospel across cultural barriers.

Congregations in diverse or multicultural areas may have special ministry to ethnic or subcultural groups different from their own. In such cases, people from non-English-speaking backgrounds or particular subcultures may be able to play a vital role in training and equipping attenders to cross the cultural barriers.

As a starting point, the church needs to apply cross-cultural principles learnt overseas to its own backyard. For instance, missionaries to other countries learn the language and study the culture, encourage people to express their faith in their own culture, and develop indigenous leadership within that culture to take the church forward. These principles apply equally to ministry within Australia.

The church today struggles to express centuries-old traditions in contemporary culture. So it should come as no surprise that this is also an issue for attenders. The young, in particular, find it hard to express faith in ordinary language. Attenders in this age group are inheriting a church culture that is distinctly different from the subculture in which they live. It is critically important that congregations help them to develop both skills and confidence in sharing their faith.

> **Discussing matters of faith is not easy. Support and training can help attenders to grow beyond the barriers that inhibit them.**
> - Seven in 10 attenders can identify reasons for feeling uncomfortable in some way about discussing their faith with others.
> - A major problem in faith sharing is being unable to answer difficult questions. Other problems are a fear of other people's reactions and lacking the knowledge to talk about Christianity.
> - Attenders of different ages have different approaches to, and difficulties with, faith sharing. One form of training is unlikely to be suitable for all attenders. Leaders need to identify and address the needs of each audience.
> - Attenders in Pentecostal denominations are more likely to have had some formal training in faith sharing than attenders in mainstream or large Protestant denominations. There is a link between receiving training and inviting someone to church.
> - A large proportion of attenders find it difficult to share across cultural barriers. This issue may need special attention if congregations are to minister effectively in diverse areas.

## Common questions

What type of questions do attenders need to be able to answer? The NCLS asked attenders what concerns about Christianity were most often raised by people in the wider community.

The most common objection to Christianity that attenders have heard is that there are too many hypocrites; that Christians don't practise what they preach (39%). The next most common issues are the problem of suffering (28%) and whether the Bible is true (24%). Around 16% have heard others say that faith is irrelevant; only 6% commonly hear that science disproves Christianity.

Many in the wider community do not appear to struggle with the concept of faith so much as reconciling faith with everyday problems. Attenders need to reflect on the issue of hypocrisy. For many outsiders this accusation may be an easy throw-away line which allows them to dismiss all church attenders in one breath. But the frequency of this response also raises the question: Is the example set by attenders all it should be?

This kind of objection underlines the importance of attenders living a consistent Christian life. Congregations, too, need to be welcoming places of compassion where Christians do practise what they preach.

Of course, the results only reveal what churchgoers perceive to be the major objections to faith held by non-churchgoers. While they may give a useful indication, a survey of the community would be needed to get an accurate picture of key objections.

Figure 6.5

**Concerns about Christianity overall profile**

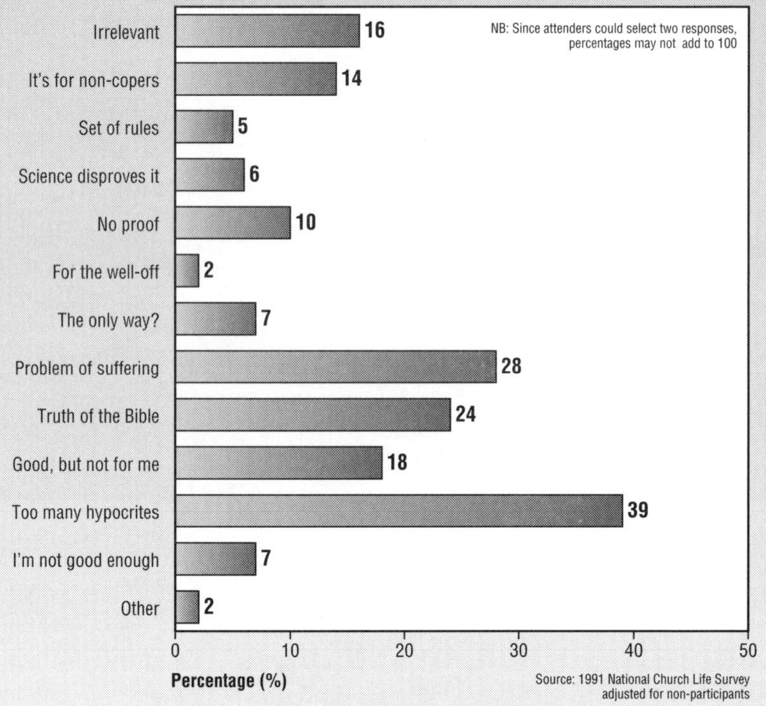

| Concern | Percentage (%) |
|---|---|
| Irrelevant | 16 |
| It's for non-copers | 14 |
| Set of rules | 5 |
| Science disproves it | 6 |
| No proof | 10 |
| For the well-off | 2 |
| The only way? | 7 |
| Problem of suffering | 28 |
| Truth of the Bible | 24 |
| Good, but not for me | 18 |
| Too many hypocrites | 39 |
| I'm not good enough | 7 |
| Other | 2 |

NB: Since attenders could select two responses, percentages may not add to 100

Source: 1991 National Church Life Survey adjusted for non-participants

It might be expected that newcomers would have a better perception of community opinion than attenders overall, in view of their recent arrival into congregational life. In fact, the perceptions of newcomers are similar to those for attenders overall.

**Who hears what?**

Since church attenders are found in all age groups and all walks of life, it stands to reason that different attenders may hear different concerns about faith, depending on their peer group. Interestingly, the statement that Christians do not practise what they preach is the key objection heard by all age groups except 15 to 19 year olds. The more common teenage concerns about Christianity include: the truth of the Bible (37%); there is no proof for Christianity (23%); science disproves it (12%); and it is a set of rules (11%).

Generally, younger attenders are more likely to encounter questions about the truth of the Bible than older attenders. Attenders with a university education are less likely to hear questions about the truth of the Bible than average (only 15%), and more likely to hear that faith is irrelevant (28%).

Men are also more likely to hear that faith is irrelevant (22%), while women are more likely to encounter the question of suffering (32%).

**Concerns about Christianity by age group**

NB: Since attenders could select two responses, percentages may not add to 100.

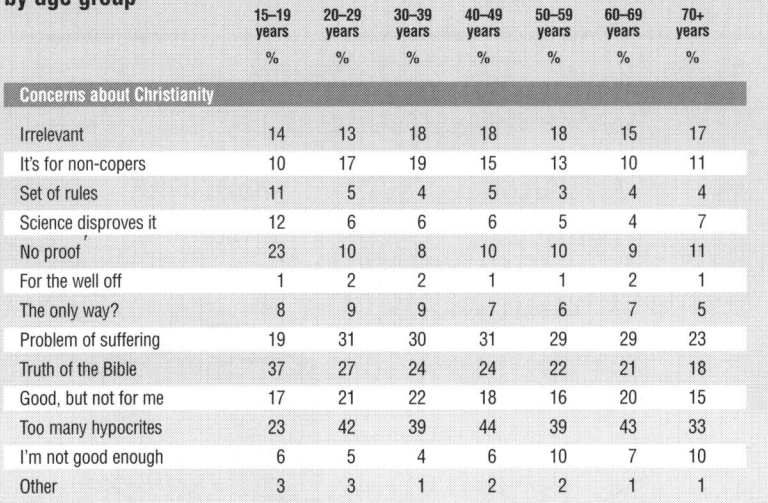

| Concerns about Christianity | 15–19 years % | 20–29 years % | 30–39 years % | 40–49 years % | 50–59 years % | 60–69 years % | 70+ years % |
|---|---|---|---|---|---|---|---|
| Irrelevant | 14 | 13 | 18 | 18 | 18 | 15 | 17 |
| It's for non-copers | 10 | 17 | 19 | 15 | 13 | 10 | 11 |
| Set of rules | 11 | 5 | 4 | 5 | 3 | 4 | 4 |
| Science disproves it | 12 | 6 | 6 | 6 | 5 | 4 | 7 |
| No proof | 23 | 10 | 8 | 10 | 10 | 9 | 11 |
| For the well off | 1 | 2 | 2 | 1 | 1 | 2 | 1 |
| The only way? | 8 | 9 | 9 | 7 | 6 | 7 | 5 |
| Problem of suffering | 19 | 31 | 30 | 31 | 29 | 29 | 23 |
| Truth of the Bible | 37 | 27 | 24 | 24 | 22 | 21 | 18 |
| Good, but not for me | 17 | 21 | 22 | 18 | 16 | 20 | 15 |
| Too many hypocrites | 23 | 42 | 39 | 44 | 39 | 43 | 33 |
| I'm not good enough | 6 | 5 | 4 | 6 | 10 | 7 | 10 |
| Other | 3 | 3 | 1 | 2 | 2 | 1 | 1 |
| Total | 100 | 100 | 100 | 100 | 100 | 100 | 100 |

Source: 1991 National Church Life Survey attender data adjusted for non participants

Figure 6.6

## CHAPTER 7

# GETTING ON WITH IT

**Discussing faith and inviting others to church**

Attenders who are involved in sharing the faith with others also have a key role in inviting others to congregational activities.

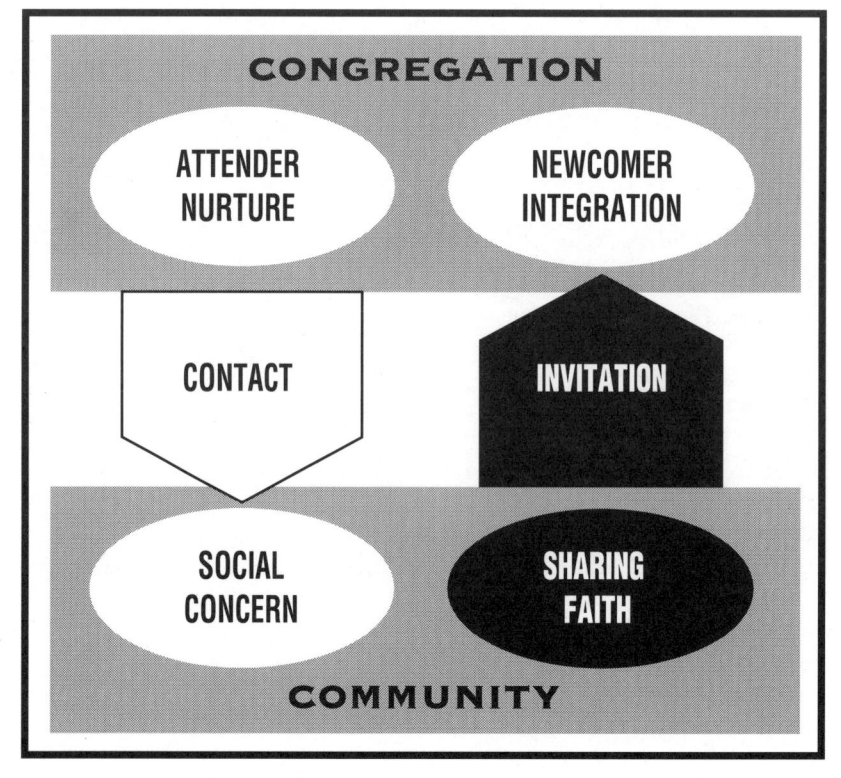

[Diagram showing CONGREGATION containing ATTENDER NURTURE and NEWCOMER INTEGRATION, with CONTACT and INVITATION bridging to COMMUNITY which contains SOCIAL CONCERN and SHARING FAITH]

# Discussing faith with others

It is one thing for Christians to believe in the importance of sharing their faith with others. It is quite another to actually do so.

This chapter focuses on the extent to which attenders are relating their faith to others. Two aspects are examined:
- whether attenders have helped others explore questions of faith in the past year;
- whether they have invited someone to church activities in the past year.

To determine the extent to which church attenders discuss their faith with others, the NCLS asked the following question.

> **In the last 12 months, have you been directly involved in helping anyone from outside your church explore questions about faith?**
> a. Yes, several people
> b. Yes, a few people
> c. Yes, one person
> d. None that I am aware of
> e. Not applicable

A number of subsidiary questions were asked to find out whether the sharing took place:
- in the community or at church;
- through a mission activity or in everyday life;
- with strangers, acquaintances, close friends or family.

The analysis of these subsidiary questions was limited only to those attenders who had discussed matters of faith with someone in the past 12 months.

## WHO TALKS ABOUT THEIR FAITH?

Nearly half of all attenders (46%) say they have helped someone explore issues of faith during the past 12 months. Just over a third (36%) have discussed faith with more than one person. Some 47% are not aware of having helped someone explore faith, and 7% consider the question not applicable.

As would be expected, attenders who look for opportunities to talk about their faith are the most likely to have actually done so. Some 78% of these attenders have shared their faith in the past year, compared to 55% of attenders who discuss their faith if the opportunity arises, 27% who find it hard to discuss their faith and 22% who do not like to talk about it at all.

Many observers might have expected the number of people who actually share their faith to be lower than this. It is particularly worth

*Attenders who look for opportunities to share their faith are more likely to have actually done so*

Figure 7.1

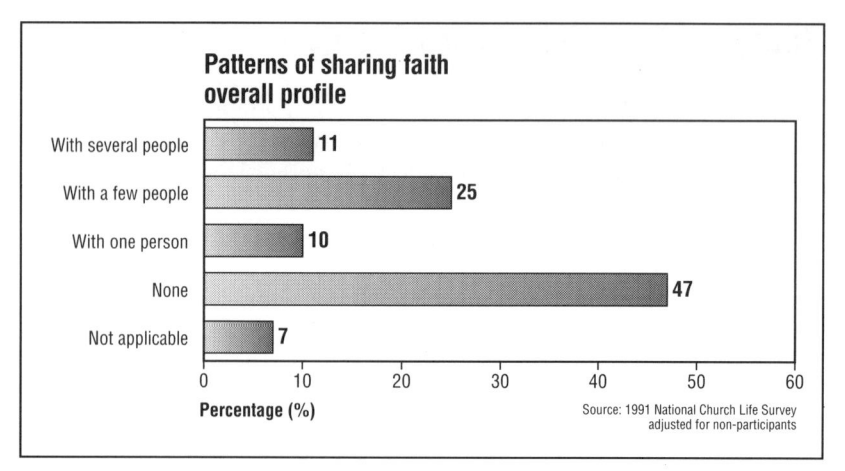

**Patterns of sharing faith overall profile**

| | Percentage (%) |
|---|---|
| With several people | 11 |
| With a few people | 25 |
| With one person | 10 |
| None | 47 |
| Not applicable | 7 |

Source: 1991 National Church Life Survey adjusted for non-participants

noting that some attenders are talking about their faith even though they find it difficult or prefer not to do so. Clearly, many attenders feel that helping others explore matters of faith is important, and they have a confidence that what they have to share is of value.

On the other hand, there is a sizeable group of attenders who are not discussing their faith with others, despite feeling at ease or actively looking for opportunities. Leaders may need to examine whether these attenders are really as comfortable with faith sharing as they claim to be, or whether they are ill equipped, lack confidence or lack wider community contacts.

*Look! It says: "Hector Drover, intent on one-to-one evangelism, froze into his current state on June 17th 1982 when he finally tried to speak to someone"*

Seven in 10 Pentecostal attenders have helped someone explore questions of faith in the past year. As will be seen later in this chapter, Pentecostal denominations also have the highest proportion of attenders who have invited someone to church – two possible reasons why they have more first-time attenders than other denominations. By comparison, 53% of attenders in large Protestant and 37% in mainstream denominations have helped someone explore questions of faith in the past year.

**Patterns of sharing faith by denomination**

Figure 7.2

| | With several people % | With a few people % | With one person % | None % | Not applicable % | Total % |
|---|---|---|---|---|---|---|
| **Overall** | 11 | 25 | 10 | 47 | 7 | 100 |
| Anglican | 9 | 18 | 9 | 56 | 8 | 100 |
| Assemblies of God | 20 | 40 | 10 | 24 | 5 | 100 |
| Baptist | 9 | 25 | 16 | 44 | 6 | 100 |
| Churches of Christ | 10 | 25 | 13 | 47 | 5 | 100 |
| Lutheran | 7 | 19 | 9 | 54 | 10 | 100 |
| Presbyterian | 11 | 23 | 11 | 48 | 7 | 100 |
| Salvation Army | 14 | 29 | 10 | 39 | 8 | 100 |
| Uniting | 11 | 20 | 7 | 54 | 9 | 100 |
| **Type of denomination** | | | | | | |
| Mainstream | 9 | 19 | 9 | 54 | 8 | 100 |
| Pentecostal | 21 | 39 | 10 | 25 | 5 | 100 |
| Large Protestant | 9 | 30 | 14 | 43 | 5 | 100 |
| Small Protestant | n.a. | n.a. | n.a. | n.a. | n.a. | n.a. |

Source: 1991 National Church Life Survey attender data adjusted for non-participants

Attenders who view the Bible as God's word to be taken literally and those who speak in tongues are more likely to have shared their faith than attenders with other theological perspectives. These relationships hold true across the denominational groups.

Chapter 1 showed that younger adults have higher levels of contact with non-churchgoers. They are also more involved in discussing their faith than older attenders. Some 57% of attenders in their 20s, 47% in their 30s, and 52% in their 40s have helped someone explore faith in the past year, compared to 39% of people in their 60s. This is true even when denominational differences are taken into account.

Younger people have more social contacts than their older colleagues and are more likely to discuss their faith with them. They are also more likely than older attenders to be in the process of forming new relationships, which provides them with further opportunities. Older people tend to have more stable relationships and may well have fully discussed their faith in previous years.

# FRIENDS, ACQUAINTANCES AND COLLEAGUES . . .

With whom do attenders mostly talk about faith? The NCLS asked the following question.

> **Were most of these occasions with:**
> a. Strangers
> b. People you would only meet in mission activities
> c. Casual friends/acquaintances
> d. Close friends/relatives

More than half of all attenders (53%) who discussed their faith with others did so mainly with acquaintances rather than close friends. A further 12% did so mainly with strangers, and 8% with people met through mission activities. Only 27% of attenders mostly helped close friends or family to explore questions of faith.

The notion of friendship evangelism, where attenders form friendships with other people before discussing faith, needs some refinement. Clearly, attenders do not need to form a close relationship with another person to discuss spiritual matters with them. Indeed, discussions of faith may be off-limits with some close friends. Attenders who don't want to jeopardise the relationship may tread more warily with close friends than with others.

### The new congregation

A new Westminster Presbyterian congregation planted on the outskirts of Perth began when two couples decided the half-hour drive to their existing congregation was too much.

'Alan and I had more contacts and are more outgoing than Fran and Bill, so getting others along was mainly up to us in the beginning', says Judy of the venture. 'We figured if we were going to have a good church for our kids we had better make one. We started by getting Friday night use of a community centre in the housing area for a youth group. Our kids invited their friends along.

'Alan and I had a pretty good reputation through the school P&C, so the other parents let their kids come. We did the usual youth fellowship thing – games, outings and talking about how God is real in day-to-day ways. I think our kids were the best evangelists. Our eldest, John, a real leader, made it almost acceptable at school to be into God. Behind the scenes was heaps of prayer.

'Then we put on a few events for the parents. Handling stress at work, help with your tax return, home decorating for beginners – our biggest success – and then we invited them to an evening to hear what we were telling their kids about "religion". A number of parents came, one couple was converted and there has been slow and steady growth ever since.'

When the fledgling congregation had six families, they asked for the services of the assistant minister from their previous congregation for two days each week. 'We agreed to work towards being able to carry that cost ourselves within two years', says Judy. 'Today we have our own building and eighty members.'

On the other hand, some measure of trust appears to be necessary. Evangelism books often include stories of complete strangers being evangelised or even converted during a chance encounter. While it does happen, such encounters are probably far from the daily reality of most attenders, whose discussions with strangers are limited to subjects such as the weather.

Pentecostal congregations sometimes pursue street and cold-contact evangelism strategies; yet they are more likely than other groups to share their faith mostly with acquaintances. The young are also more likely to share faith with acquaintances, while older attenders are more likely to explore questions of faith with close friends or relatives.

*Acquaintance evangelism* may be the way forward in the 1990s, with attenders discussing their faith with people with whom they have formed a bridge of trust and respect, rather than only with close friends.

*Acquaintance evangelism may be the way forward in the '90s*

## SHARING IN EVERYDAY CONTEXTS

For the vast majority of attenders, sharing faith is not a special event, but something that happens in everyday life. Only 19% of attenders share their faith mostly with contacts made through mission or outreach activities. The majority (81%) talk to contacts made in everyday life, such as in the workplace or with friends.

Similarly, most moments of faith sharing occur out in the community; only 10% take place on church property. These results are consistent regardless of age, denomination or attitude to faith sharing.

These results have important implications for the mission directions of many congregations. Many congregations focus their evangelistic

THIS HAPPENED EVERY TIME MARGARET LEFT HER FAITH AT HOME!

activities on their local geographic area. When a special event is planned, they letterbox the neighbourhood, inviting people to come along.

While such a local focus may sometimes be important, it is by no means the whole picture. Attenders need support and encouragement to bloom where they are planted among the people they already know – in their workplace, leisure activity or community groups. As highlighted in *Winds of Change* (p 96), many local congregations already draw attenders from well beyond their local neighbourhood. Attenders could potentially invite others to congregational activities, even if they do not live in the local area. Many congregations may find it helpful to reconsider their mission focus.

Congregations may want to augment a successful local focus with activities or groups meeting further afield, to which attenders can invite people from outside the local area. Some suburban congregations have, for instance, organised sharing or discussion groups that meet in the city centre. Others have organised small groups well away from their local area.

Such directions also underline the importance of helping attenders close the gap between belief and daily life. There are often wide gaps between holding Christian beliefs and standards, and applying these at work, at home or in leisure time (eg Banks, 1987, 42–51). Congregations need to help their attenders apply their faith to everyday issues and decision making, and equip them to talk to others about it.

## FOLLOWING UP

For some people, coming to the Christian faith is an instant thing, a moment of conversion when they step from unbelief to belief. For others, it is a gradual progression, built on many conversations about faith and the meaning of discipleship.

To gain an indication of how much faith sharing is short-term and how much it is an ongoing activity, the NCLS asked attenders who had discussed their faith with others how many people they were still supporting and encouraging.

**Q** | **How many of these people are you now still involved in supporting and encouraging?**
a. Nearly all of them
b. Most
c. Some
d. Hardly any/none

A quarter of attenders are still involved with nearly all the people with whom they have discussed their faith, and a fifth are involved with most. However, four in 10 attenders are only involved with some of the people they have spoken to about their faith, and 12% are involved with hardly any or none at all. For about half of attenders, sharing faith is more likely to be short-term than a long-term process.

There are many reasons why attenders may no longer be supporting people. Some of the contacts may have been with strangers. Other relationships, especially with acquaintances, may end because one person changes jobs or moves house. Perhaps some attenders affected their relationship with the other person when they shared their faith.

However, this may not be the whole picture. Highly involved attenders are more likely to be supporting people they have shared their faith with than attenders overall. This suggests that loss of contact may be due, in part, to attenders themselves. As noted elsewhere, patterns of discussing faith are linked to church involvement. It appears that highly involved attenders are more likely to follow up their contacts as well.

## Inviting others to church

One consequence of discussing faith may be an invitation to others to participate in the life of a congregation. Attenders may ask others to church for many reasons. Sometimes the invitation arises directly out of a discussion of faith. At other times, the invitation is low key – attenders invite friends to a baptism, special event or social activity.

To explore the links between faith sharing and invitations to church, the NCLS included the following question.

> **In the last year has anybody started attending church activities here or elsewhere as a result of your involvement with them?**
> a. Yes, as a result of discussion about the Christian faith
> b. Yes, for other reasons
> c. Both a and b
> d. No, those with whom I have shared chose not to be involved or felt uncomfortable when they tried
> e. No, I don't think I encouraged anybody to do so
> f. Don't know

One in four attenders (26%) has successfully influenced someone to attend a church activity in the past 12 months. Of these, 10% know of someone who has attended as a result of discussing faith, 11% know of

Figure 7.3

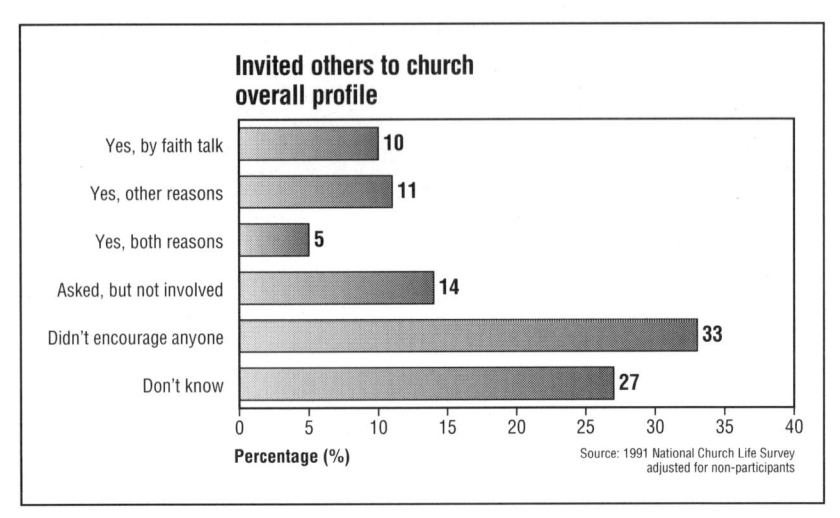

**Invited others to church overall profile**

| Category | Percentage |
|---|---|
| Yes, by faith talk | 10 |
| Yes, other reasons | 11 |
| Yes, both reasons | 5 |
| Asked, but not involved | 14 |
| Didn't encourage anyone | 33 |
| Don't know | 27 |

Percentage (%)

Source: 1991 National Church Life Survey adjusted for non-participants

someone who has come for other reasons and 5% know people who have attended for both reasons. Another 14% of attenders have invited someone to church without success; those with whom they were involved chose not to attend or felt uncomfortable when they tried.

Overall, 40% of attenders tried to invite someone to church. Of these, two-thirds report that at least some of their invitations were successful. This is not a bad record. Perhaps outsiders are more open to attending church activities than attenders expect.

However, 33% of attenders have not invited anyone to church and 27% do not know if they have influenced someone to attend church. These results may concern some leaders. Congregations need to discover why so many attenders are not inviting others to church activities.

One possibility is that attenders are unhappy with aspects of their congregational life, such as the style of worship. *Winds of Change* (pp 167–177) highlighted significant generational differences in preferred styles of worship.

Perhaps attenders are comfortable with worship, but think others would find it dull or irrelevant. This may be especially true in the context of people without a church background or who are part of subcultures that are well distanced from church life and traditions. Many of those involved in mission with such groups say that there is no way they could fit into any of the churches they know (Kaldor P and S, 1988).

Alternatively, attenders may simply lack confidence. Discovering the reasons why so many attenders aren't inviting others to church may unlock some key issues for congregations as they plan for effective mission in their own context.

Of course, encouraging someone to attend church is not the only way in which faith can be explored. Some people have many conversations about spiritual matters with Christians before they are ready for any involvement with a church. Faith sharing should seek to point people towards God, rather than being simply an exercise in recruitment.

## DENOMINATIONAL DIFFERENCES

Pentecostal denominations have the highest proportions of attenders who have tried to encourage someone to church in the past year. In all, 61% of Pentecostal attenders encouraged others to attend church activities, compared to 40% of attenders overall. Since Pentecostal attenders are more willing than average to share their faith, this result is not surprising. Pentecostal attenders are more likely to have asked someone to church as a result of discussing faith than attenders in other denominations.

A further reason could be the style of services run by many Pentecostal congregations. Attenders in these congregations may be more willing to issue invitations to non-church people because they feel the meetings are more culturally friendly. This perhaps depends not so much on Pentecostalism as on worship style. Further research will determine whether attenders in non-Pentecostal congregations that make use of non-traditional styles are also more likely to invite others.

Many of the small Protestant denominations also have a high proportions of attenders who have tried to encourage others to attend church activities, including the Westminster Presbyterian and Wesleyan Methodist Churches (50%). Other denominations in which attenders are more likely to have encouraged people to congregational activities include the Salvation Army and Congregational Churches (47%), the Churches of Christ (45%) and the Baptist Church (44%).

Attenders from some smaller denominations, in particular the Church of the Nazarene (40%), also have high success rates with invitations.

AFTER FINALLY CONVINCING HIS NEIGHBOUR TO COME TO CHURCH, STEVE STARTED QUESTIONING HIS PLAN.

Figure 7.4

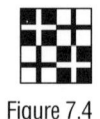

**Invited others to church by denomination**

| | Yes, by faith talk % | Yes, other reasons % | Yes, both reasons % | Asked, but not involved % | Didn't encourage anyone % | Don't know % | Total % |
|---|---|---|---|---|---|---|---|
| **Overall** | **10** | **11** | **5** | **14** | **33** | **27** | **100** |
| Anglican | 8 | 11 | 4 | 12 | 38 | 27 | 100 |
| Apostolic | 20 | 11 | 9 | 19 | 21 | 19 | 100 |
| Assemblies of God | 22 | 11 | 9 | 20 | 20 | 19 | 100 |
| Baptist | 10 | 13 | 6 | 15 | 32 | 24 | 100 |
| Christian & Missionary Alliance | 14 | 13 | 7 | 18 | 29 | 19 | 100 |
| Christian Revival Crusade | 18 | 13 | 8 | 19 | 24 | 18 | 100 |
| Church of the Nazarene | 15 | 14 | 11 | 17 | 26 | 16 | 100 |
| Churches of Christ | 11 | 13 | 6 | 15 | 32 | 24 | 100 |
| Congregational | 11 | 14 | 6 | 16 | 30 | 24 | 100 |
| Foursquare Gospel | 24 | 11 | 9 | 17 | 20 | 19 | 100 |
| Lutheran | 6 | 8 | 4 | 11 | 38 | 34 | 100 |
| NZ Presbyterian | 7 | 12 | 5 | 8 | 39 | 29 | 100 |
| Presbyterian | 8 | 10 | 5 | 13 | 36 | 28 | 100 |
| Reformed | 5 | 7 | 3 | 17 | 37 | 30 | 100 |
| Salvation Army | 12 | 13 | 7 | 15 | 26 | 27 | 100 |
| Seventh-day Adventist | 12 | 8 | 5 | 15 | 27 | 32 | 100 |
| Uniting | 6 | 11 | 4 | 10 | 39 | 30 | 100 |
| Wesleyan Methodist | 13 | 14 | 6 | 17 | 27 | 22 | 100 |
| Westminster Presbyterian | 14 | 14 | 6 | 16 | 30 | 20 | 100 |
| House Churches | 6 | 12 | 4 | 15 | 48 | 15 | 100 |
| **Type of denomination** | | | | | | | |
| Mainstream | 7 | 11 | 4 | 11 | 38 | 29 | 100 |
| Pentecostal | 22 | 11 | 9 | 19 | 21 | 19 | 100 |
| Large Protestant | 11 | 12 | 6 | 15 | 30 | 26 | 100 |
| Small Protestant | 10 | 11 | 5 | 17 | 32 | 25 | 100 |

Source: 1991 National Church Life Survey attender data adjusted for non-participants

Within the biggest denominations, there are some regional variations. For instance, Sydney Anglican attenders (41%) are more likely to have tried to invite someone to church activities than Anglicans generally (35%). In the same way, Uniting Church attenders in New South Wales and Queensland (32%) are more likely to have invited someone than attenders in other states.

Attenders influenced by charismatic (58%) or evangelical theological traditions (49%), who speak in tongues (59%) or who view the Bible as God's word to be taken literally (49%) are more likely to have encouraged someone to church activities. By comparison, only 34% of attenders who think the Bible is a valuable book have tried to encourage someone to attend church activities.

## WHO BRINGS OTHERS TO CHURCH?

Previous chapters have noted that young attenders are more likely to have contacts in the community and to share their faith than older attenders. So it should come as no surprise that they are also more likely to have successfully influenced someone to attend church. A third of 15 to 29 year olds and 30% of 30 to 49 year olds have successfully encouraged someone to attend church activities, compared to 20% of attenders in their 60s. It should be noted that this is not true in Pentecostal denominations, where older attenders are just as likely as younger attenders to invite others to church.

*Younger attenders are more likely to have successfully influenced someone to attend church*

Once again, this highlights the importance of younger attenders in a mission strategy. However, there are significant differences between 15 to 19 year olds and other attenders. Teenagers are more likely to encourage others to church for reasons other than discussions of faith. This is probably because many young attenders belong to youth fellowships with active social programs. Social activities can form an effective bridge between young people and the church.

This may provide clues for mission among older adults. While church should not become focused around its social life, some social activities may be suitable bridges for people of other ages. In an era of fractured families and relationships, some congregations may benefit from resurrecting a social calendar as a link to the wider community.

**Invited others to church by age group**

| Age group | % |
|---|---|
| 15–19 | 33 |
| 20–29 | 33 |
| 30–39 | 30 |
| 40–49 | 30 |
| 50–59 | 25 |
| 60–69 | 20 |
| 70+ | 18 |

Source: 1991 National Church Life Survey adjusted for non-participants

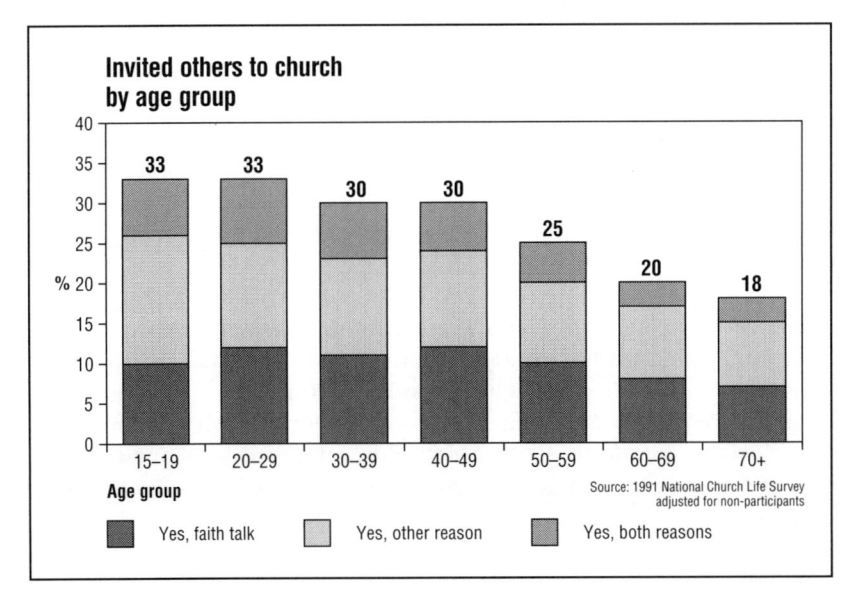

Legend: Yes, faith talk | Yes, other reason | Yes, both reasons

Figure 7.5

Attenders from non-English-speaking backgrounds are more likely to have encouraged others to church successfully (35%) than attenders from Australian-born (25%) or other English-speaking backgrounds (27%). This may be related to the important social role of churches among some non-English-speaking groups. Some churches fill a variety of needs for migrants in particular who are starting afresh socially, economically and personally in a new land (Han, 1994, Chapter 10; Lee, 1989, 44). This result may also be because, as discussed in Chapter 5, people from non-English-speaking backgrounds are more prepared to talk about their faith. This relationship holds true for each denominational group.

## FAITH SHARERS: AN ASSET

Half of attenders (53%) who look for opportunities to share their faith and 29% of attenders who feel at ease talking about their faith if the opportunity arises have successfully invited someone to church in the past year. This compares to just 14% of attenders who do not like to talk about faith and 17% of attenders who find it hard to talk about faith. Clearly, attenders are more likely to bring others to church when they are both willing and confident to discuss their faith.

Many congregations would consider those who set out to share their faith with others to be a real asset. However, some don't endorse proactive faith sharing, seeing it as inappropriate or insensitive. The NCLS cannot assess the impact of those who share their faith insensitively.

However, what is clear is that attenders who actively seek to share their faith have a vital role to play in newcomers joining the church. Congregations need to equip, train and nurture these people. One writer suggests that identifying people gifted in evangelism should be a mission strategy for denominations also (Finney, 1992a, 90–92).

## FAITH SHARING AND CHURCH GROWTH

In a study of churches in the United States, C. Kirk Hadaway found evangelistic outreach to be the most important predictor of church growth, even after accounting for factors such as demographic environment, the age profile of the congregation and the ability of the minister/pastor (Hadaway, 1991, 192).

The NCLS also explored the relationship between faith sharing and numerical church growth. Links were found to exist at a number of levels including: who attenders mostly share their faith with; how many people they share faith with; and their success in inviting others to church. For instance, some 32% of attenders in congregations which grew by more than 50% from 1986 to 1991 successfully influenced someone to go to church activities in the past year, compared to 23% of attenders in stable congregations and 22% in declining congregations.

However, these relationships appear to be confined to mainstream and large Protestant denominational groups. While the activity of individual attenders is important, there are other important factors also operating which affect church growth. More detailed analysis of these issues is taking place as part of an analysis of congregational life.

\* \* \* \*

## PUTTING THEORY INTO PRACTICE

Discussing faith and inviting others to church are the points in evangelism where the rubber hits the road. It is encouraging that so many attenders discuss their faith with others or invite others to church, but cause for concern that many don't.

A desire to talk about faith or invite others appears to reflect an overall enthusiasm about the Christian faith and congregational life. Attenders who invite others to join a church are also more likely to feel they are growing in their faith and are allowing their faith to affect their actions and priorities. They are also likely to be more involved in congregational life.

Congregations where few attenders seem willing to invite others to participate in a congregation need to evaluate this carefully. Some discussion about how attenders feel about the nature of congregational life and how helpful it is to worship and growth may be revealing.

The fact that many attenders continue to be involved with people with whom they have shared their faith emphasises that bringing people to discipleship is more commonly a process than a one-off event. This process involves listening, sowing seeds, nurturing, and joining with others. While some people may go through this process rapidly, many others take weeks, months or even years.

A congregation must be in mission not only in the wider community, but also in its own life, integrating and nurturing both current attenders and newcomers without a church background.

---

### Reaching people where they are

One of the realities of urban living is that many people spend much of their time away from their home, working in regional business districts or industrial areas. Commuting has become a way of life.

A large Anglican congregation on the outskirts of Sydney sought to reach out to men where they live and work. Apart from locally based activities, such as golf days, activities are run in the centre of the city itself, such as men's dinners and evangelistic Bible study groups.

Attenders from the church invite their non-church friends to these events. One such person invited was Ian who, after attending a golf day and a dinner, came along to a *Christianity Explained* course in the city. 'I really saw something different in the way these people related together', says Ian. 'I felt relaxed about coming to these activities and gradually felt confident to share my own experiences and to pray with the others.'

Eventually, Ian reached a point of Christian commitment. Ian recalls: 'For me, the key was getting to know about Jesus in a relaxed atmosphere. Having the opportunity to meet in the city meant that I could do so in the midst of my busy work and personal life.'

**Attenders who are involved in sharing the faith with others also have a key role in inviting others to congregational activities.**

- There is a clear link between attitudes to faith sharing and what happens in practice. Attenders who are at ease sharing their faith if the opportunity arises, are much more likely to have shared their faith in the past 12 months than attenders who don't like to talk about faith or find it hard to do so. They are also more likely to have successfully invited someone to church.
- Most faith sharing is with acquaintances, rather than with close friends or strangers. *Acquaintance evangelism* is most commonly happening.
- The vast majority of attenders who discuss their faith do so out in the community with contacts from everyday life.
- Young people and attenders in Pentecostal denominations are most likely to have shared their faith or successfully invited someone to a church activity during the past year.
- Attenders in strongly growing congregations are more likely to have discussed their faith with others or invited someone to church than those in stable or declining congregations.

PART 3

# MISSION IN THE CONGREGATION

At the beginning of *Mission under the Microscope* it was suggested that attractional and incarnational aspects of the mission of the church are both extremely important and inter-related. This part touches on some key aspects of a sustainable mission strategy that are to do with the internal life of a congregation. Many of the key results from the NCLS regarding attractional aspects of congregational life were presented in *Winds of Change* and will be only briefly mentioned in passing in the coming chapters.

As was outlined in the Introduction, when missional aspects of congregational life are considered, two key priorities emerge:

- the question of integrating and nurturing newcomers without a background in church attendance;
- the question of retaining and nurturing existing attenders and their families.

A chapter is devoted to each of these issues.

An important priority for congregations is to help attenders own their faith and explore its implications. The final chapter of this book takes a look at the place of public commitment in the process of integrating and nurturing attenders.

CHAPTER 8

# OPENING THE FRONT DOOR

## Integrating and nurturing newcomers

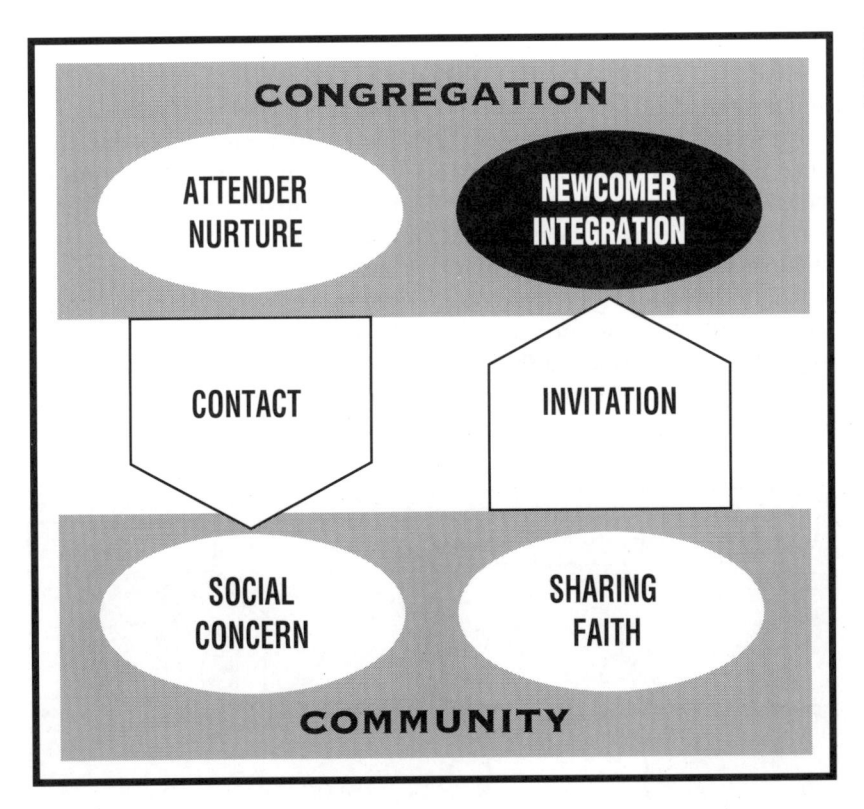

**CONGREGATION**

- ATTENDER NURTURE
- **NEWCOMER INTEGRATION**
- CONTACT
- INVITATION
- SOCIAL CONCERN
- SHARING FAITH

**COMMUNITY**

> Personal contact plays a vital role in attracting and integrating newcomers. The majority of newcomers join, are made to feel welcome and helped to fit into congregational life through personal contact with clergy and other attenders.

The desire to see the church grow in numbers is not confined to church leaders. Three-quarters of all attenders would like their congregation to be larger, either because they believe it would be more effective in ministry or because they believe it won't survive unless it grows (*Winds of Change*, p 306). However, working out how to attract and retain newcomers perplexes many congregations. (Newcomers are defined as those people who joined a congregation in the last five years and were not previously attending anywhere.)

The NCLS provides some vital clues. Some of the background information on newcomers in this chapter was provided in *Winds of Change*. Where appropriate, page references are given. More than six in 10 newcomers to church life (64%) join through some form of personal contact, including friends, acquaintances, family, clergy or a church activity. The convenience of the church (16%), its visibility (4%) and its reputation (1%) are reasons for a minority of newcomers (p 161).

In the light of these results, some congregations will need to rethink their mission strategies. Numbers will not necessarily beget numbers. Nor will large buildings automatically attract people to fill them. Activities, no matter how relevant or well organised will not, on their own, necessarily attract newcomers. Sign boards, advertisements and letterbox drops should be adjuncts to a mission program, not central to it. A broad, creative use of mass media is generally beyond the realm of most congregations and may be ineffective without personal invitation.

For many long-term attenders, this represents a new era of mission. Since the majority of attenders either grew up in their congregation or joined because it was close by, faith sharing and inviting people to church may be challenging and even threatening (p 154).

Further, an invitation to church is just one point in a process. To integrate into church life, newcomers need to feel welcome, to develop a sense of belonging, to grow in their faith and discipleship, and to make their own unique contribution to congregational life and mission. This chapter explores newcomers' first occasion at church, how they are made to feel welcome and what factors contribute to their successful integration into the church community.

## WHO ARE NEWCOMERS?

The NCLS shows that people are never too old, too young, too poor or too educated to become part of congregational life. Newcomers span the full age range and socio-economic spectrum – evidence that attenders of all ages and backgrounds need to be involved in mission. In all, 8% of attenders are newcomers; they are found in all denominations that participated in the survey.

However, newcomers are more likely than average to be in their teens, 20s or 30s and to be from blue-collar households. This is good news, since these groups are currently under-represented in the church (pp 212–224).

## THE PROCESS OF INTEGRATING NEWCOMERS

Key findings on newcomers raised in *Winds of Change* and reiterated here are:

*The style and programs of the congregation may be important.* Since most newcomers come into church life through a personal contact, congregations need to provide activities to which attenders feel comfortable inviting people and which are likely to appeal to potential newcomers. There are strong generational preferences for particular styles of worship. It is important that congregations examine their worship styles, to ensure they are appropriate for their target audience (pp 326–328). Congregations may also need to consider the quality of their children's programs, since many newcomers are people returning to church life with their young children (p 216), as well as groups or activities for those beyond youth groups, since first-time newcomers are often in their 20s (p 216).

*Newcomers are more tentative in their church involvement.* Newcomers are more likely to be tentative about congregational involvement. While they are more likely to have had a recent conversion experience and to be growing in faith than attenders overall, they are less likely to be involved in congregational mission activities, or to attend church services and other group activities. The stereotype of the newcomer 'on fire' appears to be true for only a minority of newcomers (pp 217–222 ).

*Newcomers to church life take longer to integrate.* Newcomers are less likely to feel they belong to their congregation or to have close friends in the congregation. This suggests that they need more support from the congregation (pp 220, 221) and that the process of integration may take longer than for other attenders. They are more likely to value a caring congregation than other attenders. Congregational leaders would do well to have not only welcoming procedures in place, but also ways of keeping in touch with the long-term needs of the newcomers in their midst (p 329).

*Newcomers provide a contact with other potential newcomers.* Newcomers have their own family, work and social networks, which may be totally unconnected with church. Congregational leaders need to explore this with newcomers and equip them to live out and discuss their faith with others and to invite them to join in congregational activities (p 223).

## FIRST OCCASION AT CHURCH

To explore newcomers' first occasion at a church activity, the NCLS included the following question. Some 8% cannot remember their first occasion at church; they have been excluded from the following analysis.

> **Q** **What was the first occasion you came to this church?**
> a. Worship service
> b. Christmas/Easter service
> c. Small group activity
> d. Social function or club
> e. Special outreach event/activity
> f. Baptism, wedding or funeral with which I was connected
> g. Don't remember
> h. Other

A worship service is the first occasion at church for eight out of 10 of all attenders. A further 5% first attend a baptism, wedding or funeral, and 3% a Christmas or Easter service. Only 3% of attenders first go to a small group, 2% to a special outreach activity and 1% to a social activity. Some 6% have some other form of contact. Interestingly, this pattern generally holds, regardless of denomination, congregational size, or the demographic profile of attenders.

Figure 8.1

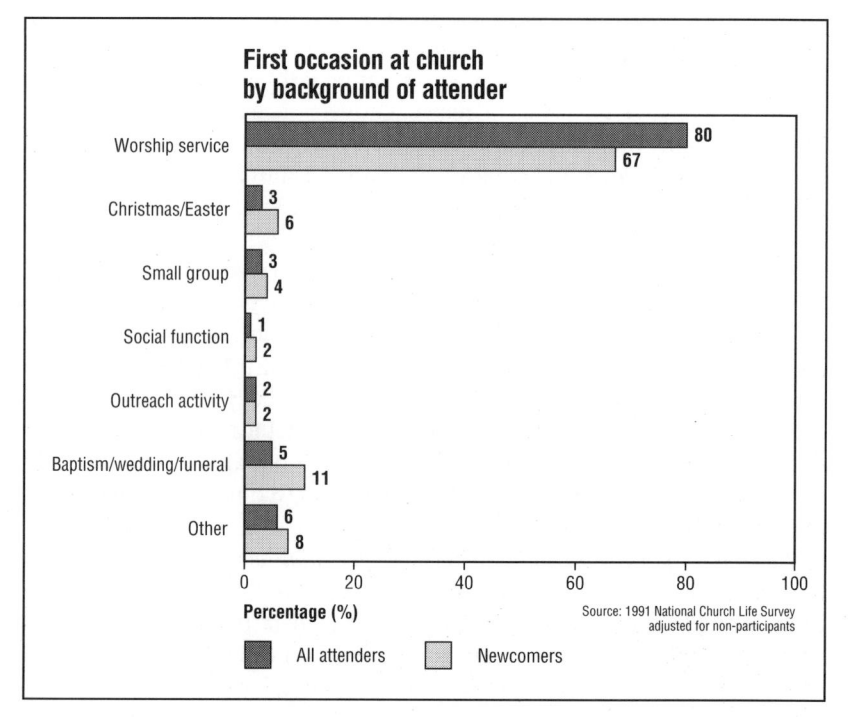

**First occasion at church by background of attender**

| Category | All attenders | Newcomers |
|---|---|---|
| Worship service | 80 | 67 |
| Christmas/Easter | 3 | 6 |
| Small group | 3 | 4 |
| Social function | 1 | 2 |
| Outreach activity | 2 | 2 |
| Baptism/wedding/funeral | 5 | 11 |
| Other | 6 | 8 |

Source: 1991 National Church Life Survey adjusted for non-participants

A worship service is also the first occasion at church for most newcomers (67%). Given that such a high percentage of newcomers start in a worship service, congregations will want to consider their needs carefully.

Congregations find many ways to deal with newcomers. Some have modified their services to be more user-friendly for newcomers, while others hold special services designed primarily for non-churchgoers. This is a difficult issue. Congregations need to meet the needs of both non-churchgoers and regular attenders.

An alternative solution adopted by some congregations is to hold meetings outside church services which can act as a stepping stone into congregational life. This approach is common among young attenders. Some 60% of 15- to 19-year-old attenders are involved in a fellowship or social group (*Winds of Change*, p 113), compared to 40% of other attenders. Congregations may want to start activities for people in other age groups as well.

Weddings, baptisms and funerals are a first point of contact for 11% of newcomers, while 6% first attend a Christmas or Easter service. These are higher proportions than for attenders generally. Such services are clearly a first point of contact for a significant group of newcomers. Congregations may want to look at how they can make the most of these events to make effective contact with others.

*A worship service is the first occasion at church for 67% of newcomers*

## MAKING NEWCOMERS WELCOME

As mentioned previously, inviting newcomers through the front door is just a first step in the process of integration. Once there, they need to feel welcomed and affirmed. To evaluate welcoming strategies, the NCLS included the following question.

> **When you first came to worship or activities organised by this church, were there any particular ways in which you were made to feel welcome? (Circle a maximum of two)**
> a. I was followed up by a visit from the minister/priest
> b. I was followed up with a visit by a member of the church
> c. I was invited to a meal
> d. I was invited to join a small group
> e. The minister spoke to me after the service/activity
> f. I was welcomed by others after the service/activity
> g. I completed an information card and was phoned up
> h. No particular ways
> i. I cannot remember

Some 14% of attenders cannot remember how they were made to feel welcome. They have been excluded from the following analysis.

Overall, attenders are made most welcome by being spoken to by others (41%) or by the minister (17%) immediately after the service, being

> *Three-quarters of newcomers felt welcome because they were spoken to immediately after a church activity*

followed up by the minister (18%) or being invited to a small group (14%). Although just one individual, the minister clearly has an important role to play.

Attenders in large congregations are more likely to have been invited to a small group: 22% were invited to a small group in congregations of more than 500 people, decreasing to 10% in congregations with fewer than 50 people. Information cards also play a greater role in larger congregations. However, being welcomed immediately after the service occurs less frequently when congregations reach 500 people, evidence that in very large congregations people can get lost in the crowd if they do not have some prior personal contact with a regular attender.

Interestingly, attenders are more likely to have been invited for a meal or welcomed immediately after the service in congregations which are growing than in stable or declining congregations. Once again, this reinforces the importance of immediate personal contact.

Being welcomed immediately after an activity is especially important for newcomers. Some 48% felt welcomed because they were spoken to straight after the activity by other attenders and 28% by the minister – figures which are higher than for attenders overall.

Church growth writers have suggested, based on experience in the United States, that visitors are more likely to return to church, and ultimately join a congregation, if they are followed up within 36 hours of

Figure 8.2

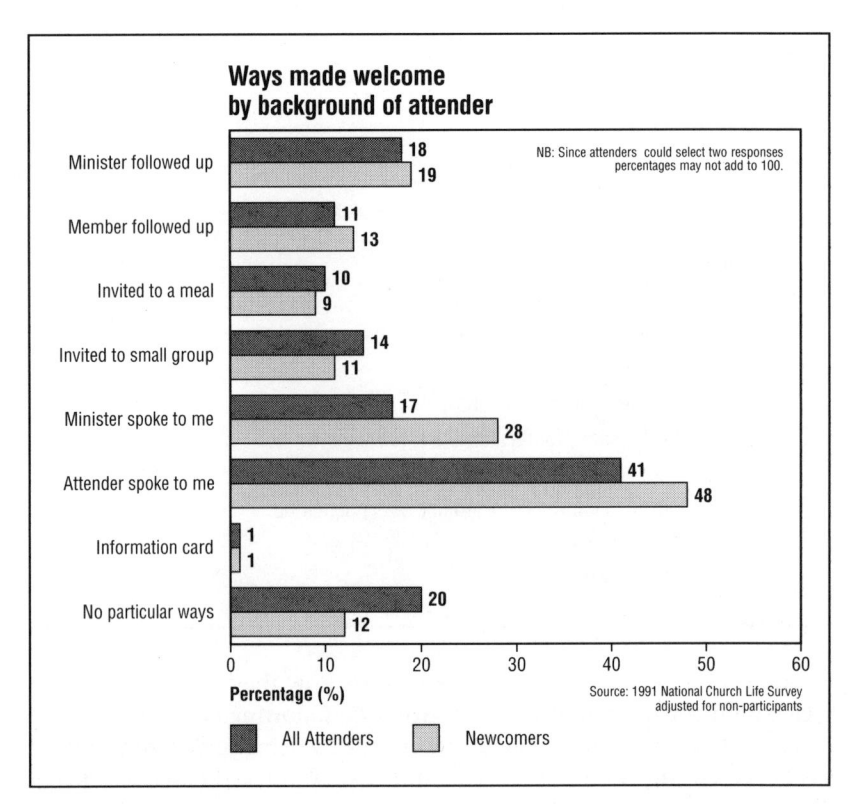

**Ways made welcome by background of attender**

| Way made welcome | All Attenders | Newcomers |
|---|---|---|
| Minister followed up | 18 | 19 |
| Member followed up | 11 | 13 |
| Invited to a meal | 10 | 9 |
| Invited to small group | 14 | 11 |
| Minister spoke to me | 17 | 28 |
| Attender spoke to me | 41 | 48 |
| Information card | 1 | 1 |
| No particular ways | 20 | 12 |

NB: Since attenders could select two responses percentages may not add to 100.

Source: 1991 National Church Life Survey adjusted for non-participants

their first visit (Miller, 1990, 81). The NCLS suggests that for most newcomers, an immediate welcome appears to be even more critical. Further research would be required in the Australian context to evaluate the importance of follow-up visits.

Only 12% of newcomers are not welcomed in any way, compared to 20% of attenders overall.

It needs to be remembered that the NCLS is a study of current attenders. There is no data on people who visited churches or were newcomers, but dropped out. The higher percentage of newcomers welcomed may reflect greater interest taken in them by other attenders or a high drop-out level of newcomers who were not welcomed by others.

## HELPING NEWCOMERS SETTLE IN

Once over the welcoming hurdle, congregations need to support newcomers through the integration process. To examine ways in which newcomers are helped to settle in, the NCLS included the following question.

> **When you first came to this church were you helped to fit in by:**
> a. Personal support from a member of the church
> b. An orientation program
> c. A course about Christianity
> d. More than one of the above
> e. None of the above
> f. Don't remember

Some 13% of attenders cannot remember how they were helped to fit in. They have been excluded from the following analysis.

Overall, 70% of attenders were helped to fit into their congregation in one of the ways suggested in the question. About half (54%) were helped to fit in through the support of other people, some 3% attended a course on Christianity and 1% an orientation program. A further 12% were assisted by a combination of these.

The small proportion of attenders who were assisted by an orientation program or a course about Christianity reflects the proportion of congregations providing such programs. Only 21% of congregational leaders say that their congregations provide orientation programs, or groups or courses for new Christians.

Three in 10 attenders were not helped to integrate into their congregation in any of the ways listed. While some may have felt welcome in other ways, the size of this group may concern some leaders. Many of these attenders may have hung on, despite not feeling especially welcomed, until they were established. Other new attenders may have slipped away unnoticed.

These results are similar for attenders in declining, stable and growing congregations, and also for attenders with different faith backgrounds. However, attenders starting in Pentecostal congregations (75%) or in congregations with fewer than 50 attenders (76%) are a little more likely to say they were helped to fit in than attenders generally (70%).

Figure 8.3

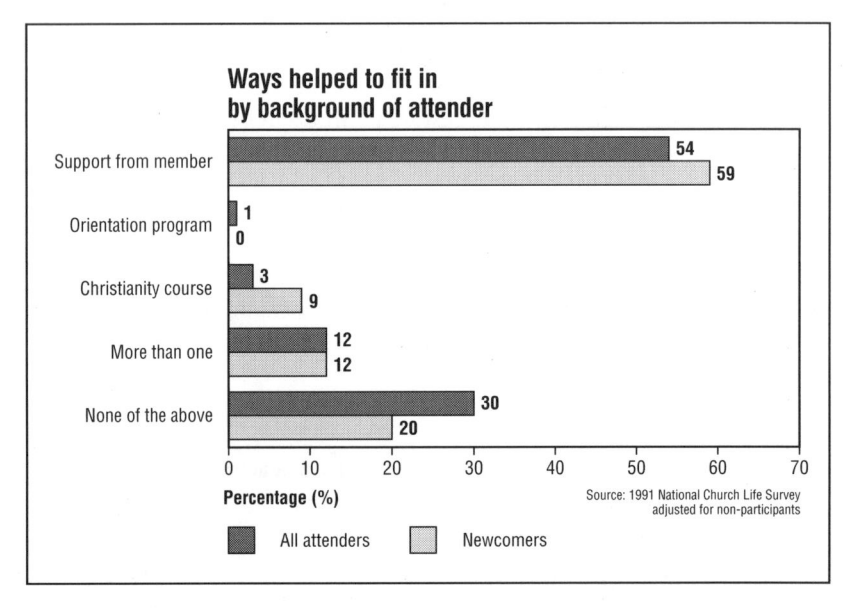

**Ways helped to fit in by background of attender**

| Category | All attenders | Newcomers |
|---|---|---|
| Support from member | 54 | 59 |
| Orientation program | 1 | 0 |
| Christianity course | 3 | 9 |
| More than one | 12 | 12 |
| None of the above | 30 | 20 |

Source: 1991 National Church Life Survey adjusted for non-participants

Personal support from another attender was important for most newcomers. Newcomers were also more likely to attend a course than other attenders. In total, 80% of newcomers were helped to fit into their congregation in some way, compared to 71% of denominational switchers and 60% of transfers.

The importance of relationships in attracting newcomers to congregations, making them feel welcome and helping them to integrate, cannot be overstated. Other kinds of programs, while of value in themselves, do not replace personal contact and support from other attenders.

The value of support from other attenders in the integration process can be seen in the strong correlation between being helped to fit in and having a sense of belonging. Four in five attenders who have a strong, growing sense of belonging were helped to fit into their congregation. In contrast, only 34% of those who wished they belonged received some kind of support.

This finding supports previous NCLS results which show that attenders with a strong sense of belonging are much more likely to have close friends in the congregation and to be satisfied at church (*Winds of Change*, p 142).

## DEVELOPING A SENSE OF BELONGING

To determine how quickly attenders feel they belonged to their congregation, the NCLS asked the following question. Attenders who grew up in the congregation have been excluded from analysis.

> **From first contact with this church, how long would you say it took you to feel as though you 'belonged' here?**
> a. It happened straight away
> b. Less than three months
> c. Three to six months
> d. Six to 12 months
> e. One to two years
> f. Over two years
> g. I still do not feel that I belong here

A sense of belonging grows over time. Only 40% of attenders feel they belonged to their congregation straight away. A third took up to six months to belong (33%), and a further 7% took up to a year. Another 7% took one to two years, while 6% took more than two years to feel they really belonged. Some 7% don't feel they belong to their congregation.

*Winds of Change* (p 141) reported that newcomers to church life are less likely to feel a sense of belonging to their congregation than other attenders. However, among newcomers who do have a sense of belonging, there is no evidence that the sense of belonging took longer to develop than for other new members such as switchers or transfers.

Pentecostal attenders are more likely to feel they belong within six months (83%) than mainstream attenders (70%).

Attenders at large congregations are just as likely to feel they belong as attenders at small congregations. However, integration into small congregations is faster. Some 51% of attenders at congregations with fewer than 50 people felt they belonged straight away, compared to just a third at congregations with more than 500 people.

Although it may take longer to belong to a large congregation, it does come. Within six months this gap is greatly reduced; 76% in the largest congregations felt they belonged within six months, compared to 82% in the smallest congregations.

Older attenders are more likely to have felt a sense of belonging straight away; 61% of attenders over 70 years felt they belonged immediately, compared to 27% of attenders in their 30s and 32% of attenders in their 20s. This difference is partly explained by younger attenders' preference for large congregations, where a sense of belonging takes longer to achieve.

However, the difference may also show differing expectations. Older attenders are more accepting of their congregation, and more likely to be loyal to it, whereas younger attenders are more likely to evaluate their congregation critically and move on if things don't work out.

Figure 8.4

**Time taken to belong by age group**

|  | Straight away % | Less than 3 months % | 3 to 6 months % | 6 to 12 months % | 1 to 2 years % | Over 2 years % | Don't feel I belong % | Total % |
|---|---|---|---|---|---|---|---|---|
| **Overall** | **40** | **22** | **11** | **7** | **7** | **6** | **7** | **100** |
| 15–19 years | 25 | 25 | 15 | 6 | 5 | 7 | 19 | 100 |
| 20–29 years | 32 | 24 | 18 | 9 | 8 | 2 | 7 | 100 |
| 30–39 years | 27 | 25 | 16 | 10 | 7 | 6 | 9 | 100 |
| 40–49 years | 34 | 22 | 10 | 8 | 10 | 8 | 9 | 100 |
| 50–59 years | 43 | 24 | 8 | 6 | 6 | 8 | 5 | 100 |
| 60–69 years | 49 | 18 | 7 | 8 | 5 | 8 | 4 | 100 |
| 70+ years | 61 | 16 | 6 | 3 | 5 | 6 | 4 | 100 |

Source: 1991 National Church Life Survey attender data adjusted for non-participants

## PROMOTING A SENSE OF BELONGING

According to Peter Wagner, there are two major ways that new members are assimilated into church life: through being assigned a task or role and through involvement in cell groups (Wagner, 1984, 206). The NCLS suggests that these and other factors contribute to effective integration (*Winds of Change*, p 141).

Overall, attenders who have a strong sense of belonging are more likely to:
- be highly involved in worship services and groups;
- be involved in mission activities;
- have a role in their congregation;
- be satisfied with the church program; and
- have close friends at church.

Newcomers who have a sense of belonging are more likely to be highly involved in congregational activities, including worship services, small study or prayer groups, or fellowship/social groups. For instance, two-thirds of newcomers who have a strong, growing sense of belonging are involved in groups, compared to only 40% of newcomers who wish they belonged.

In the light of this, some congregations need to ensure that there are small groups open to newcomers. While some groups may need to be closed for a time to encourage sharing, newcomers also need to be able to join a group without feeling like an intruder.

Some 34% of newcomers who have a strong, growing sense of belonging also have a role in their congregation, compared to just 16% of newcomers who wish they belonged. Congregations may want to reconsider how roles are allocated among attenders. While congregations need to be careful not to burden newcomers with responsibility too quickly, they also need to ensure that newcomers aren't blocked out of particular roles by attenders who 'do everything'.

### From shopping to joining

Small groups are widely recognised as a way to nurture and disciple newcomers to church life. One Pentecostal congregation takes this so seriously that special courses and small groups are provided for newcomers.

'We are careful not to integrate newcomers into existing small groups prematurely', says the senior pastor. 'Before inviting a new Christian to join one of our regular small groups we take them through a five-week *Christianity Explained* course followed by a *Church Explained* course which outlines the ministries, structure and philosophy of the church. They then join a small group with other newcomers, where issues of faith and discipleship can be explored. Only after this do they enter a regular small group.'

The pastor recognises that not all congregations would need to hold a course explaining the church. He also acknowledges that smaller congregations may not have enough new Christians at one time to form a special group. However, he recommends congregations adapt the principles to suit their circumstances.

'Without these introductory programs, we find that the newcomers' flurry of questions becomes the focus of the group to the detriment of other members', he says. 'Our system allows new Christians to explore faith while leaving longer-term members free to pursue a discipleship agenda.'

\* \* \* \*

A survey asking newcomers why they stayed proved useful at one Anglican congregation. The most common response was that they felt comfortable, followed by the relevance of the teaching.

'We try to make church as comfortable as possible', said Jennifer, who initiated the survey. 'We think about our style of music, our language, even what we wear. When we use the prayer book, we put the selected sections on overheads or handouts.'

The preachers are conscious that newcomers to church life are often puzzled by the church's stand on issues such as abortion or sex outside marriage. The teaching aims to help them explore these issues.

'It is sobering to realise that if people do actually come to church and have a bad experience they are unlikely to return and likely to share the bad news with their friends', says Jennifer. 'If we invite people to church we need to make sure that it is a positive experience for them.'

## SHOPPING AROUND

To find out whether attenders tried other churches before their current one, the NCLS asked the following question.

**Before settling with this church here, did you try other churches first?**
- a. No, I didn't
- b. I cannot remember
- c. Yes, I tried one or two others
- d. Yes, I really 'shopped around' before settling here
- e. I guess I am still shopping around at the moment

*LEAVING THE FINAL SERVICE AT BIGTOWN MEMORIAL CHURCH*

> **When greeting non-churchgoers, attenders may get no second chance**

Overall, 28% of all attenders tried another congregation before settling in at their current congregation. Certainly, the majority of denominational switchers (60%) did so. This is part of the 'shopping around' mentality which is particularly prevalent among younger attenders.

Newcomers are less likely to shop around for a congregation than attenders generally; only 23% of newcomers tried more than one congregation. Clearly, many newcomers will either settle into the congregation they first attend or not attend at all.

This has important implications for congregations. When greeting non-churchgoers, attenders may have no second chance. To ensure that newcomers are welcomed and followed up, responsibility may need to be shared by all attenders, not allocated to just a few.

\*   \*   \*   \*

## OPENING THE FRONT DOOR

In this new mission era, it is vital that congregations reflect on how to relate to those distanced from church life. The number of newcomers without a church background in congregational life provides a useful indicator of the extent to which a congregation is connecting with the wider community.

Congregational leaders would do well to evaluate the number of newcomers in their congregation and to listen to their experience of joining and becoming part of the congregation. The questions in the accompanying table may be a useful starting point for further reflection.

Leaders would also benefit by talking with newcomers who have not stayed with the congregation. Why did they leave? What difficulties did they experience? What can be learnt from them to help integrate newcomers better in the future?

> **Integrating newcomers – some questions to ask**
> - What is the overall number of newcomers to your congregation?
> - How did they first come in contact with your congregation? Were they already looking around for a church to join?
> - What was the first occasion on which they attended? How were they welcomed? Why did they choose to stay?
> - How long did it take them to feel they belonged?
> - To what extent are they getting involved in aspects of congregational life and mission? Or involved in decision making? Or growing in their faith?

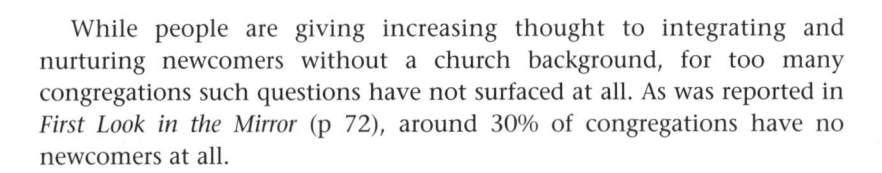

While people are giving increasing thought to integrating and nurturing newcomers without a church background, for too many congregations such questions have not surfaced at all. As was reported in *First Look in the Mirror* (p 72), around 30% of congregations have no newcomers at all.

## ALL ROADS LEAD TO . . .

All roads may not lead to Rome, but NCLS research about newcomers points to one critical issue – relationships. There is no getting around it. Personal contact plays a significant role in attracting newcomers to church, in making them feel welcome and in helping them to settle in. It should be noted that personal contact may be with acquaintances as well as close friends.

The importance of supportive relationships cannot be overemphasised. By and large, newcomers do not 'shop around' for a congregation. Consequently, the onus is on congregations to get it right first time.

Congregations that want to attract and integrate newcomers may need to rethink their priorities in the light of this information. Many attenders are already busy; indeed, many congregations rely on a core of highly involved attenders to carry much of the workload. Responsibility for befriending newcomers needs to be shared across the congregation. It may even be appropriate for some activities to be curtailed to allow relationship and community to be a priority.

Of course, developing an ethos of welcoming among all attenders doesn't excuse the congregation from being organised or proactive about it. As Peter Corney notes in *The Welcoming Church*: 'Jobs that are everybody's tend to be left to everybody else and therefore don't get done' (1992, 20).

On the other hand, greeting rosters, name tags and visitor information kits are only vehicles for community – they cannot replace genuine relationships. Congregations will need to balance the two, developing welcoming and integration strategies which promote the friendship and Christian community that newcomers value so highly.

Since a church service is the first point of church contact for so many newcomers, congregations may also want to rethink some aspects of their activities. In particular, congregations may need to rethink their use of church jargon in prayers, songs and sermons. They may also need to examine what changes to worship would be necessary for people from different ethnic or subcultural backgrounds to feel comfortable.

Congregations do not always think intentionally about these issues. The NCLS suggests that they should do so. Newcomers are a vital source of renewal for the whole church.

Holding the tension between the needs of newcomers and the needs of existing attenders will be a challenge for many congregations. However, working on some of these issues may also assist in retaining and nurturing some existing attenders. This issue is explored further in the next chapter.

---

**Personal contact plays a vital role in attracting and integrating newcomers. The majority of newcomers join, are made to feel welcome and helped to fit into congregational life through personal contact with clergy and other attenders.**

- A worship service is the first occasion at church for two-thirds of newcomers. Rites of passage events such as baptisms, weddings and funerals are the first contact for 11% of newcomers.
- The majority of newcomers were welcomed immediately after the service or activity. Some 28% were welcomed by the minister and 48% by other members.
- More than half of all newcomers are helped to settle into their new congregation through personal support from others. A fifth of all newcomers are not helped in any way.
- Newcomers who belong to a small group or have a role in the congregation are more likely to feel a strong, growing sense of belonging to their congregation.
- Personal contact is essential in attracting, welcoming and integrating newcomers. Congregations that want to retain newcomers need to rethink their programs so that attenders can form relationships with newcomers.
- Newcomers are much less likely to try different churches before settling into a congregation. When welcoming newcomers, congregations may get no second chances.

CHAPTER 9

# CLOSING THE BACK DOOR

**Retaining and nurturing the families of attenders**

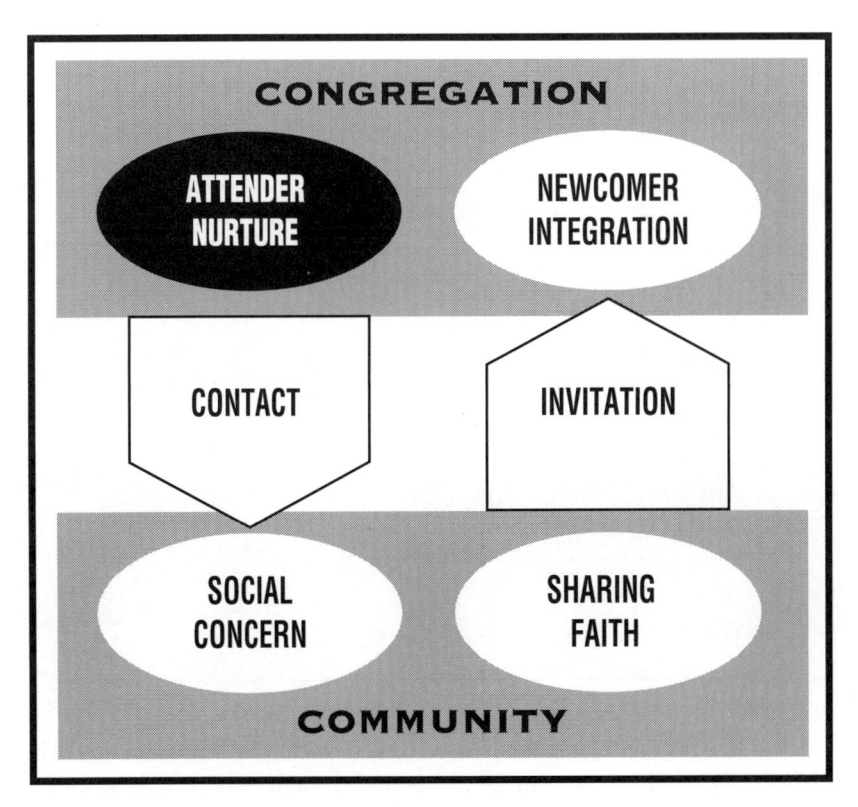

```
┌─────────────────────────────────────┐
│         CONGREGATION                │
│   ATTENDER          NEWCOMER        │
│   NURTURE           INTEGRATION     │
│                                     │
│   CONTACT           INVITATION      │
│                                     │
│   SOCIAL            SHARING         │
│   CONCERN           FAITH           │
│         COMMUNITY                   │
└─────────────────────────────────────┘
```

> 🔑 The teenage and early adult years are critical times for people to drift out of church life. Congregations need to reflect on their retention rates and the reasons for them.

113

Mission begins at home – literally. Raising children in the faith is recognised as an important ministry in virtually all sectors of the church.

Many attenders hope and pray that their children will accept Christian faith for themselves, and they actively encourage faith development, for instance, through discussions about faith, being a role model, family prayers and Bible reading. Congregations share the ministry by providing a range of children's activities, including Sunday school, kids' clubs, school holiday programs, camps and youth fellowships.

While relating to and integrating newcomers without a church background is an important aspect of mission, nurturing existing attenders is also vital. Congregations offer a range of activities, including pastoral care, small groups and social activities in an effort to support existing attenders in Christian discipleship and growth.

For the church, much rests on the continued success of its internal mission – the children of today's attenders will become the core of tomorrow's church. The church faces an uncertain future unless each generation can maintain faith in its own generation and nurture faith in the next.

## FIRST CONTACT WITH CHRISTIAN FAITH

To explore attenders' first contact with the Christian faith, the NCLS included the following question.

**Q**

**My first contact with the Christian faith was: (circle one only)**
- a. A vivid 'spiritual' experience
- b. Through my parents and/or family
- c. In a Sunday school
- d. In this church
- e. In another church
- f. In a major crusade or evangelistic event
- g. In a mission group
- h. From a workmate, friend or neighbour
- i. Scripture classes
- j. Media (eg TV, radio)
- k. Other
- l. Don't know

For the majority of attenders, first contact with the Christian faith is through their parents or family (57%) and Sunday school (20%). Older attenders are more likely to cite parents or Sunday school as their first contact with the faith; however, these are still the first point of contact for 75% of attenders in their teens and 20s. Retaining attenders and their children is clearly a critical priority.

By comparison, 10% of attenders first have contact with faith through a church, 5% through a workmate or neighbour, and 5% through major crusades, scripture teachers, or other ways. The proportion of first contacts through workmates, neighbours, or friends is higher among attenders aged 20 to 50 years than among older attenders. With the increasing need for the church to engage in adult evangelism, it could be expected that first contacts through these sources will increase.

**First contact with Christian faith overall profile**

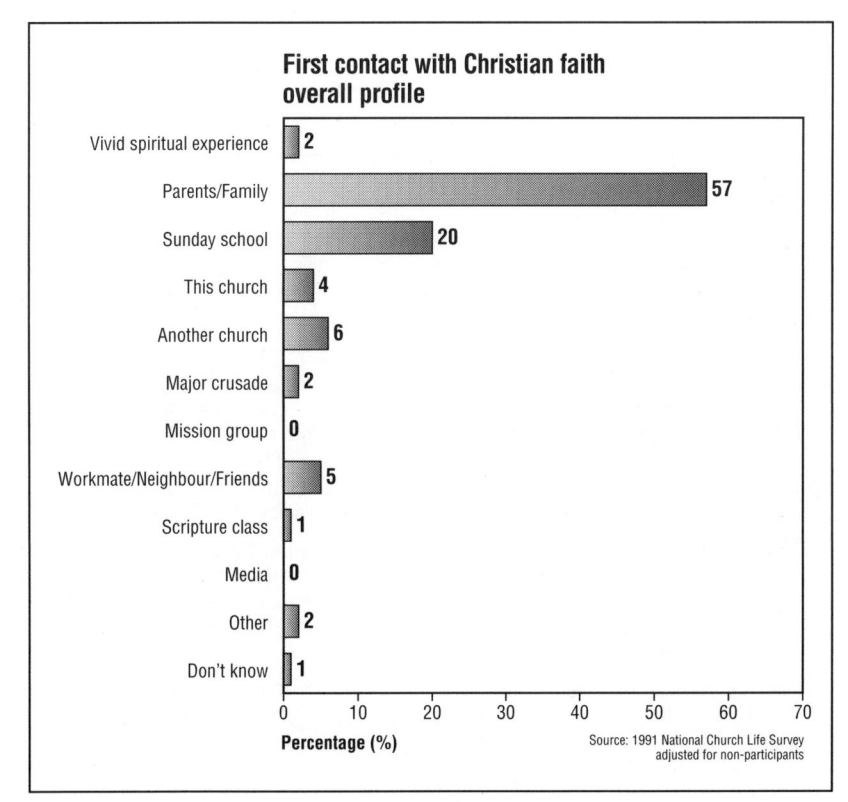

| Source | Percentage (%) |
|---|---|
| Vivid spiritual experience | 2 |
| Parents/Family | 57 |
| Sunday school | 20 |
| This church | 4 |
| Another church | 6 |
| Major crusade | 2 |
| Mission group | 0 |
| Workmate/Neighbour/Friends | 5 |
| Scripture class | 1 |
| Media | 0 |
| Other | 2 |
| Don't know | 1 |

Source: 1991 National Church Life Survey adjusted for non-participants

Figure 9.1

## HELPING ATTENDERS FIND FAITH

To determine how attenders are led to faith, the NCLS included the following question.

> **The most significant people to show me what faith was about were: (circle one only)**
> a. Parents
> b. Spouse
> c. Other family members
> d. Workmates, friends etc
> e. A mission group
> f. Sunday school teachers
> g. Scripture teachers
> h. People from this church
> i. People from another church
> j. Other
> k. No particular person
> l. Don't know

Parents and family are not only the first contact with Christian faith for most attenders, but they are also the most significant people in bringing attenders to faith. Some 41% of attenders nominate parents, 6% their spouse and 5% other family members as the most significant people to show them what faith is about.

> **A journey back to church**
>
> 'Although I regularly attended church and Sunday school as a child, I didn't think much about church as an adult', said Kate, a graphic artist in her late 20s. 'But when Steve and I split up a few years ago, I found the loneliness very difficult. I found some solace in prayer. I felt a bit like the prodigal daughter wondering if the parent still wanted to know my name. As "fate" would have it, an old friend told me about the community church I now attend.
>
> 'Many of the people here are like me; young adults, burnt out or disillusioned, looking for worship and teaching that is more relevant and contemporary. It's great here; we have teaching on topical issues, drama and lots of lay involvement. It is a church that recognises that there are greys or ambiguities in life; they allow us to be ourselves, to be different and to struggle with the meaning of faith.
>
> 'We had a meeting a few weeks ago to consider the future of our congregation. Our pastor commented that the church had originally been formed to reach unchurched people, but had become a "refuge from the roads" for those like me, disenchanted by other church experiences. He said this was fine, but we also had a responsibility to look outward.
>
> 'Someone else at the meeting said that a non-Christian friend had told her that Christians are friendly people who are too busy to be your friends. I know that is true for me; it's a major issue I'm addressing at the moment.'

These results underline the fact that the largest mission activity of parents is bringing children to faith. This should be an encouragement to parents, who clearly have a special role in helping children to discover Christian faith for themselves. In an age of specialisation, where education is increasingly undertaken in institutions, this role should not lightly be abdicated to others.

*The largest mission activity for parents is bringing children to faith*

Figure 9.2

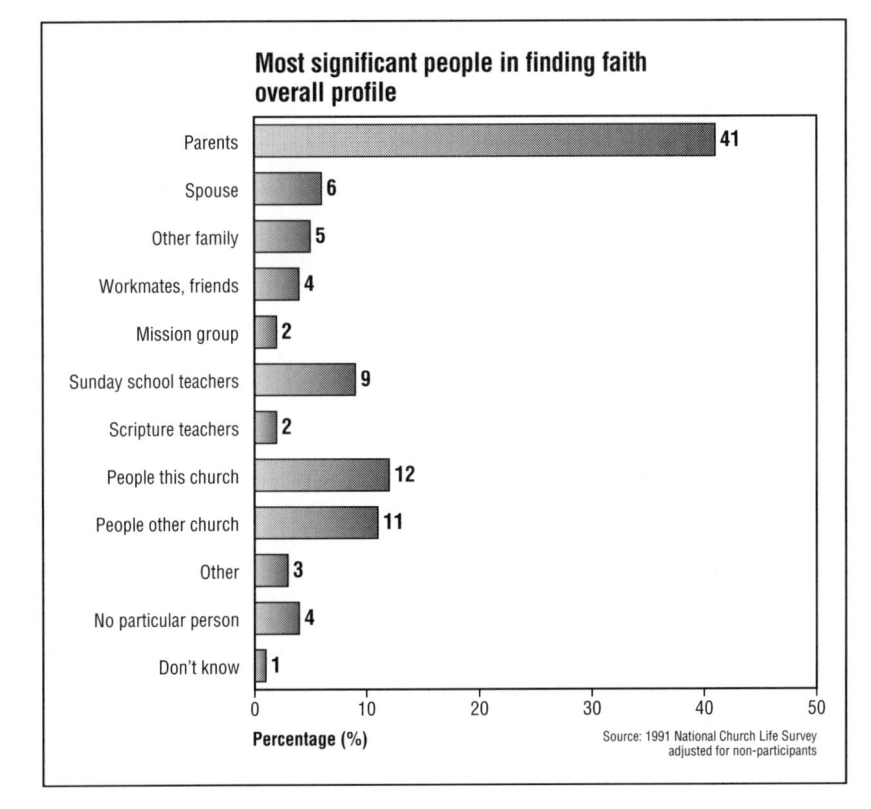

**Most significant people in finding faith overall profile**

| Person | Percentage (%) |
|---|---|
| Parents | 41 |
| Spouse | 6 |
| Other family | 5 |
| Workmates, friends | 4 |
| Mission group | 2 |
| Sunday school teachers | 9 |
| Scripture teachers | 2 |
| People this church | 12 |
| People other church | 11 |
| Other | 3 |
| No particular person | 4 |
| Don't know | 1 |

Source: 1991 National Church Life Survey adjusted for non-participants

The next most important group are people at church. More than a third of attenders say other churchgoers were significant in their finding faith, comprising people at their present church (12%), people at another church (11%), Sunday school teachers (9%), Scripture teachers (2%) and mission groups (2%).

Attenders aged 30 to 60 years are less likely to cite parents as the most significant people in their finding faith. This may be because faith is being communicated differently, or may reflect the value placed upon the words and values of parents by the baby boom generation. In the '60s and '70s, there were generational conflicts as many adolescents of the time consciously rejected the values and priorities of their parents.

Only 25% of attenders in Pentecostal denominations cite their parents as a significant influence, compared to 36% of attenders in large Protestant denominations and 48% of mainstream attenders. The influence of other church attenders is more significant for Pentecostals.

One reason for this result is no doubt the higher levels of newcomers in Pentecostal congregations. Newcomers are much less likely to see their parents as significant people in their coming to faith. Far more nominate people at their church (29% compared to 12% overall), and workmates or friends (9% compared to 4%). Parents are of less importance, with 23% nominating parents compared to 41% of all attenders.

Another reason may well be the different theological perspective of attenders. In denominations where adult conversion is more highly emphasised, attenders may view their adult experiences of faith as more significant than their childhood experiences.

Figure 9.3

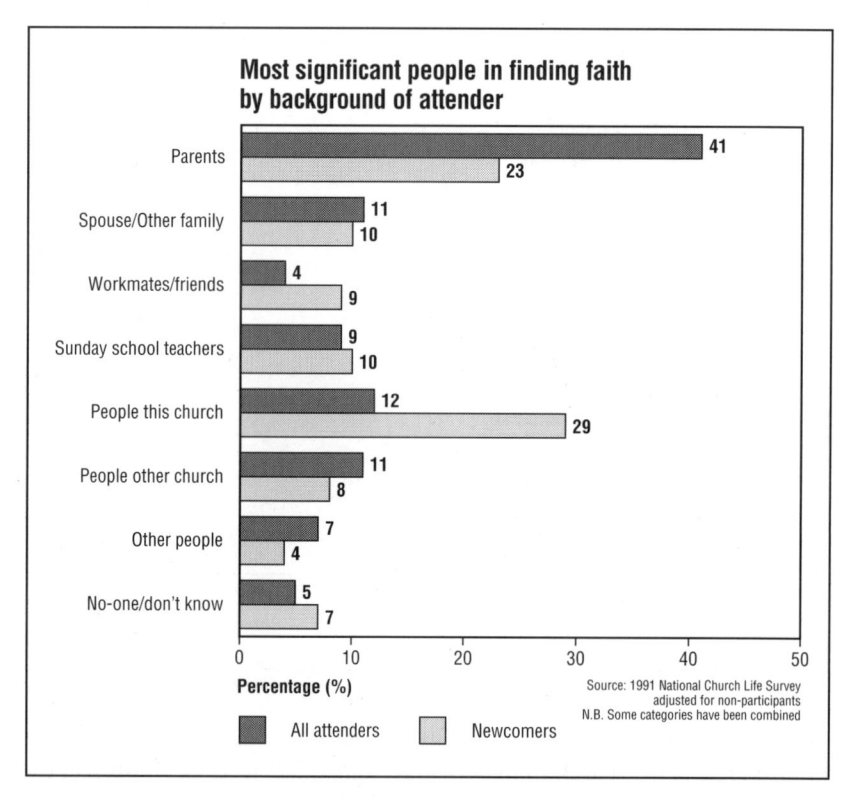

**Most significant people in finding faith by background of attender**

| Category | All attenders | Newcomers |
|---|---|---|
| Parents | 41 | 23 |
| Spouse/Other family | 11 | 10 |
| Workmates/friends | 4 | 9 |
| Sunday school teachers | 9 | 10 |
| People this church | 12 | 29 |
| People other church | 11 | 8 |
| Other people | 7 | 4 |
| No-one/don't know | 5 | 7 |

Source: 1991 National Church Life Survey adjusted for non-participants
N.B. Some categories have been combined

The results serve as a reminder that congregations face two equally important mission fields: their own families and the growing number of people who have had no or little contact with the church throughout their lives. When developing mission strategies, congregations need to consider the different needs of both these groups, devoting resources to each.

## THE PROCESS OF FINDING FAITH

For many attenders, their first contact with Christian faith was not their most significant. For instance, for 20% of attenders, the first contact with faith was through Sunday school, yet only a quarter of these attenders say that a Sunday school teacher was the most significant person to show them what faith was about. Similarly, 5% have their first contact through a workmate, neighbour or friend, yet these contacts were most significant for less than half of this group.

These results point yet again to the fact that evangelism and coming to faith is often a process, not a one-off event. Many church attenders have come to faith through more than one influence. As the Apostle Paul noted, often one person plants the seed while another waters it (1 Corinthians 3:6).

It is important that both parents and church leaders come to grips with this process. The social and mental development of children has been extensively researched. Writers such as Erik Erikson and Jean Piaget have demonstrated that children perceive and think in different ways at various stages of their lives (Erikson, 1950; Ginsburg and Opper, 1969).

Writing about the church, C Ellis Nelson and John Westerhoff III emphasised the role of the community of believers in communicating the faith to children through its life and ritual (Westerhoff, 1976). David Ng and Virginia Thomas point to the central role of parents in teaching children to worship (Ng and Thomas, 1971). Children often come to faith as part of an ongoing process as they pass through various stages of their lives; both parents and other church attenders can have a significant role.

## GENERATIONAL RETENTION

Because evangelism and Christian nurture is so often a process, parents have the opportunity to be a great influence. More than 60% of attenders who nominate parents or family as their first contact with faith also cite parents as the most significant people in showing them what faith is about.

While this indicates that parents are successfully influencing their children to faith in many instances, it doesn't measure the retention of children in church life. To gain some indication of how effectively churches are retaining children, the NCLS asked the following question.

> **Which statement best describes the level of church attendance of your children?**
> a. I do not currently have any children
> b. Most of my children are involved with this church
> c. Most of my children are involved with other churches
> d. Most of my children are not attending church anywhere
> e. I do not know whether my children attend church or not
> f. More than one of the above

Around 5% of attenders do not know whether their children attend church or believe that more than one of the options apply. These attenders have been excluded from the following analysis. The children of newcomers generally have lower attendance levels than the children of other attenders. This is because newcomers may not have brought their children up in the church, having joined perhaps years after their children were born. Consequently, newcomers have also been excluded from analysis.

To classify children according to their stage in life, the results of this question were cross-tabulated with details of the household of the respondent. Some 7% of attenders have mainly preschool children and a further 11% mainly primary school children. Of these attenders, almost all say that their children are involved in church activities.

Figure 9.4

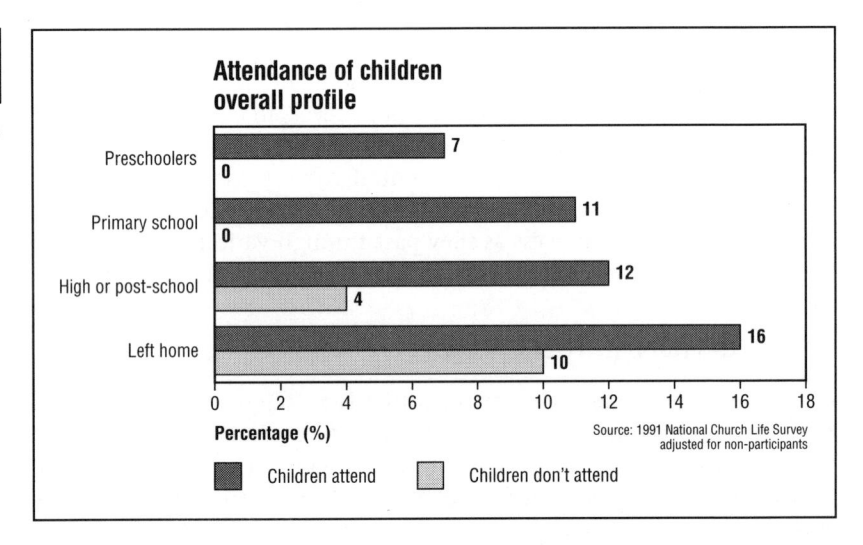

**Attendance of children overall profile**

| Category | Children attend | Children don't attend |
|---|---|---|
| Preschoolers | 7 | 0 |
| Primary school | 11 | 0 |
| High or post-school | 12 | 4 |
| Left home | 16 | 10 |

Percentage (%)

Source: 1991 National Church Life Survey adjusted for non-participants

By the time children pass through secondary school, a quarter have ceased to attend. Of the 16% of attenders who have secondary or post-school children living at home, 12% indicate that most of their children attend, while 4% say they do not. This represents a retention rate of about 3 to 1.

The main period for drifting out of church life appears to be after children have left home. Overall, 26% of attenders have children who have left home, comprising 16% who have most of their children still involved in church activities and 10% who do not. This represents a retention rate of about 1.6 to 1.

## DENOMINATIONAL DIFFERENCES

Attenders in all denominations seem to have little problem encouraging their young children to be involved in church activities. There is little difference in attendance rates of preschool and primary school children in all denominations. However, when it comes to older children and children who have left home, some denominations have better retention rates than others.

**Child retention rates by denomination**

Figure 9.5

| | Secondary/Post school | Left home |
|---|---|---|
| **Overall** | **2.9:1** | **1.7:1** |
| Anglican | 2.0:1 | 1.3:1 |
| Apostolic | 5.4:1 | 2.4:1 |
| Assemblies of God | 5.0:1 | 2.1:1 |
| Baptist | 4.1:1 | 2.1:1 |
| Christian & Missionary Alliance | 5.8:1 | 3.3:1 |
| Christian Revival Crusade | 4.7:1 | 3.7:1 |
| Church of the Nazarene | 5.4:1 | 3.6:1 |
| Churches of Christ | 3.3:1 | 1.8:1 |
| Congregational | 5.3:1 | 1.8:1 |
| Foursquare Gospel | 6.8:1 | 2.4:1 |
| Lutheran | 7.0:1 | 4.3:1 |
| NZ Presbyterian | 1.9:1 | 1.1:1 |
| Presbyterian | 3.5:1 | 2.0:1 |
| Reformed | 18.7:1 | 6.9:1 |
| Salvation Army | 4.7:1 | 2.5:1 |
| Seventh-day Adventist | 10.7:1 | 2.4:1 |
| Uniting | 1.7:1 | 1.2:1 |
| Wesleyan Methodist | 12.5:1 | 2.5:1 |
| Westminster Presbyterian | 7.2:1 | 3.4:1 |
| House Churches | n.a. | n.a. |
| **Type of denomination** | | |
| Mainstream | 2.2:1 | 1.5:1 |
| Pentecostal | 5.0:1 | 2.2:1 |
| Large Protestant | 4.5:1 | 2.1:1 |
| Small Protestant | 10.5:1 | 4.1:1 |

Source: 1991 National Church Life Survey attender data adjusted for non-participants
N.B. Newcomers and visitors excluded from above analysis.

*Mainstream denominations*

Mainstream denominations include the Anglican, Uniting, Lutheran and Presbyterian Churches. Overall, the Anglican and Uniting Churches have some of the lowest retention levels of all denominations. Their retention rates decrease significantly as children grow up; for secondary and post-school children still at home the retention rates are 2.0 to 1 and 1.7 to 1 respectively, compared to 2.9 to 1 overall. By the time children leave home, the retention rate is little more than 1.2 to 1 compared to 1.7 to 1 overall.

The question does not indicate whether the children of attenders are attending a church of the same denomination as their parents. Given the overall patterns of denominational switching detailed in *Winds of Change* (Chapter 17), it is likely that mainstream denominations not only have low overall retention rates at church, but still lower retention rates within their denomination, possibly under 1 to 1.

There are differences between Anglican dioceses. At 2 to 1, Sydney has a better retention rate of children who have left home than either Brisbane (1.6 to 1), Melbourne (1.1 to 1) or Perth (1 to 1). Similarly, there are regional differences in the Uniting Church. New South Wales (1.4 to 1) and Queensland (1.4 to 1) have higher retention levels than Victoria (0.9 to 1).

Among mainstream denominations Presbyterians fare a little better. They have a 3.5 to 1 retention rate for children living at home, dropping to 2 to 1 for children who have left home.

> *Among mainstream denominations, Lutherans have the highest retention rates*

Lutherans have the highest levels of retention of children who have left home, with a rate of 4.3 to 1. The northern European heritage of Lutheran churches may account for this in part; Lutheran churches still play an important part in their attenders' cultural identity and social networks, even though most attenders are Australian born. Among nominal Lutherans in the community, higher proportions are active church attenders than for other mainstream denominations (Black & Glasner, 1983, 20).

### Large Protestant denominations

Large Protestant denominations include the Baptist, Churches of Christ, Salvation Army and Seventh-day Adventist Churches. There is a significant difference in retention rates between denominations in this grouping. Among attenders whose teenage and young adult children live at home, retention rates are more than 4 to 1 on average. However, among children who have left home, retention rates drop to about 1.8 to 1 among Churches of Christ attenders, but are better than 2 to 1 among Baptist, Seventh-day Adventist and Salvation Army attenders. The decline in attendance levels upon leaving home is most severe in the Seventh-day Adventist Church, from 10.7 to 1 to 2.4 to 1.

### Pentecostal denominations

Pentecostal denominations have high retention rates among children living at home. On average, this rate is 5 to 1, but declines when children leave home to 2.1 to 1 for the Assemblies of God, 3.7 to 1 for the Christian Revival Crusade, and 2.4 to 1 for the Apostolic and Foursquare Gospel churches. Nevertheless, these are higher retention rates than in most mainstream or large Protestant denominations.

### Small Protestant denominations

The small Protestant denominations have the best retention levels of children who have left home, ranging from 1.8 to 1 among Congregationalists to nearly 7 to 1 at the Reformed Churches.

Generally, the smaller denominations have the highest retention rates. Such denominations tend to have a clearer identity and a more uniform theology than the mainstream and large Protestant denominations. Historically, smaller Protestant denominations have also placed more importance on regular church attendance (Bentley et al, 1992, 22). Their children are more likely to continue to attend church as adults than children in other denominations, where a lesser emphasis on the importance of church attendance will contribute to attendance being more easily seen as optional.

The high retention rates may, in part, also be due to the more recent establishment of some smaller denominations. Some of these denominations are less than a generation old; it is too soon for a fringe of nominal adherents to have formed (Gibbs, 1993, 13,14).

A slice-in-time survey such as the NCLS provides a static picture; it does not show the faith journey of individuals over time. Some people who continue in church life do not grow in faith, while others who leave the church for a time undergo profound spiritual changes before returning to it.

The denominational retention rates shown in Figure 9.5 do not evaluate levels of spirituality, nor can they predict what proportion of children will eventually return to the church. However, they do show what proportion are in church at present, and this may point to very real problems for some denominations.

Some of the children who have dropped out may have done so because of the failure of congregations to include them in decision making and to use their gifts. Others may have found that worship and activities in their church weren't geared to their tastes or needs. Still others may have felt that their church's traditions didn't offer hope and firm or relevant answers to life's questions, or they simply did not believe in the gospel message. Each denomination will need to reflect on its retention rates, the reasons for them, and whether they can be improved.

*Each denomination will need to reflect on its retention rates and the reasons for them*

## WHY DO CHILDREN DROP OUT?

The NCLS is a survey of existing attenders, so it is not possible to explore in detail the reasons the children of attenders have drifted out of church life. However, the survey does include attenders who have returned to church life after an absence of years. These returnees provide some clues as to the reasons people leave the church.

Most returnees (52%) had one or both parents who were active members of the church; a further 16% have parents who attended occasionally. Most returnees (55%) are aged under 40 years. It is likely that many of these dropped out of church life as teenagers or young adults.

*Winds of Change* (p 202) reported that 22% of returnees left because of differences over belief or loss of faith, 19% because of changing needs, 11% because of the style of their congregation and another 11% because of conflict or unhappiness with the leader. Clearly, attenders leave congregational life for a variety of reasons, not just because they lose their faith.

Four in 10 returnees left their previous congregation because they moved house. For some, moving may have interrupted a churchgoing habit which they did not re-establish at their new address. Others may have tried to find a new church, but dropped out when the new congregation did not meet their expectations or they didn't integrate as quickly as they might have hoped.

The mobility of attenders has significant pastoral implications. When moving to a new congregation, attenders may grieve for what they have lost. Congregations need to prepare attenders for the feelings they may experience on leaving and how to move beyond them. Clergy and leaders may also be able to help outgoing attenders get established in a new congregation by getting in touch with colleagues or friends in the new area and suggesting they make contact. They should also try to become aware of the reasons people leave church. Congregations should examine their welcoming procedures so that incoming attenders can be integrated more effectively.

\* \* \* \*

## CLOSING THE BACK DOOR

If congregations want to be effective in mission, it is important that, along with attracting newcomers in the front door, they close the back door and seek to retain and nurture existing attenders. The questions on page 125 may be a useful starting point for reflection.

The teenage and early adult years are critical times for people to drift out of church life. People in these age groups have specific needs which existing congregational structures may not be meeting. Ideally, congregations need to offer activities which help attenders in their faith at each stage of their life.

Retaining the children of attenders is particularly an issue in the mainstream denominations. The reasons teenagers and young adults drop out may be quite different for different congregations. Each congregation will need to find its own solutions and priorities.

> **Retaining and nurturing attenders and their families – some questions to ask**
> - What was the first contact for most attenders with the Christian faith? Who were the most significant people showing them what faith is about?
> - What has been the level of retention of the children of existing attenders? In this congregation? Within this denomination?
> - Why have people moved on or out? What can be learnt from these experiences?
> - To what extent do existing attenders feel a sense of belonging to the congregation? Or have a role? Do they own the congregation's vision for the future? Do feel they are growing in their faith?

### Parents as faith sharers

Parents have an important role to play in helping their offspring find faith. However, the high level of attenders, particularly in mainstream denominations, who do not like to talk about their faith suggests that some parents may not be willing to discuss their faith with their children. Some parents may feel embarrassed about doing so and be happy to leave this task to Sunday school teachers or other churchgoers. While these people may be important teachers for children, they are not as significant as parents themselves. Congregations should be careful not to take over the parental role, but rather to equip and encourage parents in this area.

### Parents as role models

Parents not only communicate their faith verbally, but they are also role models for their children. One important way in which they are role models is through their own attendance patterns and the priority they place on issues of faith.

The children of *highly involved* attenders are more likely to attend church than less involved attenders. The retention rate for secondary and post-school children still living at home is 4.8 to 1, compared to 3 to 1 for *involved attenders,* 2.4 to 1 for *frequent worshippers* and 1.5 to 1 for *infrequent worshippers.*

It could be argued that this retention rate is because highly involved attenders are more insistent that their children attend church activities. Whatever the reason, attendance patterns among children who have left home show a similar trend, which suggests that church attendance is not only taught but caught as well. The retention rate for children who have left home is 2.1 to 1 for highly involved attenders, compared to 1.7 to 1 for involved attenders, 1.5 to 1 for frequent worshippers and 1.3 to 1 for infrequent worshippers. This relationship is strongest among large Protestant denominations.

### Church as a role model

The church also needs to be a role model for children. *Winds of Change* (p 197) shows that parents evaluate church activities for their children and may move on if these are inadequate. Parents look for the presence of other children, of Sunday school and youth groups, of creches and church-based play groups when they seek a new congregation.

There is much congregations can do to welcome children and teenagers, provide for their needs and involve them in mission. Congregations will want to ensure that they are providing appropriate activities for children and teenagers, as well as activities which support the family as a whole.

Teenagers and young adults need mentors and role models, beyond that of the youth group leader. One of the great strengths of Christianity is that it provides a common ground between old and young. Congregations may need to do some heart searching to ensure that the role model they present to their young attenders is one that is not only attractive, but has integrity as well.

### Church as culturally appropriate

In the previous chapter the importance of expressing faith in ways that are culturally appropriate was highlighted in the context of nurturing newcomers without a church background. The NCLS suggests such matters are also important in the area of existing attenders and their families. Teenagers and young adults are more likely to prefer informal, contemporary worship to traditional hymns and liturgy. They are also much more willing than older attenders to go in search of a church which offers these.

Congregations which want to retain and nurture existing attenders and their families need to acknowledge these issues. While there may be short-term ramifications, the results of today's strategies will be evaluated in a generation's time.

---

**The teenage and early adult years are critical times for people to drift out of church life. Congregations need to reflect on their retention rates and the reasons for them.**

- Parents and family provide the first contact the majority of attenders have with the Christian faith. For more than half of attenders, they are also the most significant people to show attenders what faith is about.
- Parents need to be willing to share their faith and be a role model for their children. Congregations can be a role model of Christian values and community, as well as provide activities for teenagers and young adults.
- Anglican and Uniting Churches have among the lowest retention rates of children who have left home, with a retention rate of 1.2 to 1. Retention rates for other denominations are generally above 2 to 1, and are highest among small Protestant denominations and the Lutheran Church.
- Moving house is a major reason attenders drift out of church life. Congregations may need to help outgoing attenders get established in a new congregation and help incoming attenders to integrate more successfully.

## CHAPTER 10

# OWNING FAITH

## Conversion and public commitment

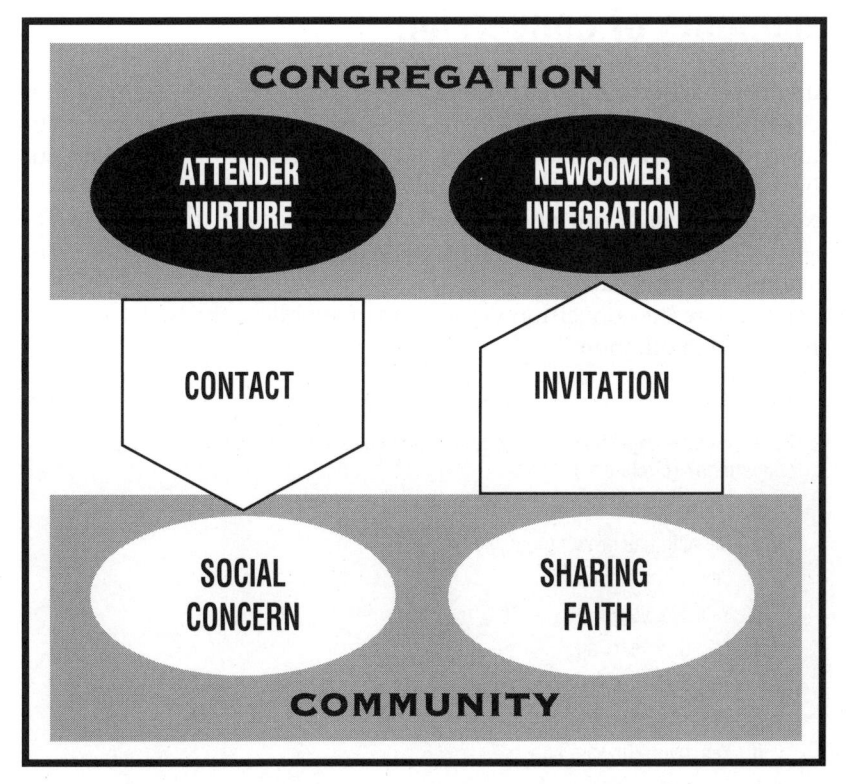

**CONGREGATION**

- ATTENDER NURTURE
- NEWCOMER INTEGRATION

CONTACT | INVITATION

- SOCIAL CONCERN
- SHARING FAITH

**COMMUNITY**

Conversion experience is linked to growth in faith and a willingness to discuss it with others. Congregations need to encourage attenders to own their faith and be publicly committed to it.

The importance of moments of decisive faith commitment or conversion is affirmed across the church. Some traditions consider conversion so important that evangelistic services are held each week. In other traditions, this is not the way things are done. The first part of this chapter explores the extent to which attenders have experienced a moment of decisive faith commitment or conversion.

Nearly all traditions have ways of acknowledging the faith of attenders and their membership in the church. Confirmation services are important opportunities for public commitment, as are evangelistic services and crusades. The second part of this chapter explores the role of public commitments of faith in the lives of attenders.

## Moments of conversion

Attenders have very different experiences of coming to faith. Many cannot remember a time when they were not a believer; they grew into faith slowly. Some remember when they did not believe, but cannot pinpoint the time when it all changed. Still others had a distinct conversion experience, a moment when it seemed they changed from unbelief to belief. They can remember the time, place and circumstances of this event vividly, even years later.

To explore the conversion experiences of attenders, the NCLS included the following question.

**Q** | **Have you ever experienced a moment of decisive faith commitment/Christian conversion? (circle one)**

a. No, not at all
b. My faith has grown gradually
c. Yes, in the last year
d. Yes, 1–2 years ago
e. Yes, 3–5 years ago
f. Yes, 6–10 years ago
g. Yes, 11–20 years ago
h. Yes, over 20 years ago
I. Yes, several times
j. Yes, but don't know when
k. Don't know

**Decisive commitment/conversion overall profile**

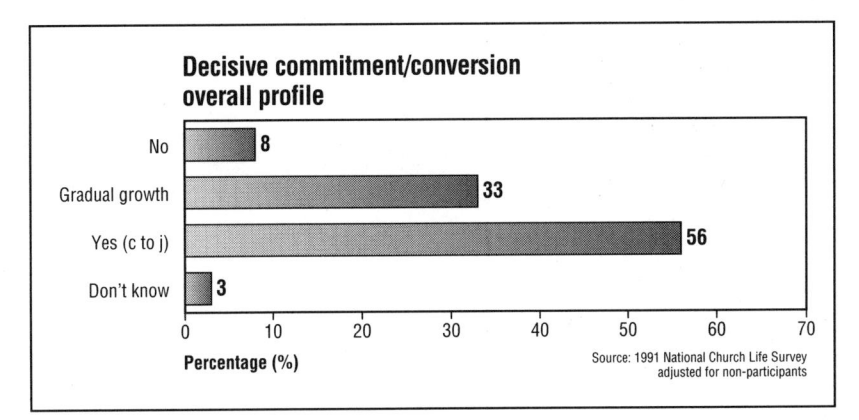

| Category | Percentage |
|---|---|
| No | 8 |
| Gradual growth | 33 |
| Yes (c to j) | 56 |
| Don't know | 3 |

Source: 1991 National Church Life Survey adjusted for non-participants

Figure 10.1

The majority of attenders (56%) have experienced a moment of decisive faith commitment or conversion. Another 41% have not had such a distinctive experience; 33% have grown gradually in their faith and 8% have never had such an experience. Only 3% are unsure.

It should not be assumed that attenders who have never had a distinct conversion experience or have grown gradually in faith do not feel they have been converted. For many raised in Christian families, faith may have always been a central dimension of their lives. Rather, they simply cannot pinpoint a particular moment at which conversion took place.

Nor should it be assumed that a distinct conversion experience does not involve a prior process of growth. Writers such as James Fowler and John Westerhoff III have suggested that people often move through a process of faith development. In relation to children raised in Christian homes, Westerhoff suggests several distinct phases as they grow towards an 'owned faith', possibly marked by a distinct conversion experience (1976, 98).

While all denominations have attenders with different conversion experiences, there are some differences between denominations. Not surprisingly, attenders in denominations that regularly invite people to make a commitment are more likely to be able to pinpoint a moment of conversion: Pentecostal (80%), large Protestant (69%), and some smaller denominations including the Christian & Missionary Alliance (81%), Church of the Nazarene (76%), Wesleyan Methodist (73%) and Congregational (71%). In contrast, only 44% of mainstream attenders and 34% of Reformed attenders have had such an experience.

Theological orientation is important. Some 73% of *literalists* have had a distinct conversion experience, compared to 57% of *contextualists* and 43% of *valuists*. Similarly, attenders influenced by charismatic (82%) and evangelical (73%) theological traditions are more likely to have had a distinct conversion experience.

Younger attenders are more likely to have had a distinct conversion experience; 63% of those in their 20s and 30s can point to a moment of conversion, compared to 50% of attenders aged in their 60s. This is true in all denominational groups except the large Protestant denominations,

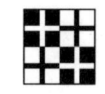

Figure 10.2

**Decisive commitment/conversion by denomination**

| | No % | Gradual growth % | Yes % | Don't know % | Total % |
|---|---|---|---|---|---|
| **Overall** | **8** | **33** | **56** | **3** | **100** |
| Anglican | 13 | 39 | 45 | 3 | 100 |
| Apostolic | 2 | 17 | 79 | 1 | 100 |
| Assemblies of God | 2 | 16 | 80 | 2 | 100 |
| Baptist | 3 | 20 | 75 | 2 | 100 |
| Christian & Missionary Alliance | 2 | 14 | 81 | 2 | 100 |
| Christian Revival Crusade | 2 | 17 | 78 | 2 | 100 |
| Church of the Nazarene | 3 | 19 | 76 | 2 | 100 |
| Churches of Christ | 4 | 23 | 71 | 2 | 100 |
| Congregational | 4 | 24 | 71 | 2 | 100 |
| Foursquare Gospel | 2 | 17 | 80 | 1 | 100 |
| Lutheran | 14 | 51 | 30 | 5 | 100 |
| NZ Presbyterian | 11 | 38 | 47 | 4 | 100 |
| Presbyterian | 10 | 39 | 47 | 3 | 100 |
| Reformed | 8 | 55 | 34 | 3 | 100 |
| Salvation Army | 5 | 25 | 68 | 2 | 100 |
| Seventh-day Adventist | 4 | 39 | 55 | 3 | 100 |
| Uniting | 11 | 39 | 47 | 3 | 100 |
| Wesleyan Methodist | 2 | 23 | 73 | 2 | 100 |
| Westminster Presbyterian | 4 | 30 | 64 | 2 | 100 |
| House Churches | 6 | 19 | 74 | 1 | 100 |
| **Type of denomination** | | | | | |
| Mainstream | 12 | 41 | 44 | 3 | 100 |
| Pentecostal | 2 | 16 | 80 | 2 | 100 |
| Large Protestant | 4 | 25 | 69 | 2 | 100 |
| Small Protestant | 5 | 36 | 57 | 3 | 100 |

Source: 1991 National Church Life Survey attender data adjusted for non-participants

> *Childhood, the teenage years and the 20s are important times for a conversion experience*

where high proportions of both younger and older attenders have had such experiences.

Childhood and the teenage years are an important time for a conversion experience; some 49% of 15 to 19 year olds can pinpoint such an experience in their lives. The 20s are also an important time for conversion experiences; a quarter of all attenders in their 20s have had such an experience in the past five years.

## WHAT DIFFERENCE DOES IT MAKE?

There are clear differences between attenders who have had a distinct conversion experience and those who have grown gradually in their faith in terms of sense of influence, discussing faith with others, inviting people to church and perceived growth in faith. The NCLS does not show that one aspect causes another; the results simply establish that a relationship exists.

AS THE YEARS WENT BY, JEFFREY WOULD HAVE NO TROUBLE REMEMBERING HIS CONVERSION EXPERIENCE

### *Influence*

Among those who have had a conversion experience, 66% feel that they have great or some Christian influence on those around them. This compares to only 49% of those whose faith has grown gradually and 23% who have not had such an experience.

### *Sharing faith with others*

There are differences between the conversion/non-conversion groups in their willingness to discuss their faith with others. Two-thirds of attenders (67%) who have had a conversion experience feel at ease talking about their faith, compared to 50% of those whose faith has grown gradually. Attenders who have had a conversion experience are also more likely to look for opportunities to share their faith. This trend holds true within each denominational group.

### *Inviting others to church*

Attenders with a distinct conversion experience are more likely to feel they have invited others to church in the past year. Some 47% of those who have had a distinct conversion experience invited others, compared to 34% who grew gradually in faith and 19% who have not had such an experience.

### *Growth in faith*

Attenders who have had a distinct conversion experience are likely to feel they have grown more in their faith than other attenders. For instance, 77% of attenders with a conversion experience have changed their priorities and actions in the past 12 months as a result of their faith, compared to 69% of attenders who have grown gradually in their faith, and only 28% of attenders who have not had any conversion experience. Again, this pattern holds true within each denominational group.

Clearly attenders who have experienced a moment of decisive faith commitment or conversion are more positive about their faith and open to talking about it with others. These results may raise issues for some leaders, particularly in mainstream denominations, where only a minority of attenders have distinct conversion experiences.

### *Involvement in congregational life*

Attenders who have had a conversion experience are a little more involved in congregational life than others. Some 19% of those who have had a conversion experience are highly involved, compared to 10% of those who have grown gradually in their faith. Many of those who have not had a conversion experience are on the fringes of church life; 17% are infrequent worshippers, compared to 7% of attenders overall.

## PATTERNS FOR NEWCOMERS

Newcomers to church life are only a little less likely to have had a distinct conversion experience than other attenders. Some 52% of newcomers have had such an experience, compared to 56% of attenders overall. It is interesting that so many newcomers have made such a commitment, given their relatively recent arrival in church life.

For many newcomers, joining a church is accompanied by a significant renewal of faith or finding faith for the first time. Some 48% of newcomers who joined a church within the past year have had a distinct conversion experience. While for some this conversion experience may have occurred a long time prior to their joining the congregation, for most the conversion experience occurred in the same year they joined their present congregation.

There is also a link between newcomers' level of involvement and conversion experience. Some 64% of newcomers who have had a distinct conversion experience are involved in small groups as well as worship in their congregation, compared to 51% whose faith has grown gradually. While these differences are not huge, they suggest that newcomers who have a distinct conversion experience may integrate more easily into congregational life.

Some newcomers are converted, then integrate into congregational life. Others join a congregation, and become integrated before a moment of conversion. For still others, these processes happen in parallel. When ministering to newcomers, congregations need to consider both processes, helping them to feel at home, but also assisting them to find and develop faith.

# Public faith commitment

For many people, the term 'public faith commitment' conjures up images of crusades and tent meetings, with preachers exhorting people to come forward and give their lives to Jesus, while the congregation sings commitment hymns such as 'Just as I am'. While the use of 'Just as I am' may have waned, many attenders still make public statements of commitment at such meetings.

However, public commitments aren't always so dramatic. Many attenders make their first commitment with friends, at a small group meeting or at a confirmation service. To explore where attenders made a public commitment, the NCLS included the following question.

**Have you ever made a public faith commitment?**
a. No, never
b. No, my faith has grown gradually
c. Yes, at the 1959 Billy Graham Crusade
d. Yes, at the 1968 Billy Graham Crusade
e. Yes, at the 1979 Billy Graham Crusade
f. Yes, at other large-scale crusades/meetings
g. Yes, at a mission/activity not described above
h. Yes, at a local church service/activity
i. Yes, at a Christian camp/conference
j. Yes, at the activities of a mission organisation
k. Yes, with friends, family or an informal group
l. Yes, at more than one of the above

A third of attenders made their public commitment at a church service or activity. Another 7% of attenders made commitments at crusades, 10% at other activities, while 6% of attenders made commitments informally among family or friends. Some 8% of attenders have made more than one public commitment.

The 1959 Billy Graham Crusade is particularly noteworthy. Between 3% and 5% of attenders in each 10-year age group over 40 years made a public commitment at this crusade. Some could have been as young as eight at the time!

Figure 10.3

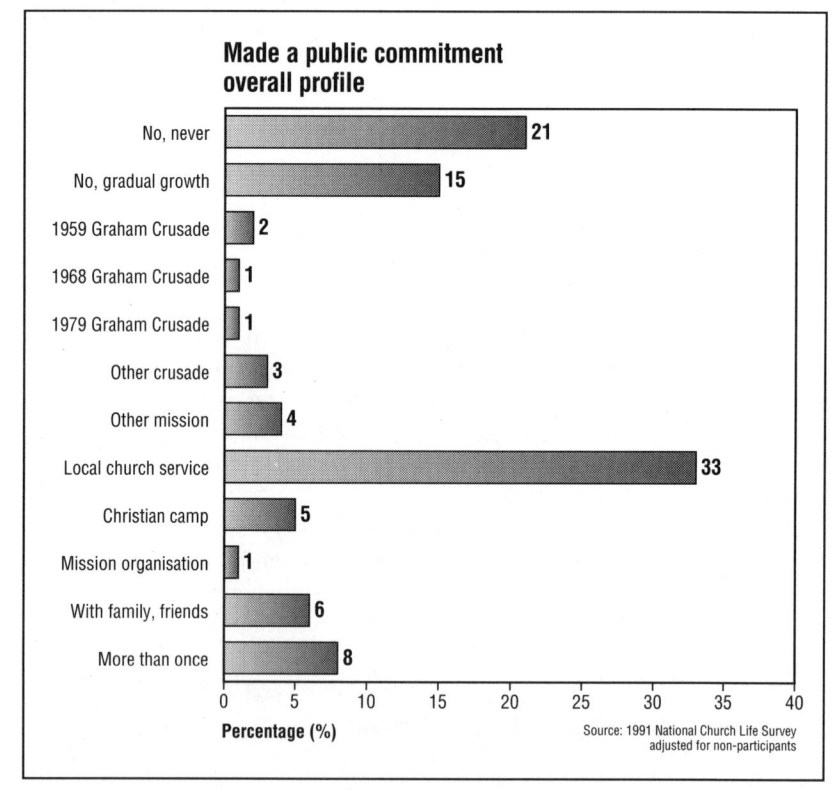

**Made a public commitment overall profile**

| Category | Percentage (%) |
|---|---|
| No, never | 21 |
| No, gradual growth | 15 |
| 1959 Graham Crusade | 2 |
| 1968 Graham Crusade | 1 |
| 1979 Graham Crusade | 1 |
| Other crusade | 3 |
| Other mission | 4 |
| Local church service | 33 |
| Christian camp | 5 |
| Mission organisation | 1 |
| With family, friends | 6 |
| More than once | 8 |

Source: 1991 National Church Life Survey adjusted for non-participants

Attendance rates at later crusades were lower than at the 1959 crusade. This is reflected in the proportions who made public commitments at these crusades. Some 1% to 2% of attenders in each age group over 30 years made public commitments at the 1968 crusade, and up to 2% of attenders in each age group over 15 years at the 1979 crusade.

About 80% of attenders who have had a distinct conversion experience have also made a public faith commitment, compared to just 44% of those who have not had a distinct conversion experience. It is likely that for some of these attenders, the conversion and public commitment were the same experience. For others, the public commitment may have been at baptism or confirmation, subsequent to a conversion experience.

## NEWCOMERS AND PUBLIC COMMITMENT

While there is little difference in the levels of conversion experience between attenders and newcomers, a larger proportion of newcomers has never made a public commitment to faith (48% compared to 36% overall). Such a difference is most pronounced in mainstream denominations, where 64% of newcomers have never made a public commitment.

Congregations need to consider whether they provide adequate opportunities for newcomers arriving into congregational life as adults to make a public commitment to their faith. This is particularly so for congregations where, apart from infant baptism and confirmation services, there is little opportunity given for adults to profess their faith publicly.

**Made a public commitment by background of attender**

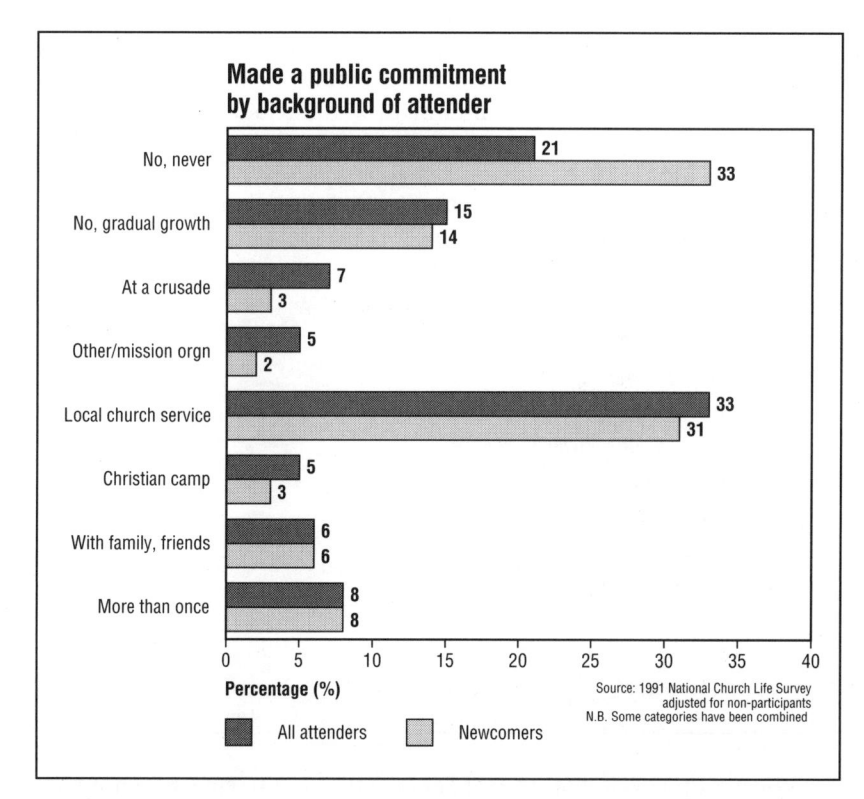

| Background | All attenders | Newcomers |
|---|---|---|
| No, never | 21 | 33 |
| No, gradual growth | 15 | 14 |
| At a crusade | 7 | 3 |
| Other/mission orgn | 5 | 2 |
| Local church service | 33 | 31 |
| Christian camp | 5 | 3 |
| With family, friends | 6 | 6 |
| More than once | 8 | 8 |

Source: 1991 National Church Life Survey adjusted for non-participants
N.B. Some categories have been combined

Figure 10.4

Almost a third of newcomers have made a public commitment at a church service or other activity, 14% at a crusade, Christian camp, mission activity or with friends, and 8% at more than one venue. These results suggest that many newcomers are making public faith commitments after starting to attend a church rather than beforehand.

This has important implications for mission strategies. As Chapter 7 showed, nearly all faith sharing takes place in the community. Yet many people make public commitments after they have begun attending a congregation. Inviting someone to attend an appropriate church activity

*Almost a third of newcomers have made a public commitment at a church activity*

or to meet other Christians is clearly a valuable way to introduce others to issues of faith. Even if attenders are uncomfortable discussing their faith, they may feel comfortable inviting others to a church activity.

The importance of relationships in the conversion process has been noted by several writers such as Hoge (1981) and McGuire (1981). Relationships can add to the attractiveness of belonging and even the plausibility of beliefs. As Meredith McGuire notes, 'The fact that a person whom one knows and likes belongs to the group attests to the normalcy or desirability of the group's way of life' (McGuire, 1981, 64).

## REASONS FOR PUBLIC COMMITMENTS

Many different circumstances lead people to make a public faith commitment, including personal crises, dissatisfaction with life, curiosity or a spiritual experience. To determine attenders' reasons for making a public commitment, the NCLS included the following question. Attenders who have not made a public commitment were excluded from analysis.

> **Were any of the following important factors for you in making such a faith commitment? (circle a maximum of two)**
> a. Death of a family member/close friend
> b. Changes in life stages (eg marriage, birth of children)
> c. The process of growing up
> d. Crises in relationships
> e. Financial crises
> f. Dissatisfaction with life/emptiness
> g. Curiosity about faith
> h. The needs of my children
> i. The life of others
> j. The wonder of life
> k. A vivid 'spiritual' experience
> l. None of the above
> m. Not applicable

Growing up (34%), life-stage changes (11%) and having an empty life (15%) are the most significant reasons for having made a public faith commitment. Attenders of all ages (apart from teenagers) have similar reasons for having made a public commitment, with a couple of notable exceptions.

Among teenagers, growing up (39%) and the life of others (16%) are more prevalent reasons. Among attenders in their 20s or 30s, dissatisfaction with life or emptiness (21%) emerges as a more important reason than for attenders generally.

Among newcomers, having an empty life (26%) and life-stage changes (21%) are the primary reasons for making a commitment. Growing up is a

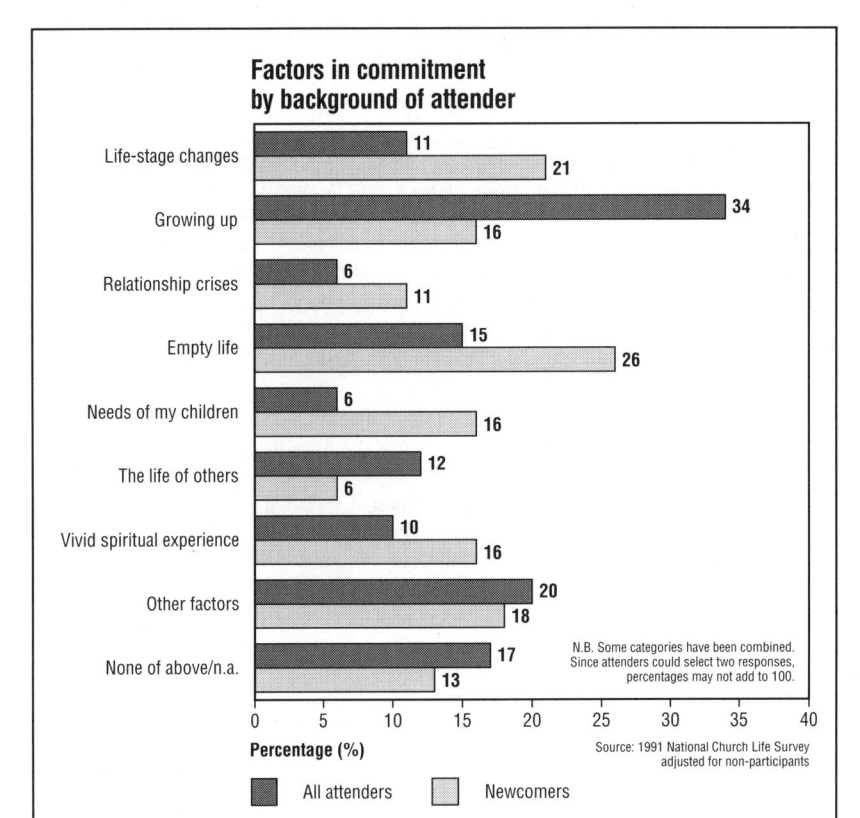

**Factors in commitment by background of attender**

| Factor | All attenders | Newcomers |
|---|---|---|
| Life-stage changes | 11 | 21 |
| Growing up | 34 | 16 |
| Relationship crises | 6 | 11 |
| Empty life | 15 | 26 |
| Needs of my children | 6 | 16 |
| The life of others | 12 | 6 |
| Vivid spiritual experience | 10 | 16 |
| Other factors | 20 | 18 |
| None of above/n.a. | 17 | 13 |

N.B. Some categories have been combined. Since attenders could select two responses, percentages may not add to 100.

Source: 1991 National Church Life Survey adjusted for non-participants

Figure 10.5

less important reason (16%). However, crises in relationships (11%), the needs of their children (16%) and a vivid spiritual experience (16%) are more important for newcomers than for attenders generally.

Social researchers have noted that personal and situational factors, such as those mentioned in the question, can predispose a person to conversion, by making them aware that their prior meaning systems are inadequate in explaining or giving meaning to events (McGuire, 1981, 63). People in such situations are therefore more open to looking at life from another viewpoint. The various transitions of life can offer entry points for the gospel.

Social issues facing Australians in the '90s include high levels of teenage suicide, marital breakdown and long-term unemployment. The NCLS suggests that many younger people and newcomers to church life are making public faith commitments because of a sense of dissatisfaction with life or crises in relationships.

## SIGNIFICANCE OF PUBLIC COMMITMENT

The importance of owning faith publicly has been an issue for the Christian church ever since 3000 people did so on the day of Pentecost. The importance of owning life values is recognised by some educationalists,

> **Many different entry points**
>
> For some, growth in faith is very dramatic. Bill, a member of a large Assemblies of God congregation, is a good example. Bill's life was in tatters through drink, loose living and purposelessness. Faith exploded into his life, recreating his priorities and values. For others the Christian pilgrimage is a slow journey. Margaret, a single mum with a 'belief in God, but not in the church' has spent a lifetime growing gradually through past hurts and misconceptions as her faith has matured.
>
> Times of crisis often create a moment of openness. Few people in hospital beds claim no religious affiliation! What may be more surprising, however, is that times of crisis in a Christian's life may be times when others can grow. In some cases people have the chance to see the difference faith makes. In others, people recognise their own brokenness.
>
> Some people grow through putting their faith into action, becoming involved in the service of others; then there are those who grow gradually as onlookers. Still others grow through reflection at an intellectual and philosophical level.
>
> People have different levels of openness at different stages of life. For example, teenagers really question the values being placed on them by society and look for alternative views of life. People moving through various mid-life crises are similarly open. Women who have been brought up to expect that motherhood would provide the ultimate meaning in their lives and meet all their emotional needs are also open to looking at questions of faith.
>
> Sue Kaldor, co-author of *Where the River Flows* (1988).

who argue that values are not really owned until they are owned publicly (Raths et al, 1966, 29,39).

However, it is also argued that many public commitments are made in the heat of the moment and not followed through; they can take place in an emotional environment, when people feel pressured to respond and make an instant decision about a long-term commitment. Such commitments ought not to a be spur-of-the-moment decision, but one that is made after all the benefits and costs of Christian discipleship have been fully understood and weighed.

To assess the significance to attenders of moments of public commitment, the NCLS included the following question.

> **If you have made such a faith commitment, how significant was it for you?**
> a. It changed the direction of my life
> b. It was significant – mainly as a moment to make a public statement about my faith
> c. I think I acted mainly from social/emotional pressure
> d. I made specific commitments but fell away. My return has been much more gradual
> e. Don't know/not applicable

On balance, giving people an opportunity to make a public commitment is a good thing. Almost half of all attenders who have made a public commitment (47%) say that it changed the direction of their life, while another 35% say that it was a significant public statement. Only 13% fell away or believe that they made an emotional response. Another 5% do not know.

The NCLS suggests that, overall, attenders who make public commitments do not feel manipulated. For most current attenders, the commitment is significant, real and enduring. However, it should be noted that the survey includes only existing attenders; it does not account for those who made commitments but later drifted out of church life.

The role of public commitment is an important issue for all congregations to consider, regardless of their existing practices. Congregations that offer attenders regular opportunities to make a commitment may want to examine their drop-out rate, and consider ways that attenders can make more measured statements of faith.

The 13% who made an emotional response or fell away are a significant minority. A public commitment is just the first step on a journey; attenders need to be nurtured and encouraged in discipleship in an ongoing way.

However, congregations that never give people an opportunity to make a public commitment may be short-changing their attenders. Opportunities for commitment need not happen only through a formal procedure such as a confirmation service. Attenders may value low-key opportunities to acknowledge their faith within the life of the congregation.

*For most attenders, a public commitment is significant, real and enduring*

\* \* \* \*

## OWNING FAITH

Everyone's Christian journey is different. Some experience dramatic moments of conversion, while others grow gradually.

For all that, making a commitment appears to be an important step in a person's faith journey. Attenders who have made such a commitment are more likely to be growing in their faith and to be at ease sharing their faith with others. This suggests that owning faith can be an important step in nurturing attenders.

Owning faith is just one part of the process of integration and nurture of attenders. It is a part that is overemphasised by some, yet forgotten by many. For congregations where it is almost forgotten, the NCLS provides a timely reminder of its value as part of the faith journey. At the same time, it ought not to be used to devalue attenders whose faith has grown gradually. Many attenders who have grown gradually in faith are also enthusiastic about their faith, highly active and outwardly focused.

Mainstream congregations, in particular, need to address the issue of providing opportunities for attenders to own their faith publicly. Some congregations, which do not have a tradition of inviting attenders to make a public faith commitment, may feel uncomfortable with this and need to explore appropriate ways within the context of their congregational culture. Confirmation services could be a useful starting point. Public commitment could also be encouraged within the context of small groups, or attenders could be encouraged to say a covenant prayer joined by all members of the congregation.

Attenders list many circumstances which prompt them to make a public faith commitment. These serve as a reminder that there are many entry points to faith. Congregations should consider these entry points and the needs and stages in life of those with whom they are in mission, in order to develop mission activities that allow people to explore faith from their particular points of need.

### Making a public commitment

'Other than the Bible, the most powerful book I've ever read is *Christ Recrucified*, written by the man who wrote *Zorba the Greek*. The book recounts the story of a Greek village which put on a play in which the man who played Jesus ends up being killed. We studied this book in a Lenten study group', said Lydia, a thirty-something professional and member of a traditional-style congregation.

'Perhaps the most life-changing thing about my encounter with this book was that it led me to talk about how much I had come to really understand the Christian message. It just clicked. I didn't just talk about it with friends, I actually got up in church and talked about it. It was like my 'coming out' spiritually, because prior to that I had sat at the back of the church and left as soon as the eucharist was over. It's strange, but I now feel confident about professing my Christian faith.'

**Conversion experience is linked to growth in faith and a willingness to discuss it with others. Congregations need to encourage attenders to own their faith and be publicly committed to it.**

- The majority of attenders can pinpoint a moment of conversion in their lives. A third say that their faith has grown gradually.
- Attenders in Pentecostal, large Protestant and some smaller Protestant denominations are more likely to have had a moment of conversion, while attenders in mainstream denominations are more likely to have grown gradually in their faith.
- Attenders who have experienced a moment of conversion are more likely to feel they are growing in their faith, to be at ease sharing their faith and to invite others to church.
- Many newcomers undergo a conversion experience about the time they commence attending church. Congregations need to be aware that the processes of conversion and integration into church life often occur in parallel.
- Most attenders who have made a public commitment of faith say that it was a significant or life-changing moment for them.

CONCLUSIONS

# MISSION UNDER THE MICROSCOPE

In every generation, mission needs to be revitalised and to adopt new forms to meet fresh circumstances. These current times are no exception.

The 1990s have been designated a Decade of Evangelism by many churches and mission groups. The 1988 Lambeth Conference of the Anglican Church, for instance, called for a 'shift to a dynamic missionary emphasis, going beyond care and nurture to proclamation and service'. There is a desire among denominations to be more intentional about mission.

Church attendance in Australia is higher in some sections of the community than others. Groups under-represented include young adults aged 20 to 40 years, blue-collar workers and their families, many ethnic groups, people who are residentially mobile, men and women heavily involved in the workforce and various subcultural and special-interest groups. Better connection with these groups is a major challenge for the churches.

In this context, congregations and attenders are pursuing a wide range of mission approaches, both in evangelism and in social concern. In modern Australia, just opening the church doors at 11 am (or 9.30 am) is no longer an adequate or effective mission strategy. Church attendance is but one option among many for Australians as they think about demands on their time.

## TOWARDS SUSTAINABLE MISSION

It is important then, as congregations seek to reach out to and serve their communities, that they identify and explore factors which contribute to effective and sustainable mission.

*Mission under the Microscope* identifies a number of key issues and how they relate to each other. These issues include:
- effective contact with the wider community;
- committed engagement with the wider community and its concerns;
- a willingness to discuss faith with others;
- a desire to invite others to participate in the life of a gathered Christian community;
- a process for integrating newcomers into the life of that gathered community;
- a concern to nurture existing attenders and their families;
- help for attenders to own their faith and develop an outward focus in its expression.

This book highlights the fact that mission is not a one-off event or something separate from the life of the congregation. The relationship between these factors indicates that coming to faith and joining the life of a church is a process.

In preparing for and evaluating their mission activities, congregational leaders need to look beyond the actual mission activities. Strategies for evangelism may be unsustainable if newcomers are having difficulty integrating into congregational life. Social concern may be short-lived if the congregation itself is not a place for nurture and building people up. Activities which create high levels of contact with those outside church life may be ineffective if attenders are reluctant to invite others to church services. Weaknesses in one area may be enough to render the mission of the congregation ineffective or unsustainable.

## EFFECTIVE CONTACT BETWEEN CONGREGATION AND COMMUNITY

One of the key themes which emerges from the NCLS is the importance of relationships. The NCLS confirms that contact with those outside church life is connected with issues such as discussing one's faith or inviting others to church. A congregation that is a completely closed system – where there is no contact with the wider community – is a congregation headed for decline. In contrast, a congregation that has become an open system – where attenders are developing relational links with others – is a congregation with potential to grow and to serve the community for which it has a concern.

The number and type of contacts attenders have vary considerably, depending on their stage of life. Younger attenders have higher levels of contact than those who are older; attenders under 30 years of age may be key sources of community contact.

## COMMITTED ENGAGEMENT WITH THE COMMUNITY

Apart from contacts in daily life, attenders have contact with people in the wider community through involvement in community groups, social action groups and congregational mission activities. These avenues not only provide opportunities for service; they are also positively linked with discussing faith and inviting others to church activities.

Attender involvement in community groups may have significant benefit for the community and, in addition, be a useful avenue for building stronger relational links. In particular, they may be a useful avenue of contact for attenders in smaller congregations, which are less likely to have the resources to organise mission activities in their own name.

Church attenders are highly involved in welfare activities. For many, this is a practical way of living out their Christian faith, seeking to make a difference for others locally and more broadly.

A survey of attenders cannot evaluate the impact attender involvement may have on the wider community. Historically such involvement has, on some occasions, been pivotal in changing the directions of society. As 'salt and light' in the community, attenders clearly have the potential to contribute significantly to shaping future directions and values. There are currently many important issues confronting Australia as a nation.

Yet denominations differ in their preferred avenues of involvement. Attenders in mainstream denominations have higher levels of involvement in community social action/welfare groups. In contrast, attenders from Pentecostal and Small Protestant denominations are more involved in congregational mission activities. While involved in meeting needs, they are more likely to prefer a congregationally based activity.

Attenders are also selective about the kind of social action they will support. Pentecostal attenders and literalists are more likely to support overseas mission and morals groups, but support environmental groups and peace or justice groups less than their counterparts in mainstream or large Protestant denominations. Attenders in mainstream denominations demonstrate less concern for overseas mission than attenders in either large Protestant or Pentecostal denominations.

While it is expected that people from different traditions will have different emphases, it is important for congregations and attenders to reflect on whether they have the balances right in this area.

The fact that younger attenders are less involved in welfare/social action activities deserves further reflection. If this represents a genuine generational difference between older and younger attenders, it will have an impact on the size of the future volunteer workforce available to churches for such activities.

## WILLINGNESS TO DISCUSS FAITH WITH OTHERS

The NCLS shows that only a little over half of all attenders feel at ease talking about their faith. The remainder either find it difficult or don't like to do so. A major challenge for the churches today is to equip attenders to be comfortable discussing their faith in natural ways.

It is not easy discussing matters of faith. Around seven in 10 attenders feel uncomfortable discussing their faith with others. A major problem for many is being unable to answer difficult questions. Others fear people's reactions or feel they lack the knowledge to talk about their faith. It should be noted that support and training are linked with having confidence to discuss faith.

The NCLS underlines the important ongoing role that congregations can play in encouraging, training and supporting attenders in this area. Congregations can be important forums for attenders to share their concerns and struggles about sharing faith and to assist each other to become more effective in this. Mission is not just an individual responsibility; attenders can do much to help each other if there is sufficient trust and openness.

Older attenders are more likely to prefer not to talk about their faith, while younger adults are more likely to say they find it difficult to do so in natural everyday ways. Younger attenders are more likely to fear other people's reactions, while older attenders are more likely to feel they cannot answer difficult questions. Congregations and trainers in mission will need to think about how to equip different age groups; one form of training may not meet the needs of all attenders.

There is a strong link between readiness to discuss faith and what actually happens in practice. Those who feel at ease discussing their faith are more likely to take the opportunity when it arises. They are also more likely to invite others to church activities.

Younger attenders are more likely to discuss their faith with others and successfully invite people to church activities. Since most newcomers to church life are under 40 years of age, younger attenders are clearly a strategic group in planning for mission.

Attenders need to realise the potential of their day-to-day contacts. People most often discuss faith out in the community with acquaintances and casual friends. Attenders need to 'bloom where they are planted'. While formal mission activities have an important place, the role of each attender in mission can extend well beyond this.

## INVITING OTHERS TO CHURCH

Some 64% of newcomers first came to their church as a result of a personal invitation from a friend or relative or through some contact with the clergy or church members. A well-timed invitation can be a very important entry point for those outside church life.

Invitations need careful consideration when congregations plan church-based activities. It is often assumed that if an activity is held, attenders will invite people to come. Leaders need to find out how many in the congregation are actually willing to invite visitors.

A range of factors may influence an attender's decision to invite someone to a congregational activity. Attenders must be comfortable with their relationship with the person they invite and comfortable about owning their faith publicly. They must also be comfortable with the activity the congregation is holding. Many congregations have modified their services or programs in order to be more 'newcomer friendly'.

Some congregations may also wish to rethink their primary focus as a congregation. Many, particularly in mainstream denominations, have inherited a tradition of thinking of themselves as 'local congregations', although attenders come from and form contacts across a much wider geographic area. Attenders may be less inclined to invite their friends and acquaintances to congregational activities if the congregation is strongly focused locally.

## INTEGRATING NEWCOMERS

If the churches are to connect with the diversity of the wider community, then congregations will need to draw in and nurture newcomers without a church background. Indeed, a useful measure of a congregation's connectedness to the wider community is the percentage of newcomers without a church background who have joined the congregation.

Most congregational leaders and attenders believe that their congregations are friendly towards newcomers. However, many may be unwittingly blind to the interests of newcomers in their midst, despite the best of intentions (Jensen and Payne, 1989, 51–59).

A key ingredient for successful integration into church life is relationships. Most newcomers join because of some sort of personal contact. The NCLS shows that newcomers to church life are more likely to have been welcomed and helped to settle into their current congregation than other attenders. They are also more likely to value a caring congregation than other attenders (*Winds of Change*, p 190).

Personal contact is essential, then, in both attracting and integrating newcomers. Newcomers are less likely than other new attenders to give unfriendly churches a second chance. The onus is on congregations to get it right first time. Congregations need to give more than an initial welcome; they also need an ongoing commitment to building relationships with the newcomers in their midst.

Many newcomers will be unfamiliar with the styles and traditions of the congregations they entering. This is such a significant issue for some cultural groups that small groups, worship services and even congregations have been developed to nurture people who are well distanced from church life. In some cases, home groups or house churches have been used as a stepping stone between the worship services of a congregation and the wider community. Others have chosen new venues, dramatically changed the shape of their worship, or held worship at unusual times in order to relate more effectively to particular groups.

## RETAINING AND NURTURING ATTENDERS AND THEIR FAMILIES

Perhaps the largest single mission work carried on by the churches is the sharing of faith with children by their parents. More than four in 10 adult attenders say that the most significant people to show them what faith was about were their parents.

But how many children now in the church can be expected to continue as adults? While levels of attendance among the preschool and primary school children of church attenders are very high, these levels drop among secondary and post-school children. Three out of four attenders with older children living at home say that most of their children still attend church. This level declines still further once children have left home; only three out of five attenders with children who have left home say that most of their children still attend. The Uniting and Anglican denominations have the lowest retention rates, while the small Protestant and Lutheran denominations have the highest, with the Pentecostal and large Protestant denominations in between.

Congregations have not only a front door through which newcomers can arrive, but also a back door out of which existing attenders leave for other congregations or leave church life altogether. The high levels of switching between denominations of attenders in their 20s and 30s suggests that retaining young adults within their existing denominations is critical, particularly for mainstream denominations.

This raises significant questions, particularly for denominations that are struggling with issues of congregational viability and wishing to attract newcomers. How can young adults be attracted to these denominations if those brought up in the church are not staying in it?

Attenders in their 20s are a good case in point. The NCLS retention data suggests that there is a high loss rate from congregational life when children leave home. Moving house is the major reason for attenders changing congregations and contributes to attenders drifting out of church life.

This raises the question of whether more can be done to prepare such attenders for changing congregations. Perhaps no more resources are needed, but greater attention to this issue may be needed. For instance, congregations could help attenders to find a new congregation in their new area. They could also prepare attenders for the grief they may feel in leaving behind a congregation that has been very important to them.

Some denominations have discovered the value of large regional congregations for younger people. Contemporary in style, such congregations are geared to the questions and concerns of young adults. Young adults have a wide, interest-based sense of community, characterised by high levels of transience and mobility. When they enter the phase of marriage and commencing families, they may again look for a local community in which to ground their lives.

In planning for the future, denominations would do well to develop plans for a wider region and help congregations understand their place in this vision. They may want to encourage the development of regional congregations or initiatives for specific groups (eg ethnic groups) to complement the more traditional local congregations within a region.

## GROWING IN DISCIPLESHIP

There is an important relationship between involvement in mission and other aspects of congregational life. Those who frequently attend church services, go to small groups, and feel they are growing in their faith, also tend to be more likely to be ready to share their faith. Encouraging a congregation towards mission will involve more than just exhortation; attention will also need to be given to spiritual nurture and growth more generally. Growth in faith may well occur through being involved in mission.

Attenders' faith journeys are unique and different. The majority of attenders can pinpoint a moment of decisive faith commitment or conversion in their lives, while for a third faith has grown gradually. Attenders who have experienced such a moment are more likely to feel they are growing in their faith, to be at ease discussing it with others or to invite others to church.

Congregations will do well to provide opportunities for attenders to own their faith and become publicly committed to it. In some traditions this is already a priority. Other congregations and denominations need to reflect on how to provide appropriate opportunities within their traditions.

## CONGREGATIONAL GROWTH

As each aspect of mission has been placed under the NCLS microscope, its relationship to other aspects has been explored. What has become clear is that each aspect does not stand in isolation, but is part of a bigger picture.

While further analysis of NCLS data is still to come, results to date suggest that a relationship exists between numerical growth and some aspects of mission. Growing congregations (which grew by more than 5% from 1986 to 1991) tend to have higher proportions of people who share their faith with others. Some 53% of attenders in strongly growing congregations have shared their faith with someone else in the past 12 months, compared to 41% in stable or declining congregations. This pattern is most pronounced in mainstream denominations. Relationships also exist between church growth and inviting others to church activities.

Interestingly, there is little relationship between church growth and the involvement of attenders in congregational mission activities, whether the activities be evangelistic or oriented towards social care/action. The key factors appear to be related to the involvement of attenders in discussing their faith in everyday life.

Considering integration into church life, attenders in growing congregations are more likely to say that they were welcomed immediately than attenders in stable or declining congregations. The growth of these congregations is likely to be linked to how well new attenders are integrated, not just how active they are in sharing faith with others.

There are also relationships between aspects of mission and congregational size. Some 64% of attenders in congregations with more than 500 people helped someone to explore faith in the past year, compared to 41% in congregations with fewer than 50 people. Attenders in the largest congregations are also more likely to have invited someone to church activities (33%) than in the smallest congregations (20%). Again these relationships are most pronounced in mainstream denominations.

## TAKING IT FURTHER

This book can assist congregational leaders both in evaluating their current mission program and in planning new mission activities.

In relation to new activities, the specific stories of congregations and the list of activities currently undertaken by congregations across Australia in Appendix 3 are a rich source of ideas. While there is always a need for new ministries beyond such a list, congregations can still learn much from the initiatives of others.

The analysis in this book underlines the importance for congregations of looking at the whole mission picture. The realities of life may not follow a neat theoretical model, but congregations should not ignore the interaction between attender involvement in the community, sharing faith, and nurturing and integrating newcomers.

By better understanding these relationships, congregational leaders can begin to identify impediments to newcomers entering into church life. They may also better understand some of the reasons for failure in mission

**Questions for congregational leaders**

- How outwardly focused is your congregation? Do the members have a particular area or group of people for whom they have a special concern?
- How well do you understand the people for whom you have a concern? Their values? Needs? Aspirations?
- What bridges of contact does your congregation have with those outside church life? How might these bridges be strengthened? How involved is your congregation in addressing the concerns and issues of those in the community you seek to serve?
- Does the congregation acknowledge, encourage and pray for attenders in their individual work, school or other situations?
- How comfortable are attenders in your congregation about discussing their faith with others? Does your congregation provide training and support for them in this area?
- Do attenders feel comfortable inviting non-church people to church activities? If there is reticence, is it to do with attenders' fears, aspects of existing activities or some other reason?
- Are there newcomers in your congregation? Why did they join? What procedures are in place for welcoming them? Do they have close friends in the congregation? What are their special needs, and are these being met?
- What proportion of the children of attenders frequently attend church activities? Have church activities been reviewed to ensure their needs and aspirations are being met?
- How does your congregation support those moving to a new area? How can you prepare them for this process?
- How are attenders encouraged to own their faith? Are there opportunities for individuals to do so publicly?
- Are attenders growing in their faith? How do the activities of your congregation help them to relate their faith to all aspects of their lives?

Conclusions **151**

> **Questions for attenders**
> - Do you have much contact with those outside church life? If not, how can you increase your contact? (In the local neighbourhood? At work? Through community groups or mission activities?)
> - How well do you understand the needs and concerns of those with whom you have contact?
> - Are there issues that concern you in your local community or wider society? What should you do about it? Are there others with similar concerns?
> - Are you able to talk about your faith if the opportunity arises? Do you get support or encouragement from your congregation in this? Would training be of assistance to you?
> - Do you feel comfortable inviting others to church activities? If not, what would need to change to make you feel more comfortable? Have you talked to others about this?
> - Have you ever publicly made a commitment of faith? How significant was that for you?
> - If you have children still at home, do you feel able to talk to them about your faith? How is the Christian faith being modelled at home? Have you ever sought the support of others in this?
> - How can you help to make newcomers welcome in church life?

or areas where improvement is required. The research can provide a basis for discussion and for moving forward on these issues.

The questions included here are designed to help both congregational leaders and attenders as they think about mission. The questions can be used in group discussion.

This book is also a resource for individual attenders who may wish to think about their own mission involvement. For this reason, questions have also been provided to assist in such personal reflection.

In a changing world there are many challenges. There are also many opportunities for growth and creativity. Congregations and attenders who prayerfully put their mission under the microscope may well find themselves moving in new and enriching directions.

# EPILOGUE

# MAKING THE MOST OF THE NCLS

Research has great value in helping congregations to plan for future mission and ministry. Good research can separate fact from fiction, by confirming or challenging assumptions. It is also essential in helping to identify the size of resources and the needs with which the church is confronted. Too often, decisions have been made without recourse to such information.

As people go about their daily lives they do research all the time. They listen for the weather report to decide what to wear. They make inquiries as to how many people are going to a meeting so that the correct number of reports and biscuits can be provided. Planning for mission and ministry is no different. It is helpful to ground planning in what is really happening.

Yet, statistical research needs to be interpreted in the light of other information. It does not stand as the only source of guidance in decision making. Statistical research does not replace the need for theological reflection. It should also be recognised that the unique socio-economic, cultural and historical context of each congregation and denomination must be taken into account.

## RESOURCES FROM THE NCLS

### Major Publications

*First Look in the Mirror* (118 pp) A summary of survey results with a focus on the relationship between congregations and the wider community. A companion volume to Congregational Printouts 1–4.

*Winds of Change* (360 pp) A comprehensive analysis of congregational life, which documents some of the major changes that are sweeping through the Protestant churches.

***Vital Stats Pack*** A summary of the key trends in *Winds of Change*, which can be photocopied for use in church bulletins or discussion groups.
***Views from the Pews*** (120 pp)  A fascinating look at what attenders think and believe on social and church-related issues.
***Mission under the Microscope*** NCLS results illuminate 10 vital issues congregations need to address in developing a sustainable mission strategy for the '90s.

*Congregational and Denominational Resources*

***Looking at Your Community*** Area profile sheets help congregations understand the nature of the community they seek to serve. The NCLS can produce an area profile sheet for the local community around a congregational centre, using data from the 1991 Commonwealth census.
***Printouts 1 to 11*** These are available to all participating congregations, and give results for questions asked of attenders in their congregations. Details as to what information is available can be obtained from the NCLS office.
***Denominational Reports*** Denominations can commission reports from the NCLS on their own denomination or region. The reports provide much information about attenders, including cross-tabulations by age, gender, education and ethnic background.
***Workshops and Conferences*** Staff from the NCLS are available for workshops and conferences to help congregations and leaders gain a clearer picture of what the survey is saying and how the printouts and results can assist their mission and planning.

*Additional Resources*

***Where the River Flows*** (192 pp)  Stories of creative ministry to different sections of society. Easy-to-read book, or a video of the TV documentary with discussion guide.
***Religion: A View from the Census*** (71 pp)  A profile of nominal religious adherance in the 1991 Census by Philip Hughes of the Christian Research Association.
***Growing an Everyday Faith*** (332 pp)  20 key leaders in Australia reflect on equipping churches for mission.
***Today's Anglicans*** A video on emerging ministry models among ethnic communities in Sydney.
***Gossiping the Gospel*** Video, cassette and/or manual designed to help people talk about faith in everyday language.

Do you want further information or resources or would you like to be kept in touch? Simply use the survey hotlines or addresses:

|  |  | **Uniting Church** | **Anglican** |
|---|---|---|---|
|  |  | Board of Mission | Home Mission Society |
|  |  | PO Box A2178 | PO Box Q137 |
|  |  | SYDNEY SOUTH 2000 | Queen Victoria Building |
|  |  |  | SYDNEY 2000 |
| Phone |  | 02 285 4594 | 02 261 9500 |
| Fax |  | 02 267 7316 | 02 261 9599 |

# APPENDIX 1

# ABOUT THE SURVEY

In August 1991, the National Church Life Survey (NCLS) invited attenders from around 8000 congregations in 19 denominations to complete a survey form during congregational activities (in fact, one of 12 different survey forms). In addition, the leadership of each congregation completed a much more detailed survey of congregational life. The design of these forms was carried out by project staff in conjunction with contact persons from participating denominations, academics and church consultants both in Australia and overseas.

**Denominations involved in the NCLS**
- Anglican
- Apostolic
- Assemblies of God
- Baptist
- Christian & Missionary Alliance
- Christian Revival Crusade
- Church of the Nazarene
- Churches of Christ
- Congregational
- Foursquare Gospel
- Lutheran
- Presbyterian Church in Australia
- Presbyterian Church in New Zealand
- Reformed Churches of Australia
- Salvation Army
- Seventh-day Adventist
- Uniting Church
- Wesleyan Methodist
- Westminster Presbyterian
- Plus some independent congregations, house churches and Christian communities

The National Church Life Survey has been an important example of inter-denominational cooperation. It is worth noting that invitations were extended also to the Catholic Church to participate. A deal of interest was shown; however several practical matters and time constraints ultimately created insurmountable barriers.

Twelve different versions of the attender survey form were designed to make the most of this opportunity. The first 35 questions were identical across all surveys. Most attenders (around 90%) in a participating congregation were given one of three primary surveys. The remaining 10% of attenders were randomly selected and given one of the remaining nine forms. In this way, random samples of between 2000 and 5000 attenders completed each of these smaller surveys. Overall, around 310 000 survey forms were processed.

Response to the survey was good: about 80% of the congregations that received forms participated.

## ESTIMATES OF DENOMINATIONAL SIZE

Each participating congregation was required to supply an estimate of the number of attenders at worship services in a typical week. Where such data was not provided, estimates were needed in order to make the overall data base representative of the denominations that took part.

Details of how these estimates were derived are provided in Appendix 3 of *Winds of Change*.

## MAKING THE MOST OF THE SURVEY

The National Church Life Survey is designed to assist congregations to reflect on their own life and involvement with the wider community, and on mission directions for this decade and into the next century. For each participating congregation, data was collected on:
- the congregation's relationship to the wider community;
- attenders' perceptions of their growth in beliefs, understanding and application of their faith;
- the nature of congregational life;
- the social context in which a congregation seeks to minister.

This data base has been set up to help congregations reflect on:
- how to be creatively involved with the different groups that make up Australian communities;
- emerging styles of congregational life in this country;
- the extent to which attenders are growing in their understanding of their faith, in their beliefs/relationship to God and in the impact that faith has in everyday life.

The data base is immense and is one of the most comprehensive data bases on congregational life in any country. To make the most of it takes patient analysis. To this end, the project team has prepared a three-year analysis time-line over three stages, each covering a different aspect of the project:

- Examining congregational life and mission
- Attender attitudes/practices
- Patterns of congregational life and openness to the community.

In the first stage, the focus has been on the relationship between congregations and the wider community. In framing the project, a model of this relationship was developed. Three publications have been released which examine different aspects of this model: *First Look in the Mirror*, *Winds of Change* and now *Mission under the Microscope*. Using this model, participating congregations were invited to evaluate their life and mission based on the survey results presented in the publications, as well as unique printouts for each congregation.

Details of attender attitudes to a range of issues in the church and wider society are provided in the publication *Views from the Pews*. Analysis of patterns of congregational life are in progress.

## SAMPLE SIZES FOR PRIMARY SURVEY QUESTIONS

Twelve different versions of the attender survey were distributed (surveys A to L). The specific survey form in which the question was asked is indicated by the prefix of the question number.

Questions which were common to all survey forms are marked by the prefix 'All'.

A Congregational Life Survey (CLS) was completed once on behalf of a congregation by one or more leaders. Questions from this survey are marked by the prefix 'CLS'.

| Survey and question no. | Description | Sample size |
|---|---|---|
| *Chapter 1* | | |
| All 31 | Number of significant contacts in a week | 309 789 |
| *Chapter 2* | | |
| H39 | Involvement in community organisations | 2011 |
| All 30 | Involvement in community social action/welfare | 309 789 |
| *Chapter 3* | | |
| H36 | Involvement in environmental groups | 2011 |
| H37 | Involvement in peace and justice groups | 2011 |
| H38 | Involvement in morals groups | 2011 |
| K47 | Involvement with people in developing countries | 2408 |
| *Chapter 4* | | |
| CLS70 | Congregational links with the community | 6330 |
| CLS67 | Congregational evangelistic activities | 6330 |
| All 5 | Involvement in congregational mission activities | 309 789 |
| *Chapter 5* | | |
| E39 | When is it right to talk about faith? | 4800 |
| E40 | Usual approach to sharing faith | 4800 |
| All 34 | Readiness to share faith | 309 789 |

*Chapter 6*

| E41 | Reasons for not talking about faith | 4800 |
| E42 | Talking about faith across cultures | 4800 |
| E49 | Getting support for sharing faith | 4800 |
| E43 | Getting training for sharing faith | 4800 |
| E38 | Concerns about Christianity | 4800 |

*Chapter 7*

| E44 | Frequency of sharing faith | 4800 |
| E47 | Shared faith with whom? | 4800 |
| E45 | Where faith shared? (1) | 4800 |
| E46 | Where faith shared? (2) | 4800 |
| E48 | Follow-up of those with whom they shared | 4800 |
| All 35 | Inviting to church | 309 789 |

*Chapter 8*

| F37 | First occasion at church | 4022 |
| F38 | Ways made welcome at church | 4022 |
| F46 | Ways helped to fit in at church | 4022 |
| F40 | Developing a sense of belonging at church | 4022 |
| F39 | Trying other congregations first | 4022 |

*Chapter 9*

| G36 | First contact with the Christian faith | 3315 |
| G37 | Significant people in finding faith | 3315 |
| All 7 | Attendance level of children of attenders | 309 789 |
| All 17 | Household type and life stage of children | 309 789 |
| A36 | Reasons for leaving church | 92 957 |

*Chapter 10*

| All 25 | Decisive moment of commitment/conversion | 309 789 |
| G38 | Public faith commitment | 3315 |
| G40 | Catalysts in making a commitment | 3315 |
| G39 | Significance of the public faith commitment | 3315 |

Results from additional questions are also referred to at various points in the book. These questions and associated sample sizes are as follows.

| B38 | Patterns of prayer | 90 628 |
| D37 | Theological traditions | 3922 |

# APPENDIX 2

# ADDITIONAL SURVEY QUESTIONS

Apart from the survey questions presented in the text, the following questions are referred to at various points throughout this book.

## PATTERNS OF FAITH

*27. Which statement comes closest to your view of the Bible?*
a. The Bible is the word of God, to be taken literally word for word
b. The Bible is the word of God which needs to be read in the context of the times to understand its implications for us today
c. The Bible is a valuable book, parts of which reveal God's word to us
d. The Bible is a valuable book with much to teach us
e. Don't know

*28. What is your opinion of 'speaking in tongues'?*
Choose the sentence which is closest to your opinion.
a. Don't know or have no opinion
b. I generally disapprove of speaking in tongues as it is practised today
c. I generally approve of speaking in tongues in most situations, but do not speak in tongues myself
d. I approve of and have spoken in tongues myself
e. Speaking in tongues is necessary for all Christians

*D37. There are many Christian traditions from which we learn and grow in our faith journeys. Select a MAXIMUM OF TWO which you believe to have been the most significant for you:*
a. Catholic/Anglo-Catholic
b. Charismatic/Pentecostal
c. Evangelical

d. Reformed
e. Liberal
f. Liberation theology
g. Eastern Orthodox
h. The tradition of the denomination I now attend
i. Other (please specify)
j. Not applicable

## CONGREGATIONAL INVOLVEMENT

The level of attenders' congregational involvement was derived from results for the following four questions.

*2. How often do you come to worship services here?*

a. Hardly ever/never
b. Special occasions only
c. Less than once a month
d. Once a month
e. Once a fortnight
f. 3 out of 4 weeks
g. Each week
h. More than once a week

*4. About how many hours would you spend in worship services and/or activities organised by this church each week?*

a. None
b. 1–2 hours
c. 3–5 hours
d. 6–10 hours
e. 11–20 hours
f. Over 20 hours

*5. Do you regularly take part in any mission activities of this church? (eg visitation, evangelism, community service/social justice/welfare)*

a. No, we don't have such activities
b. No, I am not regularly involved
c. Yes, in evangelistic activities
d. Yes, in social care/social justice activities
e. Yes, both c and d above

*6. Are you regularly involved in any group activities at this church?*

a. No, we have no such groups
b. No, I am not regularly involved
c. Yes, in small sharing, prayer or Bible study groups
d. Yes, in fellowships, clubs, social or other groups
e. Yes, in both c and d above

## BACKGROUND OF ATTENDERS

The background of attenders was derived from results for the following survey questions.

*1. How long have you been coming to worship services and/or activities run by this congregation?*

a. Less than 1 year
b. 1–2 years
c. 3–5 years
d. I am visiting from another church
e. I am visiting and do not regularly go anywhere else
f. 6–10 years
g. 11–20 years
h. More than 20 years

*8. Before you started coming here, were you participating in another congregation?*

a. No, I've come here for most/all of my life
b. No, before coming here I had not been attending church for several years
c. No, before coming here I had never regularly attended a church

*Yes, immediately prior to coming here I was attending a church which was:*

d. Anglican
e. Apostolic
f. Assemblies of God
g. Revival Crusade
h. Foursquare Gospel
i. Other Pentecostal
j. Baptist
k. Catholic
l. Churches of Christ
m. Congregationalist
n. Lutheran
o. Wesleyan Methodist
p. Methodist
q. Missionary Alliance
r. Nazarene
s. Orthodox
t. Presbyterian
u. Reformed
v. Salvation Army
w. Seventh-day Adventist
x. Uniting
y. Other

## INFLUENCE, SHARING FAITH AND INVITING TO CHURCH (CHAPTERS 2,4,5,6,10).

*33. Do you feel able to exert a Christian influence with those around you (at work, friends, local contacts)?*

a. To a great extent
b. To some extent
c. Perhaps a little
d. Not at all
e. Don't know/not applicable

*34. Which of the following best describes your readiness to talk to others about your faith?*

a. I lack faith, so the question is not applicable
b. I do not like to talk about my faith, I believe my life and actions give sufficient example
c. I find it hard to express my faith in ordinary language
d. I mostly feel at ease about expressing my faith and do so if it comes up
e. I feel at ease about expressing my faith and seek to find opportunities to do so

*35. In the last year has anybody started attending church activities here or elsewhere as a result of your involvement with them?*

a. Yes, as a result of discussion about the Christian faith
b. Yes, for other reasons
c. Both a and b
d. No, those with whom I have shared chose not to be involved or felt uncomfortable when they tried
e. No, I don't think I encouraged anybody to do so
f. Don't know

## GROWTH IN FAITH (CHAPTERS 2,4,5,6,10)

*22. Over the last year, have you grown in your understanding of the Christian faith?*

a. No real growth
b. Some growth
c. Much growth, mainly through this church
d. Much growth, mainly through other groups or churches
e. Much growth, mainly through my own private activity

*23. Over the last year, have you developed a stronger belief in or relationship with God? (circle one)*

a. If anything I have greater doubts than before
b. No real change
c. Somewhat stronger
d. Much stronger, mainly through this church
e. Much stronger, mainly through other groups or churches
e. Much stronger, mainly through my own private activity

**24. Over the last year, have you made changes in your actions and priorities as a result of your Christian faith?** *(circle one)*

a. No real changes
b. Some small changes
c. Some major changes
d. I do not feel I have a Christian faith

**B38. Which of the following best describes patterns of prayer in your daily life at present?**

a. Prayer is not important in my daily life
b. I pray mostly in times of stress, need or gratitude
c. I put aside a set time each day for prayer
d. I often move to/drift into prayer during each day
e. Both c and d above

## EVANGELISTIC ACTIVITIES AND COMMUNITY LINKS (CHAPTER 4)

**CLS67. Has this congregation undertaken any evangelistic activities in the last 12 months?** *(circle any that apply)*

a. Evangelistic services/crusades
b. Street evangelism
c. Drop-in centres
d. Evangelistic Bible studies (eg *Christianity Explained*)
e. Visitation programs (eg *Evangelism Explosion*)
f. Mission activities in shopping centres
g. Mission activities in schools
h. Other (please specify)

**CLS70. Has this congregation made links with the wider community in the last 12 months in any of the following ways?** *(circle all that apply)*

a. Use of property by community groups (eg playgroups, AA)
b. Church representation on community groups/committees
c. Participation in special community activities (eg peace marches, community fairs)
d. Provision of welfare services/facilities to meet needs (eg counselling services, second-hand clothes shops)
e. Provision of groups based on a common interest (eg. craft groups, mothers groups, adult education)
f. Civic church services
g. Community markets
h. School for seniors, aged-care activities
i. None of the above
j. Other (please describe)

## CONCERNS ABOUT CHRISTIANITY (CHAPTER 6)

*E38. Some people in the wider community have various questions and concerns about Christianity – what are the main TWO you have heard?*

a. It is irrelevant
b. It is for people who can't cope with life
c. It's just a set of rules
d. Science disproves it
e. There is no proof
f. It is a religion of the well off
g. How can it be the only way?
h. What about suffering?
i. How do you know the Bible is true?
j. Christians are good people but it's not for me
k. Christians don't practise what they preach
l. I'm not good enough
m. Other (please specify)


## WHERE SHARED FAITH? (CHAPTER 7)

*E45. Have most of these occasions occurred through contacts made through:*

a. A mission/outreach activity of this church
b. A visitation program of this church
c. A mission/outreach activity of another church or mission group
d. Everyday life activities (friends/workplace etc)

*E46. Have most of these moments of faith sharing occurred:*

a. On church property
b. Out in the community


## GENERATIONAL RETENTION (CHAPTER 9)

Retention levels for children of various life stages were derived from the following questions.

*7. Which statement best describes the level of church attendance of your children?*

a. I do not currently have any children
b. Most of my children are involved with this church
c. Most of my children are involved with other churches
d. Most of my children are not attending church anywhere
e. I do not know whether my children attend church or not
f. More than one of the above

*17. Which statement BEST describes the people who make up your household? (NB: If your household is equally divided between two age groups, please select the youngest).*

a. I live alone
b. My household consists of some adults living together
c. A married couple without children

*My household includes 2 parents and children living at home mainly of:*

d. Preschool age
e. Primary school age
f. Secondary school age
g. Post school age

*My household includes 1 parent and children living at home mainly of:*

h. Preschool age
i. Primary school age
j. Secondary school age
k. Post school age

## REASONS FOR LEAVING LAST CONGREGATION (CHAPTER 9)

*A36. If you used to go to another church, what was the* **main** *reason you left? (circle up to two)*

a. Never involved elsewhere
b. Moved to a new area
c. Got married
d. Went looking for new friends
e. Wanted a more lively church
f. It was too small
g. It was too large
h. It didn't preach the gospel
i. My needs changed
j. My family's needs changed
k. Too much conflict
l. The style/program did not suit
m. Unhappy with minister/leader
n. No-one of my age
o. I lost my faith
p. Its teaching on divorce/remarriage
q. Its teaching on female leadership
r. Its teaching was too restrictive
s. Other

# APPENDIX 3

# CONGREGATIONAL MISSION ACTIVITIES

## What the churches are doing

The following list of activities has been prepared from responses received for Congregation Life Survey (CLS) question numbers 67 and 70. The CLS was filled in by congregational leaders from 6330 participating congregations.

### 1. GENERAL EVANGELISTIC ACTIVITIES

Assisting 'Bike for Bibles' team
Baptism classes
Beach mission
Bible study (eg *Christianity Explained*)
Bibles/tract distribution
Coffee shop/Drop-in centre
Community event with evangelism
Contact with parents of Sunday school/kids club etc
Dialogue meeting
Dinner/outreach dinner
Discipleship program
Distribution of church magazine/Christian magazines/newspapers
Door-to-door surveys/community surveys
Door-to-door evangelism/door knocks
Employ new staff for evangelism
Enquirers night
Follow-up of first-time visitors/contacts
Friendship evangelism
Home meetings/using home for evangelism
Housing estate mission/public housing mission
Individual sharing/one-to-one evangelism

Interchurch missional activity
Interstate mission
Involvement with parachurch groups/agencies (eg ITIM, BCA)
Lay witness missions
Letterbox drop/mailout/letter ministry
Lunchtime meetings for business people
Newspaper column
Outreach at local show/events
Overseas missionary trip by parishioners/partnership mission into overseas country
Prayer seminars
Pub/hotel ministry/hotel visitation
Radio show
Railway station mission
Schools outreach/Scripture
Seminars/courses on relevant issues (eg family, grief)
Shopping centre outreach
Small group outreach to contacts
Stewardship program
Street evangelism
Support visiting evangelistic crusades
Supporting overseas mission
Teaching mission
Television show
Training for outreach (eg *Gossiping the Gospel*)
Vacation Bible School
Video/film series – relevant issues (eg family)
Video/film series – evangelistic (eg Jesus video)
Video outreach in secular video shops
Visit by theological students/mission group
Visit from overseas link missionaries

## 2. SPECIAL CHURCH SERVICES AND EVENTS

Annual mission day
Baptismal services
Church open day
Civic services/community Sundays/services at town hall
Community carol singing/Carols by Candlelight
Confirmation classes
Cursillo groups
Easter march
Easter/Christmas services
Easter/Christmas services in community (eg in parks, streets)
Ecumenical outreach events/ecumenical services (eg World Day of Prayer)
Ecumenical community services – Christmas/Easter/combined churches
Christmas and Easter ecumenical Bible studies

Evangelistic services (regular and occasional/crusades)
Funerals, weddings
*Growing Together in Christ* weekend
Healing services
Hospital services
Inter-church council
Inter-denominational Bible studies
Lenten studies
Mission month/mission week
Mothers Union rally
Mothers' day/Fathers' day services
Outdoor services/open air outreach
Parish mission
Peace service
Public meeting-style missions
Radio services ministry
School services
Seaman mission
Seeker services/'user-friendly' church services
Services at nursing home/aged-care units
Special services by invitation/guest services
Special mission by visiting speakers
Teaching catechism
Use of church building by other denominations
Youth services

## 3. ACTIVITIES LINKED TO LIFE STAGE

### 3a. Children

After school care/club
After school program (primary, early high school)
Chaplaincy
Child care/day care
Children's mission
Children's day camps
Christmas party for local children
Ecumenical children's ministry
Kids club/Sunday school/children's activities at church
Kindergarten/preschool
Playgroup/playtime
Run own primary school/Christian parent-controlled school
Scripture/religious education seminar at primary school
Sunday school concerts
Vacation care program/holiday program

### 3b. Youth

Annual youth events
Christian bands/rock concert

Co-op scheme (at local high school)
Coaching local school sports team
Coffee shops/drop-in centres
Community youth group
Detached youth work
Disco outreach
Ecumenical youth rally/youth activities
Extra curricula activities at high school/tutoring
Girl Guides/Boy Scouts
High school seminars/outreach programs
Links with universities
Local school functions (P & C/school canteen)
Long-term accommodation for homeless youth
Pony Club meeting
Religious education/Scripture in schools
Run youth hostel
University outreach programs/chaplaincy
Visiting youth mission
Youth group
Youth camps
Youth outreach night
Youth with a Mission
Youth chaplaincy
Youth concerts
Youth drop-in centre

## 3c. Families

Activities for non-Christian spouses
Annual musical/musical events/concerts
Caritas/mothers' outreach
Catercare – provision for single mums
Contact with families of baptised children
Family dances
Family day
Family concerts/musical productions
Family teaching days
Homemakers group for women
Ladies coffee morning
Men's breakfasts
Men's dinner
Mission to men
Parish camps/houseparties
Seminars for young families
Women's dinner
Women's breakfasts
Young mothers respite
Young mothers program

### 3d. Aged

Bus for aged to attend church
Coach/day trips for the elderly
Communion to elderly/infirm
Home nursing service
Hostel for aged care/respite day care
Housing for aged people
Meals on Wheels
Ministry to shut-ins
Ministry to veterans
Nursing home concerts/entertainment
Nursing home visitation
Senior citizens luncheons

### 3e. Ethnic groups

Aboriginal camps/ministry to Aborigines
Cross-cultural support groups
Cross-cultural radio program
Cultural activities by ethnic groups
Drop-in groups for specific ethnic groups
House for refugee families
Migrant English classes
Ministry to tourists/vacationers
National dance group
Naturalisation ceremony

## 4. LINKS WITH THE WIDER COMMUNITY

### 4a. Contacting activities

Adult fellowship evening
Bookshop/religious bookshop
Bush dance
Card evenings
City-country exchange program
Coffee party/coffee morning
Community survey
Community morning teas/luncheons/progressive tea
Community film night
Cooking evening
Craft meeting/craft centre
Display board (outside church)
Drama group
Drop-in centre
Facilities for singles (eg for worship)
Fellowship meals
Fete/arts festival/flower show/arts and crafts display
Float and street parade
Friendship centre/friendship club/social club

Fund raising
Garage sale
Gymnasium group
Historical interest in church/tours etc
Letterbox drop/mailout
Media advertising/multi-media approach
Musical groups/bands
Neighbourhood house
Newspaper column/advertising
Odd jobs in the community
Open forum (eg to hear of possible links with community)
Pool party
Radio segment/talk-back show
Reunion for people married at the church
Sporting activity (eg golf day)
Sporting clubs/teams
Street stalls/cake stall at sporting event
Street BBQ
Telemarketing/telephone canvassing
Television advertising
Trips away (eg to the snow)
Use of church property by community groups (eg Judo, Alcoholics Anonymous)
Visitation by minister or elders
Visitation group

## 4b. Caring/welfare activities

Activity centre for psychiatric patients
AIDS support group
Alcohol and drug rehabilitation
Cancer care/support
Chaplaincy to clubs, institutions
Clothing/recycling bins
Club for intellectually disabled/support group for families of people with disabilities
Communicare program
Community groups raising money to maintain church building
Counselling services/counselling centre
Court ministry (eg morning teas)
Day care
Disabled dancing
Disabled centre
Divorced ministry
Emergency accommodation/Crisis home accommodation for needy families
Emergency services
Extending a motel
Family and marriage counselling by minister

Financial and practical support for special ministries in other communities
Financial support for various activities/agencies
Food stock project for the needy/parish pantry
Food cooperative/vegetable cooperative
Foster parenting
Gay support groups
Grief support ministry
Help for flood victims/fire victims
Help for victims of drug and alcohol abuse
Help for victims of domestic violence
Hospital visitation
Hospital chaplaincy
Industrial chaplain
Involvement in community service agencies/neighbourhood centre
Involvement in Meals on Wheels/supply of meals to shut-ins
Lifeline
Opportunity shop
Overseas child sponsorship
Oversee a community service (eg home and community care)
Pastoral care/pastoral visitation
Prison ministry
Referrals to government welfare/other agencies
Refuges/hostels for the homeless
Resettlement of people with a history of long-term institutional care
Run hospital canteen
Rural crisis ministry/reaching out to those on isolated properties
Soup kitchen
Sponsor local community program (eg Skillshare)
Staffing the local community centre
Streetwork among the homeless
Stroke club
Supervision of people on community service orders from courts
Telephone care/counselling
Transport service for the disabled/welfare bus service/bus for elderly/youth
Unemployed resource group
Welfare housing
Welfare payments

*4c. Community action*

Congregational leaders becoming community leaders
Initiating community projects
Involvement in community groups/local affairs
Involvement in local politics
Protest groups on particular local issues
Protest march on wider issues (eg anti-abortion)
Resident action group
Witness against racism

**4d. Seminars/classes**

Aerobics classes
Budgeting seminar/financial advice
Business seminars
College annual summer school
Community seminar
Cooking classes
Craft lessons
Dancing lessons
Drug awareness
First-aid classes
Healthful living/quit smoking/nutrition
Lifeskills courses
Marriage enrichment/preparation courses
Migrant English classes
Parent effectiveness/family relationship courses/video series
Pregnancy classes
Public speaking
Quit smoking
Rural family seminars
Self-development courses
Specific needs seminars (eg grief, family)

# USEFUL REFERENCES

The following references provide useful material on mission in Australia and/or are cited in the text.

Bible references are from the *New Revised Standard Version*, 1989, Zondervan Publishing House, Michigan.

ABBOTT, S, 1994, *Everyday Evangelism*. Course manual. Anglican Diocese of Sydney. Department of Evangelism.

ARN, W & ARN, C, 1982, *The Master's Plan for Making Disciples*. California: Church Growth Press.

AUSTRALIAN INTERNATIONAL DEVELOPMENT ASSISTANCE BUREAU (AIDAB), 1990, *Working paper on Poverty and the Australian Aid Program*. Canberra: AIDAB.

AUSTRALIAN VALUES STUDY SURVEY, 1984, *Revised Report of International Comparisons*. Unpublished.

Awakening '94, 1994, *Mission Manual*. Series of publications on mission to different groups. Croydon: Awakening '94.

BAILEY, A, 1992, *Good News Down Under*. Sydney: Anzea Publishers.

BAKKE, R, 1987, *The Urban Christian*. Kent: MARC Europe.

BANKS, R, 1987, *All the Business of Life: Bringing Theology down to Earth*. Sydney: Albatross Books Pty Ltd.

BELLAMY, J, KALDOR, P, POWELL, R & CORREY, M, 1992, *Bible Reading Patterns among Church Attenders*. Sydney: 1991 National Church Life Survey.

BENTLEY, P, BLOMBERY, T, & HUGHES, P, 1992, *Faith without the Church. Nominalism in Australian Christianity*. Melbourne: Christian Research Association.

BIBBY, R W, 1978, *Why Conservative Churches Are Really Growing*. Journal for the Scientific Study of Religion, vol 17.

BISSET, T, 1992, *Why Christian Kids Leave the Faith*. Nashville: Thomas Nelson.

BLACK, A W (ed), 1991, *Religion in Australia: Sociological Perspectives*. Sydney: Allen & Unwin.

BLACK, A & GLASNER, P (eds), 1983, *Practice and Belief: Studies in the Sociology of Australian Religion*. Sydney: Allen & Unwin.

BLOMBERY, T, 1989, *Tomorrow's Church Today*. Melbourne: The Christian Research Association.

BLOMBERY, T, & HUGHES, P, 1993, *Faith Alive, an Australian Picture*. Melbourne: Christian Research Association.

BODYCOMB, J, 1989, *A Matter of Death and Life: The Future of Australia's Churches*. Melbourne: Joint Board of Christian Education.

BOLT, P, 1992, *Mission Minded: A Tool for Planning Your Ministry around Christ's Mission*. Sydney: St Matthias Press.

BOSCH, D J, 1991, *Transforming Mission: Paradigm Shifts in Theology of Mission*. American Society of Missiology Series, No. 16. New York: Orbis Books.

BOUMA, G D, 1983, 'Australian Religiosity: Some Trends since 1966' in Black, A & Glasner, P (eds), *Practice and Belief: Studies in the Sociology of Australian Religion*. Sydney: Allen & Unwin, pp15–24.

BOUMA, G D, 1992, *Religion: Meaning, Transcendence and Community in Australia*. Melbourne: Longman Cheshire.

BOUMA, G & DIXON, B, 1986, *The Religious Factor in Australian Life*. Melbourne: MARC.

BRIDGER, F, 1988, *Children Finding Faith*. London: Scripture Union.

CALLAHAN, K L, 1983, *Twelve Keys to an Effective Church: Strategic Planning for Mission*. San Francisco: Harper & Row.

CATHERWOOD, H F R, 1969, *The Christian Citizen*. London: Hodder & Stoughton.

CHAPMAN, J C, 1981, *Know and Tell the Gospel*. Christian Beliefs Series. Lane Cove: Hodder & Stoughton (Australia) Pty Limited.

CLAYDON, D, 1993, *Only Connect. Sharing the Gospel across Cultural Boundaries*. Sydney: Lancer Books.

COLE, G, 1994, 'Church Questions Its Welfare Role'. Anglican Home Mission Society Press Release. June 1994. Sydney.

CONN, H M, 1982, *Evangelism: Doing Justice and Preaching Grace*. Michigan: Zondervan Publishing House.

CORNEY, P, 1992, *The Welcoming Church: How to Welcome Newcomers in the Local Church*. Sydney: Anglican Information Office.

CORNEY, P, 1991, *The Gospel and the Growing Church*. Sydney: Anglican Information Office (AIO) Press.

COSTAS, O, 1982, *Christ outside the Gate: Mission beyond Christendom*. New York: Orbis Books.

CURRIE, R, GILBERT, A, & HORSLEY, L, 1977, *Churches and Churchgoers: Patterns of Church Growth in the British Isles since 1700*. Oxford: Clarendon Press.

DAYTON, E R, & WILSON, S, (eds) 1984, *The Future of World Evangelization*. California: MARC.

DEMERATH, N J, 1965, *Social Class in American Protestantism*. Chicago: Rand McNally.

ELLISON, C (ed), 1974, *The Urban Mission*. Michigan: William B Eerdmans Publishing Company.

ENGEL, J & NORTON, W, 1975, *What's Gone Wrong with the Harvest?* Michigan: Zondervan Publishing House.

ERIKSON, E H, 1950, *Childhood and Society*. Hammondsworth, Middlesex: Penguin Books.

ESCOBAR, S & DRIVER J, 1978, *Christian Mission and Social Justice*. Pennsylvania: Herald Press.

FINNEY, J, 1991, *The Well Church Book*. London: Scripture Union.

FINNEY, J, 1992a, *Church on the Move: Leadership for Mission*. London: Daybreak.

FINNEY, J, 1992b, *Finding Faith Today, How Does It Happen?* Great Britain: Biddles Ltd.

FRANCIS, L J, 1984, *Teenagers and the Church. A Profile of Church-going Youth in the 1980s*. London: Collins Liturgical Publications.

FUNG, R, 1992, *The Isaiah Vision*. Switzerland: World Council of Churches Publications.

GARVIN, M, 1992, *The New Coinage*. Sydney: Fusion Australia.

GEORGE, C F, 1991, *Prepare Your Church for the Future*. Michigan: Fleming H Revell.

GIBBS, E, 1993, *Winning Them Back. Tackling the Problem of Nominal Christianity*. Kent: Monarch Publications.

GIBBS, E, 1981, *I Believe in Church Growth*. London: Hodder & Stoughton.

GINSBURG, H and OPPER, S, 1969, *Piaget's Theory of Intellectual Development: An Introduction*. Englewood Cliffs, New Jersey: Prentice-Hall Inc.

GOODE, E, 1966, *Social Class and Church Participation*. American Journal of Sociology 72, pp 102–111.

HADAWAY, C K, 1990, *What Can We Do about Church Dropouts?* Creative Leadership Series. Nashville: Abingdon Press.

HADAWAY, C K, 1991, *Church Growth Principles: Separating Fact from Fiction*. Nashville: Broadman Press.

HALE, J R, 1977, *Who Are the Unchurched?* Washington: Glenmary Research Centre.

HAN, G S, 1994, *Social Sources of Church Growth: Korean Churches in the Homeland and Overseas*. Lanham, Maryland: University Press of America.

HOGAN, M C, 1987, *The Sectarian Strand: Religion in Australian History*. Melbourne: Penguin Books.

HOGE, D, 1981, *Converts, Dropouts, Returnees. A Study of Religious Change among Catholics*. New York: The Pilgrim Press.

HOGE, D R & ROOZEN, D A (eds), 1979, *Understanding Church Growth and Decline: 1950–1978*. New York: Pilgrim Press.

HOUSTON, J (ed), 1986, *The Cultured Pearl: Australian Readings in Cross-cultural Theology and Mission*. Melbourne: Joint Board of Christian Education.

HUGHES, P J & BLOMBERY, T, 1990, *Patterns of Faith in Australian Churches: Report from the Combined Churches Survey for Faith and Mission*. Melbourne: Christian Research Association.

HUGHES, P J, undated, *Religion and Values. Report from the Australian Values Study Survey*. Canberra: Zadok Centre.

HUGHES, P J, 1988, *The Church's Mission: Report from the Combined Churches Survey for Faith and Mission*. Melbourne: Christian Research Association.

JENSEN, P & PAYNE, T, 1989, *Fellow Workers: Discussion Papers for the Church Committee*. Sydney: St Matthias Press.

JOSLIN, R, 1982, *Urban Harvest*. Hertfordshire: Evangelical Press.

KALDOR, P, BOWIE, V & FARQUHAR-NICOL, G (eds), 1985, *Green Shoots in the Concrete*. Sydney: Scaffolding.

KALDOR, P, BELLAMY, J, POWELL, R, CORREY, M & CASTLE, K, 1994, *Winds of Change: The Experience of Church in a Changing Australia*. Sydney: Lancer Books.

KALDOR, P, POWELL, R, BELLAMY, J, CORREY, M, CASTLE, K & MOORE, S, 1995, *Views from the Pews: Australian Church Attenders Speak Out*. 1991 National Church Life Survey. Adelaide: Openbook.

KALDOR, P & KALDOR, S, 1988, *Where the River Flows*. Sydney: Lancer Books.

KALDOR, P, 1987, *Who Goes Where? Who Doesn't Care? Going to Church in Australia*. Sydney: Lancer Books.

KALDOR, P, BELLAMY, J, CORREY, M & POWELL, R, 1992: *First Look in the Mirror*. Sydney: Lancer Books.

KELLEY, D M, 1977, *Why Conservative Churches Are Growing*. New York: Harper & Row.

LARSON, R W, & BRADNEY, N, 1988, 'Precious Moments with Family Members and Friends' in Milardo R M (ed), *Families and Social Networks*. California: Sage Publications.

LEE, S T, 1989, *New Church New Land: The Korean Experience*. Melbourne: Uniting Church Press.

MACKAY, H, 1993, *Reinventing Australia*. Melbourne: Harper Collins.

MAVOR, J (ed), 1994, *Creative Life Together: Ministry in Regional Congregations*. Melbourne: Joint Board of Christian Education.

McGAVRAN, D A, 1988, *Effective Evangelism, A Theological Mandate*. Phillipsburg: Presbyterian and Reformed Publishing Company.

McGUIRE, M, 1981, *Religion: The Social Context*. Belmont, California: Wadsworth.

MEAD, L, 1991, *The Once and Future Church*. Washington: Alban Institute Publication.

MIDDLE EARTH, 1980, *Comfort or Crisis: Living Christianly in the Eighties*. Sydney: Hexagon Press.

MILLER, H, 1990, *The Vital Congregation*. Effective Church Series. Nashville: Abingdon Press.

MILLIKAN, D, 1981, *The Sunburnt Soul*. Sydney: Anzea Publishers.

MOL, H, 1969, *Christianity in Chains: A Sociologist's Interpretation of the Churches' Dilemma in a Secular World*. Melbourne: Thomas Nelson Ltd.

NEWBIGIN, L, 1989, *The Gospel in a Pluralist Society*. Grand Rapids, Michigan: Wm B Eerdmans Publishing Co.

NEWBIGIN, L, 1991, *Truth to Tell: The Gospel as Public Truth*. Michigan: Wm. B Eerdmans Publishing Co.

NG, D & THOMAS, V, 1971, *Children in the Worshiping Community*. Atlanta: John Knox Press.

OLASKY, M, SCHLOSSBERG, H, BERTHOUD, P & PINNOCK, C, 1988. *Freedom, Justice and Hope: Towards a Strategy for the Poor and the Oppressed*. Westchester, Illinois: Crossway Books.

OSWALD, R M, 1992, *Making Your Church More Inviting*. Washington: The Alban Institute.

PATRICK, P (ed), 1993, *New Vision New Zealand*. Auckland: Vision New Zealand.

PETTIFER, J & BRADLEY, R, 1990, *Missionaries*. London: BBC Books.

PIPPERT, R M, 1979, *Out of the Saltshaker*. Great Britain: Inter-Varsity Press.

RAUFF, E A, 1979, *Why People Join the Church*. New York: The Pilgrim Press.

RATHS, L, HARMIN, M & SIMONS, S, 1966, *Values and Teaching: Working with Values in the Classroom*. Columbus, Ohio: Charles E Merrill Books Inc.

ROBINSON, I, KALDOR, P & DRAYTON, D (eds), 1991, *Growing an Everyday Faith: Effective Mission in a Changing Australia*. Sydney: Lancer Books.

ROBINSON, I, 1992, *Gossiping the Gospel. Leaders Manual*. Sydney: Uniting Church in Australia, NSW Board of Mission.

ROOF, W C, 1978, *Community and Commitment: Religious Plausibility in a Liberal Protestant Church*. New York: The Pilgrim Press.

ROOZEN, D A, & HADAWAY, C K (eds), 1993, *Church and Denominational Growth: What Does (and Does Not) Cause Growth or Decline*. Nashville: Abingdon Press.

ROOZEN, D A, McKINNEY, W & CARROLL, J W, 1984, *The Varieties of Religious Presence: Mission in Public Life*. New York: Pilgrim Press.

ROSE, L L & HADAWAY, C K, (eds), 1982, *The Urban Challenge*. Nashville: Broadman Press.

SAMUEL, V, and HAUSER, A (eds), 1989, *Proclaiming Christ in Christ's Way*. Oxford: Regnum Books.

SCHALLER, L E, 1978, *Assimilating New Members*. Creative Leadership Series. Nashville: Abingdon Press.

ST MATTHIAS PRESS, 1989, *Two Ways to Live Personal Evangelism: Leaders Manual*. Sydney: St Matthias Press.

STROMBERG, J, 1983, *Mission and Evangelism: An Ecumenical Affirmation*. A study guide. Geneva: World Council of Churches.

TROELTSCH, 1960, *The Social Teachings of the Churches*. New York: Harper Books.

WAGNER, C P, 1984, *Leading Your Church to Growth*. California: Regal Books.

WALKER, C C, 1988, *Connecting with the Spirit of Christ: Evangelism for a Secular Age*. Nashville: Discipleship Resources.

WARREN, M, 1976, *I Believe in the Great Commission*. London: Hodder & Stoughton.

WESTERHOFF III, J H, 1976, *Will Our Children Have Faith?* San Francisco: Harper & Row Publishers.

WILLMOTT, P, & YOUNG, M, 1960, *Family and Class in a London Suburb*. London: Routledge & Kegan Paul.

# THE NATIONAL CHURCH LIFE SURVEY TEAM

*Peter Kaldor*

Peter has had many years' experience with mission groups and churches in different denominations. For the past 10 years he has been researching aspects of church life for the Uniting Church Board of Mission, providing congregations with valuable information about mission possibilities. He is committed to helping churches relate more effectively to the many diverse groups in Australian society. With this book, Peter has provided an overall framework, written some chapters and provided support to John in his coordinating role.

*John Bellamy*

A town planner by background, John is the staff person from the Anglican Home Mission Society most involved in the research side of the NCLS. He is currently completing a Masters Degree with the University of New England, which includes community survey work, exploring the relationship between the church and the community. John believes creative research has a vital role to play in developing effective mission strategies. John has been the primary researcher and coordinator in the production of this book.

*Sandra Moore*

A member of the NCLS staff team for a little over a year, Sandra's journalistic and administrative skills have been a great gift to the project. Press releases and short articles have usually been the result of her work. Sandra has been a major contributor to both the research and writing of this publication.

*Ruth Powell*

Ruth has a background in psychology and statistics. A staff member of the Uniting Church Board of Mission, she has had previous involvement in welfare and experience with many different subcultures. Currently involved in post-graduate research into generational differences in the churches, Ruth is committed to ensuring that the church relates to all the different groups in society. Ruth is a primary researcher and writer with the NCLS.

*Merilyn Correy*

Merilyn has been involved in helping churches relate to their local communities for about a decade and is the main NCLS presenter at workshops and conferences. Her background in psychology and social work, augmented by her gifts in communication, allows her to lead congregations sensitively yet efficiently through processes of change. She is committed to seeing change occur at a grass roots level, as well as in church agencies. She has brought together the material for most of the ministry stories in this book.

*Keith Castle*

Keith has been employed by the Anglican diocese of Sydney as an urban planner for the past four years to assist congregations and diocesan leaders. He believes that focused research is an essential component in helping the church to review the past and plan for the future. Keith has had an important and ongoing role in survey design, analysis and the production of resources for congregations.

*Joy Sanderson*

Joy provides administrative coordination for the NCLS team. While she may be too modest to acknowledge it, Joy keeps the whole project moving forward.

*Bob Moin*

Bob is the administration and accounting backbone of the NCLS. A member of the Anglican Home Mission Society, Bob provides advice and wisdom to both staff and Steering Committee on where the project is heading.

\*　\*　\*　\*

The NCLS team has been greatly blessed by a stability of membership over four years. An important member of the team in its early years was **Jane Ford**, who played a vital role in the design of the survey.

Some others are so vital to the project that they feel like part of the team: **Phil Mackay** (and his computer expertise), **Chris Morgan** (and his cartoons), **Jeanette Scott** and **Corylanne Vandyke** (for their office support).